D0851992

p 980

812

SEARCH FOR THE
FIRST AMERICANS

For my children, Emily and Ethan Meltzer

SMITHSONIAN
EXPLORING THE ANCIENT WORLD
JEREMY A. SABLOFF, Editor

SEARCH FOR THE
FIRST AMERICANS

By DAVID J. MELTZER

St. Remy Press • Montreal

Smithsonian Books • Washington, D.C.

EXPLORING THE ANCIENT WORLD
was produced by
ST. REMY PRESS

Publisher	Kenneth Winchester
President	Pierre Léveillé
Managing Editor	Carolyn Jackson
Managing Art Director	Diane Denoncourt
Production Manager	Michelle Turbide
Administrator	Natalie Watanabe

Staff for *SEARCH FOR THE FIRST AMERICANS*

Editor	Michael Ballantyne
Art Director	Philippe Arnoldi
Contributing Art Director	Chantal Bilodeau
Picture Editor	Christopher Jackson
Contributing Editors	Daniel McBain
	Brian Parsons
Researcher	Olga Dzatko
Photo Researcher	Andrea Reithmayr
Photo Assistant	Geneviève Monette
Designers	Hélène Dion
	Sara Grynspan
Illustrators	Maryse Doray
	Robert Paquet
	Maryo Proulx
Systems Coordinator	Jean-Luc Roy
Administrative Assistant	Dominique Gagné
Indexer	Christine Jacobs
Proofreader	Judy Yelon

THE SMITHSONIAN INSTITUTION

Secretary	Robert McC. Adams
Assistant Secretary for External Affairs	Thomas E. Lovejoy
Director, Smithsonian Institution Press	Felix C. Lowe

SMITHSONIAN BOOKS

Editor-in-Chief	Patricia Gallagher
Senior Editor	Alexis Doster III
Editors	Amy Donovan
	Joe Goodwin
Assistant Editors	Brian D. Kennedy
	Sonia Reece
Senior Picture Editor	Frances C. Rowsell
Picture Editors	Carrie F. Bruns
	R. Jenny Takacs
Picture Research	V. Susan Guardado
Production Editor	Patricia Upchurch
Business Manager	Stephen J. Bergstrom

© 1993 St. Remy Press and Smithsonian Institution
All rights reserved. No part of this book may be reproduced or utilized in any form or by any means, electronic or mechanical, including photocopying, recording, or by any information storage and retrieval system, without permission in writing from the publishers.

Library of Congress Cataloging-in-Publication Data
Meltzer, David J.
    Search for the first Americans / by David J. Meltzer.
        p. cm. -- (Exploring the ancient world)
    Includes bibliographical references and index.
    ISBN 0-89599-035-0
    1. Indians--Origin. 2. Paleo-Indians. 3. Indians--History.
4. America--Antiquities. I. Title. II. Series.
E61.M398   1993
970.01--dc20   93-29453
                                      CIP

Manufactured and printed in Canada.
First Edition

10 9 8 7 6 5 4 3 2 1

FRONT COVER PHOTO: *The cast of a tool found at the Murray Springs site in Arizona, this implement is believed to have been made from mammoth bone and used to straighten the foreshafts of spears.*

BACK COVER PHOTO: *This Clovis point, discovered at the East Wenatchee site in Washington State, is made of agate, perhaps from the Columbia River gravels.*

CONTENTS

EDITOR'S FOREWORD

The questions of who peopled the New World, when, and how, have generated much interest and considerable controversy for more than two centuries—theories argued by Thomas Jefferson and his contemporaries are still debated today. Even though, as readers will see in the pages that follow, there currently is some scholarly agreement about answers to the "who" and "how" questions, the question of "when" is just as contentious now—if not more so—than it was in the last century. This volume by Professor David Meltzer thus addresses one of today's most active archaeological debates.

In keeping with the rationale of the *Exploring the Ancient World* series, Professor Meltzer describes the history of the search for the first inhabitants of the Americas and puts readers at the cutting edge of modern archaeological thinking. Readers will learn not only where the field has been, but also where it is today and where it appears to be going. Discoveries at controversial sites throughout the Americas—Monte Verde and Meadowcroft Rockshelter, for instance—are analyzed and assessed, and the implications of the acceptance or rejection of their early dates are explored. Moreover, Professor Meltzer's discussion goes well beyond narrow questions such as "Which is the oldest archaeological site in the Americas?" to examine the nature of the environments which the early inhabitants of the New World confronted and the different means by which the first Native Americans adapted to and exploited these varied and changing environments, as well as to elucidate the broader cultural lifeways of these people. The archaeological record left by these early hunters and gatherers is carefully outlined by Professor Meltzer, and the methods used by scholars to date and interpret this record are clearly presented. In addition, the strengths and weaknesses of different approaches are critically but judiciously appraised.

Given the widely disparate and highly partisan nature of much of the literature on the early settlement of the Americas, general readers will not find a more readable, succinct, and level-headed discussion of the state of the art of archaeological thinking on the first Native Americans than this volume, nor will they find a more intellectually stimulating and provocative interpretation of current data on the topic than that provided by Professor Meltzer. The scholarship that forms the foundation of this book is obviously quite wide-ranging and impressive.

Professor Meltzer is eminently qualified to write this book. He is an Associate Professor of Anthropology at Southern Methodist University and received his doctorate from the University of Washington. He is internationally recognized as an authority on the first inhabitants of the New World, and has published widely on both that subject and the history of American archaeology. Professor Meltzer also is the co-editor of several books, including *Environments and Extinctions*, *American Archaeology: Past and Future*, *The Archaeology of William Henry Holmes*, and *The first Americans: search and research*. He is particularly appreciated by his colleagues as a scholar who can provide a fair overview of the debates on the peopling of the Americas and is not viewed as a partisan polemicist.

This book is especially exciting to me because it places its discussion of the settling of the New World in a variety of contexts—the intellectual history of the scholarly debate surrounding the topic, the broad development of Native American cultures until the time of European invasions, and the environment at the close of the Pleistocene Age. Moreover, it provides readers with criteria with which to judge claims for early sites, claims that frequently appear on the front pages of the local newspapers or in national magazines.

The book also allows readers to share the fascination of this rapidly changing area of interest and gives them insights into the thought processes of the principal archaeologists involved in the scholarly debates. Finally, it shows how these disputations are not esoteric dead-ends, but are relevant to current concerns about European impacts on Native American populations and the great demographic tragedy that occurred in the Americas after Columbus' voyages.

Jeremy A. Sabloff
University of Pittsburgh

IN THE END

In November 1519, Hernán Cortés and his army marched into the Aztec capital of Tenochtitlán—now Mexico City—and quietly seized its ruler, Moctezuma. Cortés commanded the uneasy city for six months, before hastening away to meet an armed force under his would-be rival Pánfilo de Narváez. Spanish authorities had sent Narváez to arrest Cortés, whom they suspected of undue profiteering. Left in charge of an unsavory lieutenant during Cortés' absence, Tenochtitlán erupted in battle, sparked by the Spaniards' unprovoked slaughter of 600 unarmed worshippers in the latter part of May 1520. The natives, led by Moctezuma's brother Cuitlahuac, pinned down the resident Spanish force and were on the verge of annihilating it.

Cortés defeated Narváez, then hurried back to Tenochtitlán as soon as he heard of his soldiers' desperate plight. He reentered the city on June 24, 1520 with 1250 Spaniards—including many of Narváez' men—and 8000 allied native (Tlaxcalan) warriors. Seven days later Cortés and his forces were decisively beaten and forced to flee under cover of darkness after suffering dreadful casualties. With the tattered remains of his small army—the Spanish adventurer lost perhaps two-thirds of his men—Cortés retreated from the Valley of Mexico, taking refuge with friendly natives on the far side of the mountains flanking Tenochtitlán.

Despite the devastating defeat, Cortés returned to lay siege to Tenochtitlán within the year and, after another round of bloody battles, conquered the Aztec state. It was an astonishing victory against overwhelming numbers, coming so close on the heels of utter disaster. How did Cortés manage it? Some point to his superior weaponry and horses, and the surprise and terror these created in foes who had seen neither. Others speak of his missionary zeal, his courage, and military genius—including the use of naval power on inland Lake Texcoco.

Zeal and courage Cortés had in abundance, but then so did his adversaries. They did not possess his weaponry, but did firearms, a dozen cannon, and a couple of dozen horses really make the difference? Hardly. Cortés' arms advantage certainly hadn't helped him much that last disastrous week in June 1520. Besides, once the tactical surprise of such weapons wore off—as it very quickly did—the Aztecs with their large numbers and razor-sharp obsidian weapons (soon mounted on long pikes to disable horsemen) were at least a match for the Spaniards.

Moctezuma, the Aztec ruler of
Tenochtitlán, was captured by Hernán
Cortés in 1519. Six months later the
Aztecs roundly defeated the Spaniards.
But the diseases brought to the New
World by Cortés and his soldiers
devastated the Aztecs and within a
year they were unable to hold out
against the Spanish.

Cortés may indeed have been a great general, but what brought him victory at Tenochtitlán was neither strategy nor tactics. It was smallpox, considered nothing more than a childhood disease back in Europe. One of Narváez' men was infected, and once the disease took root amongst the natives it spread with such indiscriminate force that it decimated the Aztec population, young and old. While Cortés and his beaten troops were licking their wounds in the late summer of 1520, smallpox claimed Cuitlahuac and a host of other Aztec leaders. They never knew what hit them. By the time Cortés regrouped and returned in the spring of 1521, the pestilence had wracked Tenochtitlán. The siege was merely the final blow. The city fell.

The fall of Tenochtitlán was unusual, but only because the devastation by introduced epidemics was so militarily decisive. What was not unusual at all was the appalling effect of Old World diseases on New World peoples. Over the next few centuries Native American groups were repeatedly decimated by waves of smallpox, measles, influenza, plague, and other introduced epidemic diseases against which they had little, if any, immunity. Indeed, it has been said that in the four centuries after Columbus more Native Americans died every year from European diseases than were born. Overstatement, maybe.

But we now know, quite certainly, that these imported pathogens caused native deaths in fearful numbers—mortality across the continent may have ranged upward from 75 percent to well over 90 percent of the native population.

The immediate cause of this post-Columbian population disaster was that native peoples lacked immunity to European diseases. But why was this so? Why were Native Americans of all ages so vulnerable to European childhood diseases? Why had they no epidemic diseases of their own, diseases that might even have devastated Europeans and checked their advance into America?

The answers to these questions have little to do with events after 1492. They have a great deal to do with events that took place well before 1492.

They have everything to do, in fact, with the story of the first Americans, which began more than 11,500 years ago.

Sunset gilds the view to Siberia over the Krusenstern Lagoon and Chukchi Sea, near Cape Krusenstern, Alaska. Near this place, some 11,500 years ago, a band of travelers may have been the first to cross the land bridge from Asia into North America.

1

OVERTURE

Sometime before 11,500 years ago, a group of hardy Stone Age Siberian hunter-gatherers pushed eastward over a vast northern steppe, slipped across the unmarked border separating the Old World from the New, and one day found themselves in an infinitely trackless land. It was a world rich in plant and animal communities that became ever more exotic as the wayfarers moved south. It was a world where great beasts lumbered past on their way to extinction, where climates were frigidly cold and extraordinarily mild. In their New World, glaciers extended to the horizons, the Bering Sea was dry land, the Great Lakes had not yet been born, and the ancestral Great Salt Lake was about to die.

But the first humans to set foot in America were surely unaware of what they had achieved: Alaska looked little different from their Siberian homeland and there were hardly any barriers separating the two.

Even so, that relatively unassuming event, the move eastward from Siberia to Alaska and the turn south that followed, is one of the great triumphs of human prehistory, and one of the great questions and controversies of American archaeology. Those first Americans could little imagine our intense interest in their accomplishment thousands of years later, and would almost certainly be puzzled at how the details of their coming sparked a wide-ranging, bitter, and long-playing controversy (now in its fifth century!) that ranks among the greatest in anthropology and perhaps in all the sciences.

Here are the bare and least controversial facts of the case. The first Americans successfully colonized the last remaining major continent of the earth. They did so during the Pleistocene or Ice Age, a time when the New World appeared vastly different than it does today. Tilts and wobbles in the earth's spin, axis, and orbit reduced the amount of incoming solar radiation, cooling Northern Hemisphere climates and triggering glacial growth. Immense ice sheets almost two miles (three kilometers) high, blanketing the northern reaches of the continent and high mountains throughout the mid-latitudes, changed the climate and environment in still more profound ways.

While it was colder during the Ice Age, winters across much of the land paradoxically were warmer. The jet stream, displaced southward by glacial ice, brought rainfall and freshwater lakes to what is now western desert, and today's Great Lakes were then mere soft spots in bedrock that were being excavated by millions of tons of glacial ice grinding slowly overhead. Rivers cut deep to meet oceans and seas that had fallen 325 to 500 feet (100 to 150 meters), and were then hundreds of miles beyond modern shorelines.

A whole zoo of giant mammals, soon to become extinct, roamed this landscape. There were the American elephants—the woolly mammoth and the mastodon—ground sloths, measuring nearly 20 feet (6 meters) and weighing upwards of 3 tons, and dozens of other plant eaters including the exotic glyptodont, a clumsy and slow-moving mammal encased in a giant turtle-like carapace, weighing upwards of a ton, and bearing an uncanny resemblance to a 1966 Volkswagen. Feeding on these herbivores were a gang of formidable predators: huge lions, sabertooth tigers, and giant bears. All of these mammals were part of a richly mixed faunal community in which Arctic species browsed and grazed side by side with animals of the forests and plains.

This was no fixed stage. From 18,000 years ago, at the frigid depths of the most recent glacial period, until 10,000 years ago when the Pleistocene came to a close, the climate, environment, landscapes, and seascapes of America were

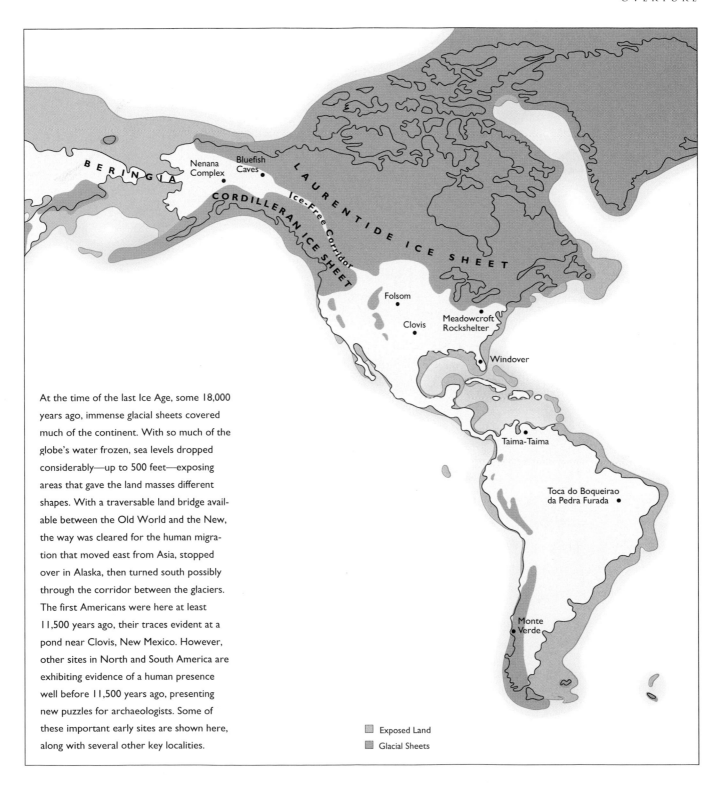

At the time of the last Ice Age, some 18,000 years ago, immense glacial sheets covered much of the continent. With so much of the globe's water frozen, sea levels dropped considerably—up to 500 feet—exposing areas that gave the land masses different shapes. With a traversable land bridge available between the Old World and the New, the way was cleared for the human migration that moved east from Asia, stopped over in Alaska, then turned south possibly through the corridor between the glaciers. The first Americans were here at least 11,500 years ago, their traces evident at a pond near Clovis, New Mexico. However, other sites in North and South America are exhibiting evidence of a human presence well before 11,500 years ago, presenting new puzzles for archaeologists. Some of these important early sites are shown here, along with several other key localities.

Exposed Land
Glacial Sheets

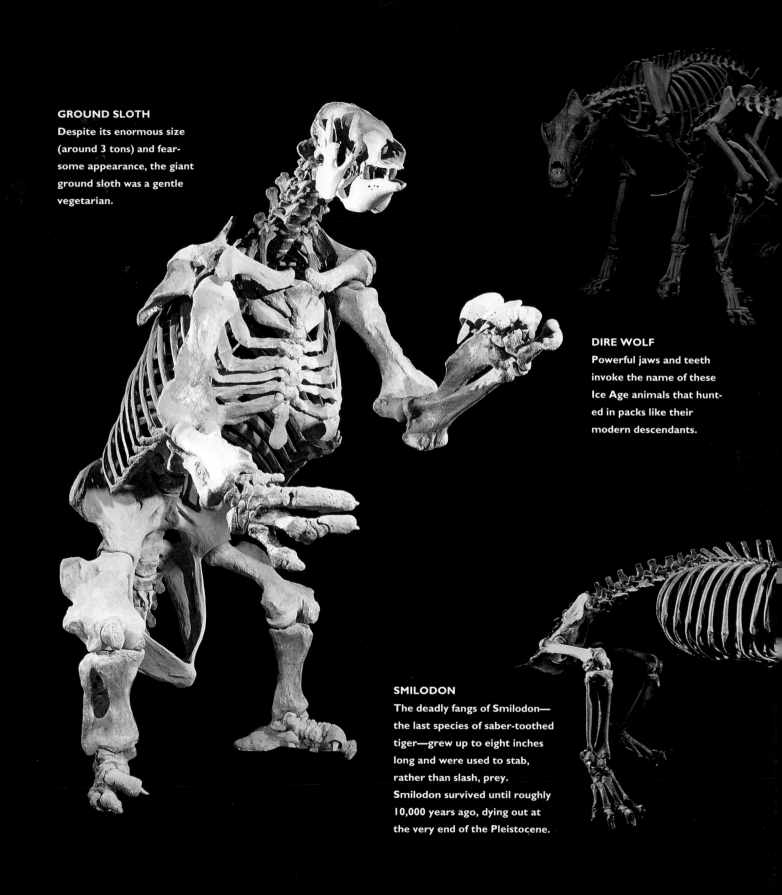

GROUND SLOTH
Despite its enormous size (around 3 tons) and fearsome appearance, the giant ground sloth was a gentle vegetarian.

DIRE WOLF
Powerful jaws and teeth invoke the name of these Ice Age animals that hunted in packs like their modern descendants.

SMILODON
The deadly fangs of Smilodon—the last species of saber-toothed tiger—grew up to eight inches long and were used to stab, rather than slash, prey. Smilodon survived until roughly 10,000 years ago, dying out at the very end of the Pleistocene.

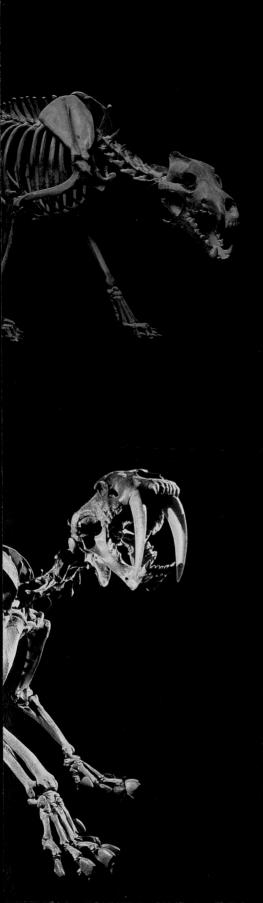

changing. Many changes were imperceptible on a human scale, others not. Certainly, however, the world of the first Americans was unlike anything experienced by human beings on this continent since that remote time.

But precisely when did the first Americans enter the scene? Here is where the controversy begins. In 1927, after centuries of speculation and 40 years or so of intense debate, archaeologists finally demonstrated that the first Americans had arrived during the Pleistocene. As best matters could then be determined these Paleoindians, so named to recognize their great antiquity, arrived during the final millennia of the Ice Age. The oldest Paleoindians, the Clovis groups (named for the New Mexico town near which their artifacts were first recovered), possessed a distinctive stone-tool technology. Their artifacts were found across North America, while signatures of their technology were spotted on artifacts scattered through South America, as far distant as Tierra del Fuego.

The precise antiquity of the Clovis Paleoindians would have to wait on chemist Willard Libby's Nobel Prize-winning development of radiocarbon dating in the 1950s. But by the early 1960s, the Clovis occupation was securely fixed at between 11,000 and 11,500 years before present (hereafter, B.P.). The dates could not have been better. They coincided beautifully with the breakup of the northern ice sheets that, it was widely believed, had jammed the migration route of the first Americans and had forced them to lay over in Alaska.

By the early 1950s there were already indications of a much earlier human presence in America. Those hints would become broader as the years went by, until today scores of purportedly ancient sites have appeared, some with estimated ages upwards of 200,000 years. Each new candidate for great antiquity brings with it fresh claims, but the outcome remains the same. Skeptics ask hard questions. Debate ensues. The claim is accepted by some, rejected by others, while the remainder wait and see. So far at least, the Clovis barrier remains intact. A pre-11,500 B.P. human presence in America does not now exist.

Still, there may be cracks in the Clovis wall. Sites are now appearing—some in far South America—with the best evidence yet for a human presence in the Americas before 11,500 years ago. The age of these sites ranges from 13,500 B.P. to upwards of 48,000 B.P., but even if they are no older than their youngest date, they demand reckoning. For no matter how fast the first Americans traveled, and they may have traveled very fast, they could not have arrived in southern South America 2000 years before they left Alaska.

The antiquity of the first Americans captures our attention, and is a lightning rod for controversy, but our inquiries go well beyond this question. Where, we also ask, did the first Americans come from? What triggered their migration? What routes did they travel and what obstacles did they overcome to reach this land? Was the initial peopling of the New World accomplished by a single hardy band, or were there multiple migratory pulses?

If Clovis Paleoindians were the first Americans, then they colonized the length and breadth of the hemisphere in a matter of a few hundred years.

That's a stunning achievement for any human group, but especially one of hunter-gatherers in a novel and exotic setting. What was life like in Ice Age America? What adaptive strategies keyed their colonization of continents as complex and diverse in habitat and landscape as North and South America?

Understanding Paleoindian adaptive strategies has even more than the usual significance, because of the still-unexplained events that happened on their watch. The first Americans were witness to the extinction, by 10,800 years ago, of that extraordinary zoo of large mammals—some 35 separate genera. All seemingly vanished in a geological instant from a landscape where they had thrived for tens and hundreds of thousands of years.

Those extinctions were, of course, coincident with the end of the Pleistocene. Surely the climatic and ecological changes that marked that event are sufficient to explain this massive extinction. Perhaps. But isn't it odd, if ecological changes triggered extinctions, that the horse, which disappeared from North America at the end of the Pleistocene, flourished on the very same ground when reintroduced by the Spaniards 10,000 years later? Isn't it odd too that the plants comprising the diet of the western giant ground sloths would today be common outside the very caves these animals once frequented and long after they became extinct?

Could it be mere coincidence that such attractive game animals vanished just about the time the first Americans arrived? Hardly, accusing voices have declared. The first Americans are charged with killing or, more properly, overkilling—the Pleistocene megafauna.

If they did so, then the first Americans behaved unlike any other known hunter-gatherer groups before or since. Yet we do not know what members of our own species—*Homo sapiens sapiens*—might have done on a virgin landscape teeming with game never before hunted by human predators. Perhaps the rules that govern hunter-gatherers in other times and places do not apply here. The first Americans were unique in many ways—this may be another.

The effort to understand the prehistory of the first Americans—just what they were up to, and what they were responsible for—traditionally has been the bailiwick of archaeologists, with help from Pleistocene geologists. Archaeology provides the direct record of the first Americans' artifacts and structures, their subsistence activities and settlement systems, as well as the number, nature, and timing of their migrations into the New World and their adaptations once here. Above all, it is from archaeological sites that we obtain the essential materials—charcoal, bone, shell, soil—by which we can determine, through a variety of dating techniques, their antiquity.

Pleistocene geologists, from whose ranks many early American archaeologists were drawn, in turn contribute vital data relating to the landscape of the first Americans. Our knowledge of the Ice Age stems from their fieldwork and laboratory studies, and from them we understand the environments traversed and the ecological challenges faced by the first Americans.

PREVIOUS PAGE: **Unaware of the significance of their journey at least 11,500 years ago, a small band of Asian hunter-gatherers crossed the land bridge into unknown territory.**

Yet the days of scientific hegemony are long past. Archaeologists and geologists have relinquished their exclusive claim to the study of the first Americans (and we did so graciously, with only modest grumbling about scientific poaching, and only when the interlopers deserved it!). Today, linguists, physical anthropologists, and molecular biologists are also major players in the field.

And for good reason. While archaeological evidence speaks directly to the questions of when, where, and how the first people came to the Americas, it struggles mightily with the question of who these people were, and precisely how they relate to contemporary Native American populations. The non-archaeological evidence promises to complete the circle between the most ancient Americans and the most modern. By grouping together similarities in the words and grammar of many hundreds of modern native languages, similarities in nuclear and non-nuclear DNA (deoxyribonucleic acid), and similarities among attributes from prehistoric and historic teeth, it should be possible to unravel the complex relationships and ancestry of modern native peoples, and then go the next step and infer the number and timing of their ancestors' migrations to the New World.

It hasn't been easy. Compounding the evidence has also compounded the controversy. Besides archaeologists arguing amongst themselves, we have linguists, physical anthropologists, and geneticists haggling amongst themselves, and all of us arguing with one another. There is a good reason for that, too. On this question of questions, linguists, physical anthropologists, and geneticists speak with no more unanimity than archaeologists, nor is it easy to bring together such radically different kinds of evidence. Not that we haven't tried.

One group of linguists, for example, argues that all native languages fall into just three broad families, the descendants of three separate migrations to America. Some physical anthropologists and geneticists, looking at their own data agree and, measuring the linguistic, dental, and genetic distance among the different groups, even arrive at an estimate of the relative order and absolute age of each migration.

Yet any hoped for convergence among these independent lines of evidence is short-lived, dissolving in the face of harsh criticism from within and without. In the end, we have many scenarios for the number, relative timing, and antiquity of migrations to America, and no easy choice among them.

Ultimately, much of the dispute over the first Americans, and many of the questions we ask about them, would evaporate if we could at least resolve when they arrived. Since the North American landscape and climate changed so dramatically in the millennia before 11,500 years ago, knowing when they arrived would help identify what routes they may have taken (certain routes were not available at certain times), and the kinds of environmental challenges they faced as they crossed into the Americas and began to settle down. Knowing when they arrived would help calibrate rates of genetic, dental, and linguistic change, and determine the speed with which Paleoindians—or their distinctive

Early Americans left evidence of their presence over a long period of time at the Meadowcroft Rockshelter, near Pittsburgh, Pennsylvania. Artifacts have been unearthed at the cave that may date back as far as 14,250 B.P.

technology—spread across the continent. It might even clear them of wrong-doing in Pleistocene extinctions.

But the question of when, though easily asked, has stubbornly defied an easy answer for a very long time. Attempts to answer the question quickly become entangled in disputes over the site's artifacts, geology, and dates, disputes that spiral into point-counterpoint matches that run without closure, ending untidily only when the participants (or journal editors) weary of them.

Remarkably—given all the heat—the implications of a pre-11,500-year-old migration are important but not necessarily profound. Knowing that the first Americans may have arrived 14,250 years ago, as the artifacts deep within Meadowcroft Rockshelter, near Pittsburgh, Pennsylvania, suggest, only tells us that American prehistory is a few thousand years older than we used to think. If that's the case, we will need to adjust the way we think about the first Americans; for example, about how fast they moved across the landscape and how long it took for specific evolutionary and technological changes to occur.

Antiquity on the order of a Meadowcroft, or even of Chile's Monte Verde site (at its earliest, perhaps 33,000 years old), will not radically alter our understanding of human evolution. But if the first Americans arrived 200,000 years ago, as those excavating the Calico site, near Yermo, California, have claimed, the ante is upped considerably. We have long assumed, and have no reason to doubt, that the Americas were colonized by our own species, *Homo sapiens sapiens*. Yet, 200,000 years ago *Homo sapiens sapiens* were only first emerging on the African Plains, and were nowhere near Eastern Asia, let alone Siberia or America. If Calico's evidence is valid, then either our hard-won understanding of human evolution is wrong, and our species appeared earlier and spread faster than we have ever thought, or else the Americas were indeed colonized by evolutionarily earlier humans (for which we have never found any evidence). That is, if Calico is valid (an issue to which we shall later return).

Antiquity on the order of a Calico site is, however, more the exception than the rule. Mostly, the debate concerns sites declared to be a few thousand to a few tens of thousands of years older than the earliest accepted date of 11,500 B.P. At any rate, there is no reason the first Americans could not have arrived well before 11,500 years ago, nor why this is anything but a low stakes claim in the grand scheme of our understanding of human history on the globe.

Curiously, this controversy over deep human antiquity is uniquely American. Archaeologists here have long looked with interest—envy, too—at the study of the first Australians. We are interested because of the strong similarities in the prehistory of the two continents. As Australian archaeologist John Beaton reminds us, both continents were colonized about the same time from East Asia by highly mobile people possessing stone-age technologies, who found new and fantastic landscapes with naive native fauna, and who apparently spread quickly through virtually the entire land mass.

We are envious because of the very different archaeological history of each continent. It has been more than 60 years since we first demonstrated a late Pleistocene arrival date for the first Americans, but since that time the first Americans have grown no older. A late Pleistocene human presence was first documented in Australia in 1965. In just the last 28 years the first Australians have grown older in 10,000 year jumps—their antiquity now hovers around 35,000 years ago, and may settle at 50,000 years B.P. Now, consider the circumstances. In the American Southwest alone, there may be as many archaeologists at work as in the whole continent of Australia. And in any one year there is more earth moved and more ancient deposits exposed in America than in many years in Australia. Yet, the antiquity of the first Australians has been pushed back quickly, easily, and without controversy. Does this imply the first Americans will grow no older? Some would certainly think so.

Or consider the situation in Africa. Humanity's earliest fossils and oldest stone artifacts come from there. Those simple and primitive tools are the first tangible evidence of the stirring of human culture, what would ultimately distinguish us from all other life on this planet. Just three decades ago such artifacts were a respectable 2 million years old. Since then, still older finds have been made, and the antiquity of human tool making has been pushed back in time in breathtaking 100,000 year plunges, back as far as 2.6 million years ago. And again, it all happened with nary a murmur of protest.

Why is it that folding back the prehistoric envelope of the very first human behavior in Africa half a million years generates no controversy, while the announcement of the Meadowcroft radiocarbon dates—a scant 3000 years older than we expect—are met with profound skepticism? Why is it that the controversy persists in the face of an impressive array of converging evidence from

This unusually large example of a Clovis point was found at the East Wenatchee site in Washington State. Clovis points are named after the New Mexico site where they were first discovered in 1932. Since that time these projectile points have been found all over North America. Generally made from fine-grained or glass-like stone, such as obsidian, chert, or chalcedony, the points were three to four inches long and highly practical when used as points or knives. This particular point is of agate, perhaps from the Columbia River gravels.

fields as diverse as linguistics, genetics, physical anthropology, and Pleistocene geology—as well as archaeology? Why does the question remain unresolved in the face of a regular crop of purportedly ancient assemblages and archaeological sites, and an almost annual harvest of books and papers on the topic? Why all the fuss?

There are a number of reasons, not the least of which is that the origin and antiquity of the first Americans is a scientific problem in which opinion far outpaces, and often outweighs, the meager available facts. In any science, disagreement always moves in quickly to fill the void between fact and opinion.

And this is a problem compounded by too many false alarms. Scores of sites have been advertised as possessing great antiquity. But on closer inspection, each has failed to live up to its advance billing. *Caveat emptor.* Archaeologists have long memories—it's part of our business, after all—so it is hardly surprising that under such circumstances any and all new claims for great antiquity in the Americas are met with skepticism bordering on cynicism. The response may not be commendable, but it is understandable.

Then too, this is a scientific problem that is fundamentally under-determined. We cannot identify, let alone control, all the essential variables that might lead to a solution. Compounding this lack of control, University of Kentucky archaeologist Tom Dillehay argues, is the nature of archaeological research. We destroy our data in the process of recovering it, making replication and confirmation of findings no easy task. And so controversy over the first Americans will likely always be with us.

Recognizing this essential fact, the story of the first Americans told here will be two interlocking stories. The first is the story of what we know of the first Americans—about when we think they arrived, and how. About the climatic and ecological conditions of the terrain they traveled and the landscape they encountered. About their adaptive responses to the challenges of an Ice Age world. About the speed with which they moved across their world. About their effect on the native fauna of the Americas, and about the evolutionary processes and pathways they blazed in American prehistory.

The other is the story of how we know what we know about the first Americans. It is about the methods and techniques archaeologists, geologists, linguists, physical anthropologists, and geneticists are bringing to bear on the problem. About why archaeologists are in the best position to know something about the number and timing of migrations to America, but as yet cannot say, and why non-archaeologists are in a position to say something on that score, but as yet cannot know. It is about why, despite evidence from so many fields, fundamental disputes over the first Americans stubbornly resist resolution.

This is also the story of why these questions about the first Americans are among the most controversial in American archaeology. But before telling the stories, we first need to set the Pleistocene stage, then tour the environments in which initial migration and colonization occurred.

Like a bumpy white highway, Alaska's Mendenhall Glacier stretches into the distance. Some 20,000 years ago, two even more enormous ice sheets world's water locked up as ice, sea levels fell, exposing a land bridge between Siberia and Alaska over which the first Americans likely crossed.

covered much of North America. With much of the

2

THE GREAT ROUTE

In a scene akin to Dante's *Inferno*, candles and torchlight flickered over a thousand rapt faces in a smoky underground cavern. It was early Victorian England, the summer of 1839, and the masses huddling in the dank chamber were listening intently to a lecture on geology. A German chemist witnessing the event was dumbfounded: by the speaker, the Reverend William Buckland, professor of geology at the University of Oxford, in top hat and academic robes; by the audience that had been cramped in those

The Reverend Dr. William Buckland, professor of geology at Oxford University and Dean of Westminster, propounded a decidedly theological and chauvinistic view of both nature and geology.

Swiss geologist Louis Agassiz was the first to propose, in 1837, that much of Europe had been covered by glaciers during an ice age.

close quarters for hours; and especially by Buckland's jingoistic message that God had heaped iron and coal near the earth's surface in order to make Britain the richest nation in the world. Small wonder that when he finally finished, Reverend Dr. William Buckland led his listeners back to daylight singing *God Save the Queen*.

Buckland's theological view of Nature was not unusual in early 19th century geology. Nor, particularly, was the fact that he saw far more in God's "other" works—those written in the earth—than just patriotic pap. Geology, it appeared, bore silent witness to one of the most dramatic of all the Biblical events. There were "immense deposits of gravel," Buckland reported, throughout England, Northern Europe, and North America. He was certain these gravels were water borne, and this "diluvium" must have come from "a transient deluge, affecting universally, simultaneously, and at no very distant period, the entire surface of our planet." When? Five or six thousand years ago, he felt, judging by the condition of animal bones embedded within the diluvium. And this was not just any flood. It was Noah's.

Granted, the gravels lacked the remains of those human beings who had perished in the flood, and in retrospect Buckland's Cambridge counterpart, Adam Sedgwick, admitted that that fact alone should have given Buckland pause. Nevertheless, the Oxford scholar found an explanation for the absence of human bones: In Noah's time humans lived only in the "Asiatic" region. Their remains did not belong in the diluvium of northern latitudes.

As it happens, Buckland was doubly wrong. There were human remains in the diluvium (as we will see in Chapter 3); and the diluvium was not the result of a universal flood.

AGASSIZ IN THE ALPS
Inhabitants of the Swiss Alps had long been familiar with the way their giant mountain-top tongues of ice moved, leaving gravelly trails of debris in their wake. In the 1830s, Swiss geologist Jean de Charpentier had codified a glacier's telltale signs: scored and smoothed bedrock, piles of gravel debris (tills and moraines), and boulders that had moved great distances (erratics).

Then, a one-time student of de Charpentier's, fossil fish expert Louis Agassiz, went a step farther. Agassiz saw those distinctive glacial signs—on a much larger scale—far below Alpine valleys, on the low-lying plains of Northern Europe. Without question, the presence there of erratics and moraines spoke just as clearly of glaciers as they did when found alongside mountain glaciers. And what they told was that an immense, unbroken sheet of ice had once covered the whole Northern Hemisphere. "Since I saw the glaciers," Agassiz crowed in 1838, "I am quite of a snowy humor, and will have the whole surface of the earth covered with ice."

Although glaciation was not quite as extensive as he thought, in the main Agassiz was correct, and Buckland proved a willing convert, happily giving up

Geologists in the mid-1800s soon learned to recognize the telltale signs left by advancing or retreating glaciers. Glacial erratics, huge boulders that have been moved great distances *(above left)*, and striations and gravel debris *(above right)* were quickly accepted as having been left by moving ice sheets. But since one moving glacier eradicates signs of a previous one, concurrence on how many glacial episodes there had been took another hundred years.

his floods for glaciers. Soon, Agassiz' Ice Age was linked with the Pleistocene epoch of the eminent Scottish geologist, Sir Charles Lyell. Lyell's Pleistocene, a geological period independently defined by fossil shells, seemed to correspond perfectly with Agassiz' glaciers.

Almost immediately, in 1839, traces of the Ice Age were spotted by American paleontologist Timothy Abbott Conrad in western New York. By the 1870s, American geologists realized that layers of plant material sandwiched between sheets of glacial till, and the differential weathering of moraines, were clues that there had been multiple episodes of glacial advance and retreat within the Ice Age itself. The Glacial Division of the United States Geological Survey (USGS), under the aegis of Thomas C. Chamberlin, spent the last decades of the 19th century and first decades of the 20th century mapping and naming those separate episodes. Some resisted the USGS efforts: Oberlin College geologist and theologian, the Reverend George Frederick Wright, doggedly insisted there had been but a single glaciation. His was a losing cause, but its aftershocks rocked the early debates over the first Americans.

Discerning the number of glacial episodes proved no easy task, given the unfortunate tendency of later glaciers to bulldoze traces of earlier ones. Nonetheless, by the turn of the century four distinct glacial stages, separated by long interglacials (warm periods), had been identified. The names given to the stages identify places where the deposits left behind by these episodes are especially well represented. They were, beginning with the oldest, the Nebraskan, followed by the Aftonian interglacial; Kansan, followed by the Yarmouth interglacial; Illinoian, followed by the Sangamon interglacial; and the Wisconsin, followed by the Holocene interglacial, which we are now in.

DANCES WITH PLANETS

Just as the four-stage model of Pleistocene glaciation was embraced, Milutin Milankovitch, a Serbian mathematician, laid the groundwork to render it

In 1911, Serbian mathematician Milutin Milankovitch began work on creating a mathematical model of global climates. He spent decades attempting to reconstruct on paper the variations in climate that had taken place across space and time. His goal was to link his record of the changes in solar radiation to periods of glaciation. His model demonstrated that the number of glacial episodes during the Pleistocene far exceeded what had been previously acknowledged. ·

obsolete. In 1911, Milankovitch set himself the intimidating goal of creating a mathematical model of the world's climates. Well-meaning colleagues tried to dissuade him. Who needs a model when weather stations around the globe provide actual data? Milankovitch paid them no mind. With a model, he would be able to predict climatic variation across space, and perhaps even through time, both future and past.

Driving the earth's climates, Milankovitch knew, was solar radiation, or insolation. Insolation varies by latitude and season, as the relative position of the earth and the sun shift over the annual cycle. It also varies over much longer time spans. As the earth orbits in the Newtonian cotillion around the sun, it is jostled by the gravitational tug of the sun and other planets. That jostling alters the shape or eccentricity of the earth's orbit, the tilt of the earth's axis, and the precession of the equinox (which varies as the earth wobbles on its axis, like a top, and the elliptical orbit of the earth rotates). These variables are altered in predictable cycles. Over a 100,000-year period, eccentricity ranges from a near perfect circle to something closer to an ellipse; in 41,000-year cycles the earth's tilt swings between $21.8°$ and $24.4°$ (it is now at $23.5°$). Equinoxes shift completely every 22,000 years or so (winters in the Northern Hemisphere today occur when the earth is closest to the sun, but in the past have occurred when the earth was farthest from the sun).

Long before computers made such efforts commonplace, Milankovitch tackled the task of calculating changes in insolation (by season and latitude) over very long periods of time as a function of such orbital cycles. The work took him decades, though he worked away at it steadily—even while a prisoner of war in late 1914. Milankovitch, a non-combatant, had been captured by the Austro-Hungarian army while visiting his hometown, but was released soon thereafter when sympathetic colleagues in Budapest learned of his plight.

All along, Milankovitch aimed to tie the record of changing insolation to glacial episodes. The link, he and others realized, lay in changes of summer insolation at high latitudes. Glaciers are created and fed by snow that, by slightly melting, condensing, and recrystallizing, becomes ice. A glacier rises depending partly upon how much snow accumulates during the winter, but mainly on how much is lost by melting the following summer. When summer insolation is reduced and temperatures are cooler, snow from the previous winter stays frozen on the ground. The next winter, more snow accumulates and builds the mass higher. If it does not melt back the subsequent summer, the mass grows even larger the following winter. And so the process continues. That accumulating mass of snow is steadily converted into dense glacial ice, and begins to move (from a few inches to a few yards a day).

Milankovitch's detailed calculations identified times in the past when lowered summer insolation favored glacial growth. But his model called for dozens of glacial episodes over the Pleistocene, when geologists had found only four. The discrepancy turned out to be more apparent than real, with the blame

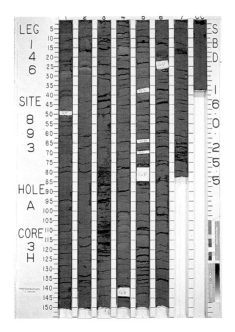

The advent of deep sea drilling and coring technology brought answers to some of the questions of prehistoric climate. Samples, such as the one at top brought up from the sea bed in the Santa Barbara Basin, span thousands of years of history and provide a detailed record of glacial and interglacial cycles—complete with evidence of natural phenomena. Skeletal remains of planktonic animals called foraminifera, above, also are found in the cores and provide readings on the composition of ancient seawater.

squarely at the doorstep of the geological record. Successive advances of ice had obliterated previous glacial traces more than anyone had ever realized. Just how many glacial advances had occurred on land would be learned in, of all places, the ocean deep.

Seawater molecules have two isotopic forms of oxygen—a light form (^{16}O) and a heavier form (^{18}O). When seawater returns to the clouds as vapor, it contains a greater proportion of ^{16}O, simply because these lighter water molecules evaporate more readily. During non-glacial periods the moisture in the clouds that falls over land is relatively quickly returned to the ocean. But when the water that falls on land becomes frozen in massive glaciers, the ocean becomes progressively depleted of the lighter water molecules. Thus, the relative amount of ^{16}O to ^{18}O in the oceans provides a measure of how much ^{16}O-rich water molecules are locked up on land (^{18}O-to-^{16}O ratios are largely driven by ice volume, but to a lesser degree—so far unknown—may also reflect water temperature). But how can we know the relative proportion of these light and heavy water molecules of the past?

Within the calcareous skeletons of the planktonic animals called foraminifera, oxygen is fixed in proportion to the ^{18}O-to-^{16}O composition of seawater at the time the organisms were alive. Sediment cores extracted from the sea floor containing foraminifera's skeletal remains thus provide a history of relative changes in oxygen-isotope ratios, and hence of ice volume on land. These deep-sea cores record at least 10 major glacial-interglacial episodes (of varying intensity) over the last one million years alone, and probably as many as 15 to 20 over the entire Pleistocene.

The timing of these glacial-interglacial events roughly matches the cycles predicted by the Milankovitch theory, with enough variance in the details to suggest that other factors are at work, and thus to challenge the next generation of climatologists. Milankovitch's orbital-driven insolation changes proved to be the ultimate force behind Agassiz' continental glaciation. But Agassiz' Ice Age and Lyell's Pleistocene, tightly bound since the 1840s, must now go their separate ways. Glaciation began some 2.5 million years B.P.; the Pleistocene—as Lyell defined it—began only 1.65 million years B.P. Strictly speaking, the Pleistocene covers only the latter part of the Ice Age.

And what of the traditional four glacial stages? These turn out to have been based on a hodgepodge of debris from many glaciers of different ages. The younger stages (such as the Illinoian and Wisconsin) retain some currency, insofar as they can be linked with specific isotope stages. Still, even the Wisconsin encompasses three oxygen-isotope stages which are correlated, but not coincident, with glaciation:

1) Early Wisconsin, isotope Stage 4, a cooler period marking the onset of this last major glacial episode (80,000 to 65,000 B.P.);

2) Middle Wisconsin, isotope Stage 3, a relatively warmer period, with glaciers much reduced (65,000 to 35,000 B.P.);

3) Late Wisconsin, isotope Stage 2, with expanded glaciers that reached a maximum between 20,000 and 18,000 years ago (35,000 to 10,000 B.P.).

With the final retreat of Late Wisconsin ice, our present-day interglacial—the Holocene (isotope Stage 1)—began. We remain in it today.

A STAGE FOR THE FIRST AMERICANS

On one point virtually all the most passionate boosters and hard-boiled critics agree: The first Americans arrived during the Wisconsin period. Exactly when in the Wisconsin is another matter altogether. The "Clovis-first" money and even some of the recent "pre-Clovis" claims are on a Late Wisconsin arrival. Others, however, are betting on the meager and hotly disputed archaeological evidence from Middle and even Early Wisconsin contexts. A very few others place the arrival of the first Americans in the Illinoian—still, unless radically new evidence is forthcoming, this last possibility seems extremely unlikely.

An environmental picture of these periods would considerably enhance our understanding of the corresponding archaeology, especially since these were ecologically complex times. As the vast Wisconsin ice sheets waxed and waned, they radically altered North America's landscape, climate, and environment, opening and closing possible entryways for the earliest Americans.

Unfortunately, however, our knowledge of paleoenvironments diminishes as we retreat in time. A great deal is known of Late Wisconsin environments, far less of the environments of the Middle and, especially, the Early Wisconsin. Much of the discussion of the earlier periods is thus framed in terms of the later period. So it shall be here.

ICE

The North America of the Late Wisconsin period would be unrecognizable to us today. Much of Canada and the northern third of the contiguous United States was buried beneath the vast Laurentide and Cordilleran ice sheets.

The Laurentide was by far the larger, comprised of ice spreading from at least three major centers lying over Foxe Basin (on eastern Baffin Island), the Keewatin Uplands (west of Hudson Bay), and Labrador. As these sheets came together and moved southward, they covered much of Eastern and Central North America, extending from above the Arctic Circle (75° North) all the way down to mid-Ohio (40° North), and from the eastern coast of North America (64° West) roughly to the present western border of Alberta (120° West). The Laurentide ice sheet may have reached 1.2 to 1.9 miles (2 to 3 kilometers) in thickness near its sources, thinning toward the edges.

The Cordilleran ice sheet in the West was a blend of mountain glaciers and stretched along the west coast from Alaska, through Western Canada, to the Puget Lowland of Washington State. Isolated alpine glaciers existed farther south, down the Sierra Nevadas and Rockies. The Cordilleran reached a thickness of 1.5 miles (2.5 kilometers), overwhelming the northern Cascade Range, and burying all but its highest summits. On its seaward edge, the glacier extended beyond the present coastline, and calved into the Pacific Ocean.

Today, so little remains of these vast glaciers—mostly small patches of ice at high latitudes and on northwestern mountaintops—that their monumental size is best measured on a more tangible scale: the glaciers that all but bury the continental masses of Greenland and Antarctica.

Glaciologists in Alaska extract a snow core in order to measure the density of the snow. The composition of glacial ice can provide scientists with a picture of weather patterns from the past.

GLACIAL ICE, NOW AND THEN

	Today		Late Wisconsin maximum
Greenland	1.73 million km²	Cordilleran	2.37 million km²
Antarctica	12.53 million km²	Laurentide	13.39 million km²
Cordilleran	.076 million km²	Greenland	2.30 million km²
Laurentide	.147 million km²	Antarctica	13.81 million km²

Only during the Early Wisconsin were ice sheets possibly as extensive as they were in Late Wisconsin times, though the geological and oxygen-isotope records disagree: The latter imply less glacial ice than the former. Undoubtedly, Early Wisconsin glaciers were present throughout Eastern Canada and the northeastern United States, and extended onto the Atlantic continental shelf. They blanketed the western mountains, and moved down onto the Plains. But whether the eastern and western ice sheets joined, as they did in the Late Wisconsin, is far from certain.

Middle Wisconsin times saw far less glacial ice. It was warmer then (though still cooler than today), and glaciation was extremely spotty, limited to small areas of Eastern Canada and high elevations in the far western mountains.

OCEANS AND SHELVES

When the ice sheets were extended, they created an avenue over which the first Americans journeyed from Asia. Ice sheets the size of the Laurentide and Cordilleran (and their Northern European and Asian contemporaries) freeze a tremendous amount of water, nearly all of which comes from the oceans, where 97 percent of the world's water is stored. Raising glaciers on land lowers sea levels.

During the Late Wisconsin, roughly 5.2 percent of the world's water was locked up as ice (about half in the massive Laurentide ice sheet alone). That was enough to draw down global sea levels roughly 325 to 500 feet (100 to 150 meters) below what they are today. The Atlantic shore in Late Wisconsin times was hundreds of miles seaward of its present position. Small wonder, then, that the bones and teeth of large land mammals—such as mammoth and mastodon—are occasionally dredged from the ocean floors where they once walked. Along the Pacific Coast, where the continental shelf is narrower, the coastline was still some 30 miles (50 kilometers) beyond its present position. Across the globe the fall in sea level increased exposed land by about eight percent.

Far less is known of earlier changes in sea levels. Oxygen-isotope records suggest that sea levels fell in Early Wisconsin times perhaps as much as they did in the Late Wisconsin, with a minimum of 280 feet (85 meters) below present sea level reached around 70,000 B.P. Sea levels rose thereafter, hitting a high of about -180 feet (-55 meters) around 50,000 B.P., then declined again to the Late Wisconsin nadir.

BERINGIA

In far Northwestern North America, these lowered oceans exposed the shallow continental shelf beneath the Bering and Chukchi Seas. This shelf, stretching some 930 miles (1500 kilometers) north to south, was transformed into a broad land mass known as Beringia that connected Alaska and Siberia. Beringia was a vast, flat, almost featureless highway, and it trafficked for millennia in plants, animals, and people.

Beringia was dry land whenever seas fell 150 feet (46 meters) below their present levels, but when those depths were first plumbed is uncertain. By the oxygen-isotope evidence, Beringia should have surfaced in Early Wisconsin times, then been flooded during the Middle Wisconsin high stand. At 40,000 B.P. sea levels were not far below their present position, and began to decline steadily. Certainly by around 25,000 years ago the Beringian plains were exposed, and from then until roughly 14,400 B.P., there was uninterrupted dry land from the Old World to the New. After 14,400 B.P., rising water severed Beringia, but from then until perhaps 10,000 B.P., the sea was still narrow enough to freeze in winter, remaining seasonally traversable.

Traversable it was, but hospitable it may not have been. While Beringia proper was not buried under glacial ice, it was a cold, dry, inhospitable landscape, with few trees or lakes, but with extensive dune fields and loess (wind-blown silts), and tracts of permafrost, which would indicate a mean annual air temperature below 21 to 17 Fahrenheit degrees (-6 to -8 Celsius degrees).

Oddly, animal bones recovered from Eastern Beringia (today's western coastal plain of Alaska), show an apparent abundance of large grazers—mammoth, horse, and bison. That evidence bespeaks a land surface covered by dry, yet rich, grassland, which paleontologist R. Dale Guthrie calls the "Mammoth Steppe." However, evidence of the contemporary vegetation, recorded in pollen-bearing deposits from higher elevations, suggests instead that there was sparse vegetation, and that Beringia more closely resembled a polar desert. This is the so-called "Productivity Paradox"—lots of animals, but nothing for them to eat. Or so it seems. But the burden of proof, Guthrie argues, must be on the palynologists, the pollen experts. There were simply too many grazers on the landscape for too long for it to have been barren. The Mammoth Steppe obviously was not productive in all spots, but generally it must have been a relatively rich grassland.

The Laurentide and Cordilleran ice sheets spread toward each other. If each reached its maximum extent simultaneously, they would have joined along a nearly 1250-mile (2000-kilometer) stretch and formed an impenetrable barrier to the movement of human or other life. But did they reach maximum size simultaneously, or was there always a passage between them? So far, the answers to these questions have eluded us.

Naturally, with the uncertainty surrounding the extent and age of Early Wisconsin glaciation, it's impossible to do more than speculate about the nature and condition of the ice sheets at that time. Without question, however, the absence of glaciers on the Western Canadian plains during Middle Wisconsin times eliminated any possible ice barriers. If humans had been in Alaska then, they could easily have moved farther south.

Some have suggested that the region has stayed ice-free ever since, even during the Late Wisconsin maximum, a notion that only recently would not have been taken too seriously. Nevertheless, based on admittedly scanty evidence, there likely was a space between the ice sheets throughout the Late Wisconsin (the Cordilleran and Laurentide sheets, it seems, did not reach their fullest extent simultaneously). If the Cordilleran and Laurentide sheets did join, it was only for a few thousand years, perhaps around 20,000 B.P.

Still, the mere presence of a corridor, however long- or short-lived, is not in itself evidence of a viable passageway. Physically separate ice sheets may still constitute a barrier. Large meltwater lakes would collect alongside the ice margins in low-lying areas, and the dry terrain would be rendered inhospitable by cold winds draining off and around the ice. All of which nicely explains why, even though glacial ice was absent, palynologists and paleontologists have found scant evidence of much plant or animal life in the corridor region from 20,000 B.P. until sometime after 14,000 B.P.

JUST HOW COLD WAS LATE WISCONSIN NORTH AMERICA?

During glacial periods it was colder than it is today: wetter, too, in some places, but drier in others. How much colder and how much wetter or drier is a complex by-product of insolation, ice sheet mass, sea-surface temperatures, snow cover, and a host of less-important ingredients. These factors control atmospheric circulation, precipitation, and airmass dominance, which in turn are modified seasonally and locally by elevation, proximity to mountains, oceans, ice sheets, and so on. Temperatures and rainfall from past times can be simulated by complex mathematical models and measured, more or less directly, in the fossil and geological records of plants, animals, sediments, and lake levels.

Results of paleoclimate studies, which until now have been devoted almost entirely to the Late Wisconsin, indicate full glacial temperatures averaged 9 to 12.6° F (5 to 7° c) below modern values. Close to the ice sheets, temperatures may have been 18° F (10° c) cooler than today; on top, as much as 45° F

(25° c) cooler, though we have no record of whether the first Americans were hardy enough to venture onto the ice.

At their fullest extent, the glaciers modified weather patterns. An anticyclone developed over them and cold, katabatic (downslope) winds flowed off the ice, chilling adjacent land areas. That produced a dry, irregular permafrost zone up to 125 miles (200 kilometers) wide along the southern edge of the Laurentide and Cordilleran ice. In the Pacific Northwest, the easterly track of the anticyclone displaced moist Pacific air and dried the region considerably; in the far Northeast, conditions were cold but slightly wetter, a result of storms along the border of ocean and glacial ice.

In other areas climatic conditions were strikingly different. At times of full glaciation, the westerly flow of the polar jet stream was split by the ice sheet, with branches of the jet flowing along its northern and southern edges. The northern (weaker) branch brought relatively warmer air across Alaska and the northern edge of the ice sheet. In Alaska, at least, full glacial climates were only a few degrees cooler than at present. The southern branch brought cooler, moist air into the American Southwest, producing rainfall much heavier than at present (and perhaps on different seasonal schedules), and lower evaporation. As a result, innumerable pluvial lakes, some quite large, formed in what are now the arid and semi-arid Great Basin and Southern High Plains.

The largest of those was in the Great Basin: Pluvial Lake Bonneville covered about 19,800 mi^2 (51,300 km^2) of northeastern Utah, about the size of modern Lake Michigan, and was 1220 feet (372 meters) deep. This vast inland sea hit its high-water mark between 16,000 and 13,000 B.P., and provided ample watering and feeding areas for a variety of plants and animals, perhaps even people. Today we have, relatively speaking, only tiny puddled remnants of pluvial Lake Bonneville: Great Salt Lake, Utah Lake, and Sevier Lake, which together comprise no more than six percent of the ancestral lake. The Bonneville "salt flats," and the prominent wave-cut ridges on the slopes east of Salt Lake City, for example, mark the floor and beaches of the ancient lake.

The climatic situation was quite the reverse in the Southeastern United States. Driven by a southward expansion of polar waters, sea-surface temperatures around the globe were lowered in Late Wisconsin times. On average, ocean temperatures were 4.1° F (2.3° c) cooler than they are today. In some places, the drop was even more dramatic. Atlantic Ocean temperatures off the coast of New England were as much as 25° F (14° c) lower than today. Cooler oceans, of course, give up less water to evaporation, reducing the moisture available for rainfall on land. Florida and the southeastern states, as a result of the cooler ocean, were a great deal drier in the Late Wisconsin than they are today.

While average annual temperatures south of the ice sheet were cooler at glacial maximum, the swings in temperature from summer to winter may not have been as pronounced then as now. Today's severe winters are a consequence of frigid polar air masses that sweep down from Northern Canada and

The Bonneville Salt Flats stretch into the distance at Great Salt Lake, Utah. Between 16,000 and 13,000 B.P. this was the floor of a vast inland sea, 1220 feet deep, covering an area about the size of modern Lake Michigan and supporting a great variety of life. Changes in the jet stream sent cool moist air down into the Great Basin, causing enough rainfall to create these huge pluvial lakes.

reach deep into the United States. In full glacial times, polar air was trapped in the Arctic basin by the looming presence of the nearly 2-mile-thick Laurentide ice sheet. Blocking that air mass lessened the seasonal swings in temperature and, as a result, Pleistocene climates were more equable than today, with cooler summers and relatively milder winters.

ENVIRONMENTS WITHOUT ANALOGUE

Late Wisconsin plant and animal communities are well known in some areas (Eastern North America, the Southwest, and the Southern High Plains), less well known in others. But in all cases they appear unlike any existing today.

Biotic communities, Illinois State Museum paleontologist Russell Graham contends, are individual plants and animals co-occurring under particular climatic and environmental circumstances. Change those circumstances, and the communities dissolve, to reform with new members. Bring on continental glaciers and the climatic changes that accompany them, and plant and animal communities will not merely shift south en masse, but instead will come apart. Individual species set off on their own, moving in accordance with their specific ecological tolerances. Some moved very far: In Late Wisconsin times, spruce trees grew in Georgia, and reindeer (or caribou) grazed in Tennessee.

As Arctic and boreal plants and animals moved south ahead of the expanding ice sheet, they were integrated within existing temperate communities, and lived alongside species with which they are now ecologically incompatible. Co-habiting Clark's Cave, Virginia, in Late Wisconsin times, for example, was the cold-loving yellow-cheeked vole *(Microtus xanthognathus)*, whose present range extends no farther south than the Canada-United States border; the thirteen-

33

lined ground squirrel *(Spermophilus tridecemlineatus)*, which today inhabits the American prairie and plains; and the pine vole *(Microtus pinetorum)*, which now lives in warm southeastern pine forests.

Climatic equability allowed the intermingling of species that today must live far apart. Nowadays, it is the seasonal climatic extremes that chiefly limit plant and animal distributions. (The tundra-boreal forest boundary across Canada, for instance, roughly marks the mean summer position of the Arctic air mass, while the southern boundary of the boreal forest marks the winter position of the air mass.) Dampen those extremes by blocking Arctic air and summers south of the ice sheet became cool enough to support northern plants and animals, while winters were not so very cold that they prohibited southern forms. All that made for species-rich Pleistocene environments lacking modern analogues. The Late Wisconsin "tundra," for example, supported many of the same plants and animals living today in the high Arctic, but it included others which did not, and could not, survive the rigors of our modern tundra winters.

When glaciation was at its height during the Late Wisconsin period, environments varied considerably across space, as well as through time. In very broad-brush strokes, a treeless zone of tundra plants and animals intermingled with a few southern and prairie forms, skirted the southern edge of the Laurentide ice sheet from New England through the Midwest and discontinuously into Montana. The zone also stretched south along the top of the Appalachians. In the Pacific Northwest, areas along the ice margin were largely treeless, but more as a result of the drying effects of the shifted jet stream than the permafrost conditions caused by nearby ice.

A highly diverse forest covered much of Eastern and Central North America south of the treeless zone, dominated by spruce in the northern Midwest and northern pines toward the Northeast. Farther south, oak, ash, hickory, as well as other temperate and deciduous trees, increased in abundance. In these forests, cold-loving shrews, lemmings, and voles lived alongside warmth-loving armadillos and tapirs, chipmunks and ground squirrels, as well as a host of now-extinct mammals. Naturally, the relative number of cold-loving species decreased as the temperate species increased from north to south.

Farther west, on the Central and Southern Plains, was a relatively cool, treeless landscape dominated by sedges and grasses, and in low-lying and wetter areas, open forest or wooded parkland. Antelope and bison grazed on this landscape, alongside mammoth, horse, and camel. On the eastern and western edges of the Plains, these species overlapped with woodland species from adjoining parklands. Little is known of the Northern Plains environments, but there must have been species hardy enough to withstand cold and windy conditions.

So, too, in the Pacific Northwest, where the environment was too dry and cool for substantial forests, but where occasional spruce and lodgepole pine grew in the unglaciated portions of the Puget lowland (Puget Sound itself was buried by ice). In the mountains of the West and Southwest, alpine snowlines and treelines dropped perhaps 3300 feet (1000 meters) below their present elevations. Trees now restricted to higher elevations—such as juniper and pine woodlands—reached down into what are now desert basins. Other high elevation plants and animals moved downslope, where they lived alongside plants such as evergreen oaks, yucca, lechuguilla and shadscale, and adapted to warmer and drier climes.

MEGAFAUNAL MENAGERIE

Dozens of large, now-extinct mammals lived in all these settings. Among them were two species of mammoth, distant relatives of the modern elephants, standing nearly 12 feet (3.6 meters) high at the shoulder, with tusks extending 13 feet. They grazed the vast grasslands of Pleistocene North America, Europe, and Asia, and surprising numbers of their freeze-dried carcasses have been unearthed in Siberia and Alaska, where, in the last century, their thawed flesh was fed to dog teams. None of the dogs was reportedly worse off for the experience.

Even more distantly related to the elephants was the American mastodon, shorter but stockier than the mammoth. Unlike its grazing relative, the mastodon browsed on twigs, leaves, grasses, and moss in the vast Pleistocene forests of Eastern North America, where its bones have been unearthed for centuries. One very early report came from Puritan Cotton Mather who, weak in human anatomy but adept at identifying witches in 17th-century Salem, Massachusetts, mistook mastodon bones as proof of the Biblical passage, "There were giants in the earth in those days." Right size, wrong animal.

There were four genera of ground sloth, distant and considerably larger relatives of the tree sloths now inhabiting Central and South America. Fat tree sloths may weigh 20 pounds (9 kilograms). The largest Pleistocene ground sloth—the *Eremotherium*—probably weighed 3 tons (2700 kilograms), and reached a length of 18 feet (5.5 meters). A giraffe, by comparison, is a mere 15 to 16 feet (4.5 to 4.9 meters) tall.

Distantly related to the ground sloths was the glyptodont, a cumbersome, semi-aquatic animal nearly 10 feet (3 meters) long and 5 feet (1.5 meters) tall, encased in a turtle-like carapace with an armored skull and tail, weighing upwards of a ton (900 kilograms). Rounding out the list of herbivores was a giant beaver *(Castoroides)*, weighing more than 200 pounds (90 kilograms), with incisors 8 inches (20 centimeters) long; horses, tapirs, peccaries, camels, deer, pronghorns, musk-ox, and assorted bit players such as Harrington's mountain goat, the capybara, and *Dasypus bellus,* "beautiful armadillo," two to three times larger than its modern counterpart.

Preying on these herbivores were Pleistocene lions, tigers, and bears. The lions were larger than their modern African counterparts, but like their living relatives also fed on the animals which inhabited open grasslands. Amongst the tigers was the sabertooth, aptly named *Smilodon fatalis.* This huge cat, with its

Charles R. Knight, a turn-of-the-century New York artist who had a keen interest in animals, revolutionized the process of conceptualizing the great creatures of prehistory. He worked with leading paleontologists to sculpt and paint the extinct animals, always imbuing them with a sense of movement and life. During his 50-year career working with leading American museums, he produced such works as this portrayal of a Pleistocene water hole near the site of Los Angeles. Smilodons and carrion-eating birds gathered at such pools to feed on the carcasses of mired animals.

protruding 6-inch (15-centimeter) upper canines—serrated front to back and compressed side to side—probably fed on the young of mammoths, or other slow-footed herbivores, biting their necks or bellies to produce suffocation, heavy bleeding, and death. The remains of the massive dire wolf are often found beside sabertooth bones, but not because it was part of the meal plan. Rather, dire wolves were career scavengers, cleaning out the leftovers from sabertooth meals. On occasion, however, the wolves must have showed up too early for their meals. A dire wolf skull, penetrated by a broken *Smilodon* saber has been found.

The bears included the giant short-faced bear, 30 percent larger, substantially more carnivorous (perhaps feeding on bison), and faster than our largest living carnivore, the Alaska brown bear. Rounding out the carnivores were other Pleistocene cats and dogs, wolves, and the short-faced skunk *(Brachyprotoma obtusata)*, larger and more carnivorous than any modern skunk.

What is most astonishing about these animals, aside from their size, is their dramatic disappearance. After living through multiple glacial events, they all vanished at the end of the Late Wisconsin, just about the time Clovis Paleoindians appeared.

An increase in insolation heralded the end of glaciation, and around 14,000 B.P. the vast ice sheets began to retreat. By 13,000 B.P. the area of the Laurentide had decreased by 20 percent, its volume by 50 percent (the sheet thinned more rapidly than its area shrank). By 11,000 B.P. the Gulf of St. Lawrence opened; by 9500 B.P. the ice front had withdrawn north of the Great Lakes; by 8200 B.P. the once great Laurentide was calving into Hudson Bay. Its last major segment melted over Baffin Island 5000 years ago. On the other side of the continent, the Cordilleran was retreating rapidly, 325 to 650 feet (100-200 meters) per year in some places, and by 11,000 B.P. the ice was north of the United States-Canada boundary.

A Soviet scientist studies the remarkably well-preserved remains of a baby woolly mammoth found in 1977 beneath the permafrost in a creek bed by workers in the goldfields of Eastern Siberia. The 40,000-year-old calf was preserved by the extreme cold and the high levels of tannic acid in the surrounding marshy land.

As the glaciers withered, water from melting ice returned to the oceans (much of the Laurentide meltwater rushed down a swollen Mississippi River into the Gulf of Mexico), raising sea levels. By 10,000 B.P., waters were within 165 feet (50 meters) of the present level, and rising less than half an inch a year. Modern sea levels were reached around 5000 B.P., the timing varying by area.

The steady rise in insolation, which peaked around 11,000 to 10,000 years ago, and the attendant breakup of the ice sheets, profoundly changed North American environments. With a decrease in the cooling effects of the ice, the unleashing of the Arctic air mass, and the increase in summer radiation, climatic equability gave way to more severe seasonal extremes: hotter summers and warmer winters. Peak summer warmth was not reached until between 9000 and 6000 B.P. owing to the ameliorating effects of the diminishing ice sheet.

Between 12,000 and 9000 B.P., biotic communities changed rapidly. Had the process been recorded in time-lapse photography, then viewed at high speed, it would have resembled a Keystone Kops routine, with plants and animals bumping and jostling one another to reach new habitats. They left their Pleistocene communities the way they had entered—as individual species, whose movements were timed and directed by the speed with which they traveled, by inter-specific competition, their location during full glacial times, the availability of suitable habitats, and a host of other factors.

By 9000 B.P., the tundra-like band (along with the permafrost) had all but disappeared in the Eastern and Central United States, the victim of a diminished anticyclone and flagged katabatic winds. With it went the Arctic mam-

The Exhumation of the Mastodon was painted by artist Charles Willson Peale in 1806 to record his own excavations in August of 1801. The first museum keeper in the U.S., Peale was always looking for items to exhibit. When he heard that a farmer in Orange County, N.Y., had found some bones, Peale went to excavate, but found that the skeleton was in a swampy area. Undaunted, Peale devised this ingenious system of pumping out water. The artist painted himself into his picture. He is seen at right, pointing into the pit.

mals. The deglaciated terrain left in the wake of the retreating ice was initially colonized by tundra-like vegetation, soon replaced by boreal and northern forests. Farther south, oak-hickory forests spread from the Southeast into the central and northern Midwest. These new regimes wrought changes in the animal communities, which by 10,000 B.P. had become essentially modern.

On the Western Plains, grasslands expanded at the expense of woodland and parkland, which survived piecemeal in moist and protected river bottoms. The grasslands became dominated by warm-season rather than cool-season grasses. The Plains fauna took on its modern appearance more slowly than its eastern counterpart, perhaps a reflection of the lingering cooling effect of the dwindling ice sheet. But by 9000 B.P. it, too, was modernized.

In the Pacific Northwest, deglaciation brought warmer temperatures, and more humid conditions initially, and an increase in the number of temperate trees such as western hemlock, Douglas fir, and alder. In the far Southwest, vegetation changes became most pronounced after 11,000 B.P., when cooler summers and moist winters gave way to hotter and drier climates, accompanied by a shift to more seasonal rainfall. Alpine species began their upward retreat, piñon-juniper woodlands giving way to more warm-loving oak-juniper woodlands by 10,000 B.P. By early Holocene times, desert scrub occupied lowlying, inter-mountain valleys of the Southwest and Great Basin, leaving many boreal mammals, which in cooler and wetter times had been able to scurry from peak to peak, forever stranded on the mountaintops.

An aerial view of the Chippewa moraines in Chippewa County, Wisconsin, reveals an Ice-Age landscape of kettle lakes and moraines. Glacial meltwater filled the hundreds of depressions that were left behind as the retreating glaciers gouged out bedrock.

That drying trend was caused by the repositioning of the jet stream, and it in turn lowered lake levels throughout the West and Southwest. By 10,000 B.P., most of the lakes were on the way to drying up completely.

Simultaneously, new lakes began to form farther north. Meltwater filled the bedrock depressions left by the retreating glaciers, creating a land of lakes in the upper Midwest. Hundreds of thousands of these survive, although the largest— the Great Lakes—are together still smaller than glacial Lake Agassiz, which 9900 years ago covered about 135,135 mi² (350,000 km²) of Saskatchewan, Manitoba, and Ontario, and the upper Midwest. Humans visited the area in the latest Pleistocene, but mostly to hunt game that was attracted to lakes. Fishing had to await natural postglacial stocking.

And in the far Northwest, ice retreat drained rather than filled a lake. In Late Wisconsin times, Glacial Lake Missoula, once about the size of Lake Ontario, formed behind a dam of Cordilleran ice across an upper reach of the Columbia River. When the dam failed, as it did repeatedly in late glacial times, floodwaters would burst across the neck of Idaho and much of eastern Washington, some-times rushing 10 times faster than the world's fastest rivers today. When the water plunged back into the Columbia River in central Washington, it created falls seven times wider and five times higher than Niagara, and tore deep gashes into the bedrock—Grand Coulee, for instance, at 50 miles (80 kilometers) long, at least a mile (1.6 kilometers) wide, and nearly 1000 feet (300 meters) deep.

A spectacular flood, this one. Buckland would have been pleased. But the Lake Missoula dam-burst was merely one in a long chain of radical changes in the land-scape, climate, and environment of Wisconsin-period North America. Sometime and somewhere along the way, humans appeared. But where, and when?

Embedded between the bones of an extinct bison, a flint spearpoint, bearing a distinctive groove or flute, shows unmistakable signs that a was unearthed near Folsom, New Mexico, in 1927, and helped establish solid proof of an early human presence in the New World.

prehistoric hunter had been at work. The find

3

A HISTORY OF CONTROVERSY

In the fall of 1780, the Governor of Virginia received a letter from the Secretary of the French Legation in the newly declared American nation, inquiring about the political institutions, natural history, and native peoples of the state. But the question was posed at an awkward time. The Revolutionary War was reaching its crescendo, and hostile British forces under Lord Cornwallis were already advancing on the governor's home. He was obliged to postpone his answer until the following summer, after the with-

Title page of the 1801 printing of Thomas Jefferson's volume, *Notes on the State of Virginia*, in which the future American president examined the origins of the native peoples of his state. Written some years before at the request of the secretary of the French Legation in Philadelphia, Jefferson's miscellany describes the excavations he carried out near his home at Monticello, which represented the continent's first genuine archaeological excavation.

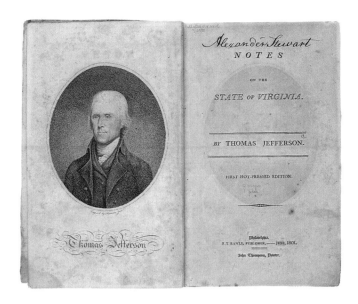

drawal of British forces from tidewater Virginia, and the end of his term of office. "Great question has arisen," Thomas Jefferson then replied, "from whence came those aboriginals of America."

There were (and, sadly, still are) balmy claims about the natives' being descendants of wandering Romans, Egyptian colonists, seafaring Phoenicians, "Hindoos" (those other Indians), survivors of the Lost Continents of Mu or Atlantis, or descendants of the Ten Lost Tribes of Israel. This last was perennially popular, explaining as it did two great mysteries: who the Native Americans actually were, and where the Israelites had been lost all those years.

Yet few capable thinkers, and Jefferson was an extraordinarily capable thinker, paid these theories any mind. Diverse as the Native Americans were, Jefferson realized they shared a common ancestry. Judging from their appearance, their homeland was Eastern Asia. He reasoned that they had arrived in America speaking one language, and that once here, their language had divided a thousandfold, until the continent was peopled by tribes speaking radically distinct tongues, few of which were mutually intelligible or bore any resemblance to their ancestral Asian language. To Jefferson the conclusion was inescapable: Such linguistic and physical divergence from a common origin required "an immense course of time; perhaps not less than many people give to the age of the earth."

The views of Jefferson, which were published in 1787 as *Notes on the State of Virginia*, sparked a firestorm of criticism. His outraged critics called him a "howling atheist" who was mounting a thinly veiled attack on the Bible and the sacred Mosaic chronicles. The earth itself might turn out to be very old, perhaps tens of thousands of years old as astronomers and geologists were

In the mid-19th century, excavations at Brixham Cave in Southwestern England uncovered human artifacts that were associated with Pleistocene fossils. These discoveries convincingly established the scientific fact that human ancestry pre-dated recorded history. They also marked the beginning of prehistoric archaeology.

then already insisting, but Jefferson's detractors demanded that human history go back no farther than the 6000 years allotted in Scripture.

And for at least another 72 years, it didn't.

THE DISCOVERY OF DEEP TIME

Before 1859 the Bible served as history, chronology, and ethnography—a detailed and sacred account of human genealogy from Adam downward, linking modern life to the very creation of heaven and earth. Well, almost to the Creation.

During the 18th century, Edmund Halley (of comet fame), the French naturalist Georges de Buffon, and others began clamoring for a longer time period for earth history. They knew that physical evidence required an earth more than 6000 years old, but, not daring to reject Genesis entirely, they compromised by treating the first "days" of Creation as allegorical only, supposing "the chronology of Moses relates only to the human race."

Uncoupling earth history from human history was a splendid idea in a world fast becoming inconceivably old. Humanity's best hope for its own uniqueness and importance in God's ultimate design lies in the affirmation of the Bible. Here, fortunately, Genesis and geology seemed to agree: Humans themselves were the most recent and crowning creation.

So geologists got busy. From the strange fossils brought to light by exploring expeditions and the rapacious mining that fueled the Industrial Revolution, Georges Cuvier and others reconstructed the wonderfully exotic and often extinct plant and animal life of earlier pre-human periods of the earth's history. The most recent of those earlier periods, the Pleistocene,

A 19th-century caricature of Charles Darwin confronting an ape *(above)* bore the caption: "It is a wise father that knows his own son." Darwin's views, expressed in his 1859 *Origin of Species*, met with opposition, but gained acceptance as they were bolstered by the newly found archaeological evidence of deep human antiquity. The American physician Charles Conrad Abbott (1843-1919) *(below)* began collecting artifacts near his Trenton, New Jersey, home in the early 1870s, hoping to establish a link with European Paleolithic sites. His discoveries—later discredited—raised a storm of protest.

just preceded the appearance of the modern world, and was inhabited by huge mammals—mammoth, mastodon, and the like. No human remains were expected in Pleistocene deposits, and for good reason: Whatever its age in absolute years, the Pleistocene was old, relative to people. This was a period unknown to human history, beyond the range of the Mosaic chronicles, and thus had become a base line against which human antiquity could be measured.

Naturally, when human artifacts or bones occasionally popped out in Pleistocene gravels or alongside the bones of extinct Pleistocene animals in the early 19th century, they were dismissed as accidental intrusions, or ignored. After 1859, they couldn't be.

The summer before, excavations at Brixham Cave in Southwestern England by Britain's finest geologists (Sir Charles Lyell among them) had uncovered stone tools in direct association with Pleistocene fossils. That could only mean one of two things: Either the excavation had been botched (and no one there was willing to admit that!), or the theologically disconcerting was true—human ancestry predated recorded history.

Brixham Cave's revelations prompted another look at the long-standing claims of the French antiquarian Jacques Boucher de Perthes, who for decades had been collecting stone tools and Pleistocene fossils in the valley of the Somme. A parade of geologists and antiquarians made the pilgrimage to Boucher de Perthes' home in Abbéville and, in the summer of 1859, Charles Lyell himself, foremost among those who had challenged any and all claims of great human antiquity, offered his *mea culpa*. Humanity, he admitted, had been around in the Pleistocene, had seen Agassiz' glaciers, and had preyed on Cuvier's fauna.

The Paleolithic or Stone Age occupants of Brixham Cave and the Somme Valley represented prehistory, a part of the human past about which the Bible said absolutely nothing. The Paleolithic was knowable only through its silent artifacts and skeletal remains—only through archaeology.

That *annus mirabilis*, 1859, in fact bore two intellectual revolutions: the discovery of deep human antiquity and the debut of prehistoric archaeology, and the publication of Charles Darwin's theory of evolution by natural selection in the *Origin of Species*. The two events had independent origins, but would ever after be linked. For while Darwin's *Origin* had no more to say about the evolution of the human species from our animal forebears than the understated one-liner, "Light will be thrown on the origin of man and his history," everyone knew what *that* meant: a shared ancestry with other primates, and earlier human ancestors deep in time. One could scarcely accept Charles Darwin's views of human evolution without the evidence of deep antiquity that prehistoric archaeology granted. As Darwin himself later insisted: "The high antiquity of man has recently been demonstrated ... and this is an indispensable basis for understanding [human] origins."

The studies of anthropologist and archaeologist William Henry Holmes helped to undermine the claims of Paleolithic antiquity made by Abbott and his colleagues. This 1892 letter neatly captures his low opinion of Abbott's archaeology and the tone of this often-harsh feud.

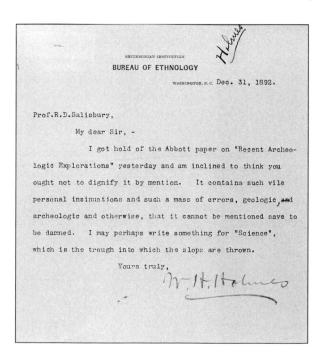

THE RISE AND FALL OF THE AMERICAN PALEOLITHIC

These discoveries fired the imagination of American scientists. Why couldn't American prehistory reach back as far as the European Paleolithic? The idea was appealing, since the geology of the two continents seemed so alike. But archaeologists quickly learned that in America there were no deeply stratified river valleys or caves in which human artifacts were indiscriminately mixed with Pleistocene fauna.

No matter. American archaeologists soon had another inspiration: Find artifacts that looked like the "rude" tools of the European Paleolithic, and they were likely to be the same age. The catalyst for these studies was Charles Conrad Abbott, a New Jersey physician who began collecting artifacts around his home near Trenton in the early 1870s (and, coincidentally, was the nephew of Timothy Abbott Conrad who, as previously noted, first spotted traces of Agassiz' Ice Age in America). The artifacts Abbott found looked "rude" enough, rather like those from the European Paleolithic sites. Better still, on occasion they came from geological deposits that hinted they might be very old.

We now know, based on a great deal of archaeological work done at the Abbott farm since, that the artifacts he found were not old at all, but rather post-Pleistocene in age. But Abbott never knew this, nor did most of his peers. In February 1877, Harvard geologist Nathaniel Shaler went over the Trenton ground with Abbott and pronounced the artifact-bearing deposits Pleistocene in age. In his diary that night, Abbott excitedly recorded his triumph: "I have discovered glacial man in America."

Heady stuff, this, and it inspired Abbott's compatriots. Harvard's Frederic Ward Putnam hired a Trenton man to walk the railroad cuts and sewer line trenches of the town, watching for more of these "Paleolithic" artifacts. The search was on throughout the eastern states, and soon Paleolithic artifacts were reported from dozens of different sites. On occasion these artifacts came from geological settings suggestive of a Pleistocene antiquity, but that hardly mattered; since the artifacts so readily mimicked European paleoliths of undeniable antiquity, they must be as old. As George Frederick Wright put it: In Paleolithic times, as today, American fashions followed the Paris line.

By the end of the 1880s, Abbott and his colleagues had the proof they needed that the first Americans had arrived thousands of years earlier when northern latitudes lay shrouded in glacial ice. Their evidence of the American Paleolithic was displayed in symposia, feature articles, and books, and Abbott himself was lionized as "America's Boucher de Perthes." Everyone believed the first Americans had arrived in the Pleistocene. The only lingering question was how much further back in time American prehistory might ultimately extend.

Harvard University's Frederic Ward Putnam (1839-1915), here ruminating over his field notes, helped Charles Conrad Abbott in his enthusiastic search for "Paleolithic" artifacts.

Yet, scarcely a year later the American Paleolithic came under withering fire from USGS geologists and archaeologists at the Smithsonian Institution's Bureau of Ethnology (later to become the Bureau of American Ethnology, or BAE). Over the winter of 1889, the archaeological community first heard the rumors that BAE archaeologist William Henry Holmes' excavations at a prehistoric stone quarry along Piney Branch Creek in Washington, D.C., would undermine the very foundations of the American Paleolithic.

In late January 1890, Holmes fired his opening salvo. Its message for Paleolithic proponents was devastating: Artifact form had no chronological significance whatsoever. The Pincy Branch quarries taught Holmes that an artifact might appear "rude" merely because it was unfinished, a "failure" in the manufacturing process, and not because it was ancient. The fact that "rude" American artifacts mimicked truly ancient European paleoliths only served to convince Holmes that analogies between American and European artifacts were utterly misleading. The age of an artifact must be determined independently, by its geological context.

Abbott had heard whispers of this before, and he was not impressed with their re-telling. After all, he could not see how Holmes' "so-called failures" were the same as the "true" Paleolithic implements of the Delaware River Valley, which Abbott believed occurred in genuine, undisturbed Pleistocene deposits. Even if geologists did quibble over the precise age of his Trenton gravels, such "traces of man must possess a very great antiquity."

When Abbott visited Holmes at Piney Branch that spring, he was unmoved. Holmes may well be correct on the archaeological significance of Piney Branch, Abbott admitted, but he failed to see that this had any bearing on the question of human antiquity in America. Still, on departing he politely told Holmes, "I have learned more arch[aeology] in three hours than ever before in three months." Holmes was first content to think of Abbott's remark "as a pleasant compliment," but from his "subsequent studies and increased wisdom I concluded [Abbott] probably meant what he said."

The battle lines were drawn. The Great Paleolithic War began had begun.

From 1890 to 1893, Holmes visited, then attacked in print, each alleged Paleolithic site in Eastern North America, starting with Abbott's Trenton gravels. Mistakes had been made, Holmes gravely reported. In each case, the alleged paleoliths were actually failures of manufacturing with no appreciable antiquity. They were merely the debris of historically known Native American groups. None, in Holmes' view, belonged in Pleistocene-aged deposits, and those allegedly found there must have fallen through rodent burrows or cracks in the earth, fortuitously settling in the older deposits. As to those actually retrieved from "Pleistocene" gravels, Holmes could say, on the supreme authority of the USGS' Thomas Chamberlin, that the gravels were not Pleistocene at all.

Proponents of the American Paleolithic were flabbergasted. They howled that Holmes' comparison of Native American manufacturing failures with

George Frederick Wright (1838-1921) *(above)*, an ally of Abbott's, who also argued in favor of the American Paleolithic, was vilified by opponents as a "betinselled charlatan." Geologist Thomas C. Chamberlin (1843-1928) *(below)* was one of Wright's critics. "No one is entitled to speak on behalf of science," he said, with Wright in his sights, "who does not really command it."

their Paleolithic artifacts utterly misrepresented the true nature of the American paleoliths. And they disputed Holmes' claim that younger artifacts had fallen (undetected) into older strata, protesting that it was specious and irrelevant without any actual demonstration on Holmes' part that such mixing had actually occurred. "You are all off your base," George Frederick Wright assured Holmes. Abbott retorted with doggerel:

> The stones are inspected,
> And Holmes cries "rejected,
> They're nothing but Indian chips."
> He glanced at the ground,
> Truth, fancied he'd found,
> And homeward to Washington skips.

Then, in late 1892, the controversy grew ugly, when USGS and BAE scientists rose up against Wright's just published *Man and the Glacial Period*. Wright's wrongs were obvious enough: he had spoken in favor of the American Paleolithic; he had challenged one of Chamberlin's (and by extension the entire USGS Glacial Division's) intellectual monuments—the demonstration there had been multiple glacial events—and, worst of all, he had written a book for a popular audience. "No one," Chamberlin thundered, "is entitled to speak on behalf of science who does not really command it." The BAE's W J McGee, an especially bloodthirsty critic, called Wright a "betinselled charlatan whose potions are poison. Would that science might well be rid of such harpies."

The vicious assault on Wright thinly veiled a proprietary dispute in which BAE and USGS scientists, seeking to revolutionize archaeology and geology, used Wright as a whipping post for their claims on American prehistory, and their certain knowledge that there had been multiple glaciations. Wright and Abbott were "mere amateurs," unfit to judge fundamental questions of science. Because BAE and USGS scientists were richly funded, and supported by the power of the federal government at a time when the government bureaus dominated American science (the balance of power would shift to universities only in the 20th century), the atmosphere became charged with accusations that heavy-handed federal scientists were conspiring to crush state and local practitioners and recreate science in their own image. With the return volley, the discussion degenerated in a blistering crossfire, its repercussions reaching into the Halls of Congress at a time when the USGS and BAE—their budgets threatened by fallout from the economic Panic of 1893—could ill afford the bad press.

After savaging each other at meetings and in print, the antagonists suspended hostilities in late 1893, both sides hardened beyond compromise. They met again in the summer of 1897, first in the field at Trenton, later in Toronto at a joint meeting of the American and British Associations for the Advancement of Science. There, American Paleolithic advocates suffered their most devastating blow: Sir John Evans, the doyen of the British Paleolithic, was given a set

Aleš Hrdlička (1869-1943) was a young physician-turned-anthropologist when he began to challenge the skeletal-based claims made by champions of a deep human antiquity. An enthusiastic traveler, the Czech-born immigrant collected human bones from all over the world and was instrumental in setting up the Smithsonian Institution's collection.

of Trenton artifacts, only to dismiss them as not Paleolithic at all. The critics gloated. Proponents were badly shaken. Only the true believers went away undaunted, Abbott grumbling about Evans' being "so misled by the unfortunate Toronto business." He blamed Harvard's Putnam.

The active search for the deep past continued, although after that landmark summer no more "paleoliths" were found in America. Two years later they were hardly missed. In December 1899, Putnam's hired hand in Trenton found a human femur (upper leg bone) deep in the "Pleistocene" gravels. With renewed hope and new evidence the controversy took a sharp turn.

BONES TO PICK

"We must not make any blunder about it," Putnam warned, and for good reason: Government critics had already reacted with "scorn and contumely" to the fast traveling news of the find. Putnam turned the bone over to Aleš Hrdlička, a young physician-turned-physical anthropologist. Hrdlička was none too impressed by the skeletal material, which looked rather like the bones of recent Native Americans. Perhaps, he suggested, the geology of the find site might shed light on its age. Wright had examined the geology, and thought the facts "were so clear that there was scarcely anything to discuss." Wright, however, was hopelessly optimistic. By then, the Trenton gravels had such notoriety that any agreement on their age was altogether futile.

The Trenton femur proved to be the first of many human skeletal parts found over the next 25 years in apparent Pleistocene-age deposits. During that period Hrdlička would emerge—after 1903 in the employ of William Henry Holmes at the Smithsonian—to challenge each and every claim "like Horatio at the land bridge between Asia and North America, mowing down with deadly precision all would-be geologically ancient invaders of the New World," as one wag put it.

Hrdlička's position was this: If the earliest Americans arrived in the Pleistocene, they should look like a Pleistocene-age people—like Neanderthals, say—not like the historic inhabitants of the region. In structure this was no more than Abbott's argument (if it's old, it should look primitive) applied to skeletons. But there was one big difference: The argument worked for Hrdlička. Hrdlička was fast becoming the premier physical anthropologist of his day, and few could challenge his considerable knowledge of human variability and evolution. To claim a human skeleton was Pleistocene in age, one had to play by Hrdlička's rules. So, were there Neanderthals in America?

Along the Missouri River just outside Lansing, Kansas, in February 1902, brothers Michael and Joseph Concannon were digging a tunnel to store fruit and vegetables on their father's farm. Seventy feet into the hillside on which the farmhouse sat, and 20 feet beneath the surface, they shoveled into two human skeletons. The bones were pushed aside—there was a tunnel to be dug—but after a few months, word of their discovery reached the City Public Museum in nearby Kansas City.

The Museum's curator visited the Concannon farm and, seeing that the bones lay beneath a layer of apparent loess, he alerted geologists Warren Upham and Newton Winchell of the Minnesota Historical Society, who rushed to Lansing. The two men were stunned by what they saw: The bones were definitely lying beneath Pleistocene-Age loess. Within days of his return to St. Paul, Upham drafted a paper announcing that Lansing proved a human presence in the New World prior to the last episode of ice advance in North America. In round numbers, perhaps 30,000 years before the present.

To Wright, Upham happily chirped that Lansing confirmed the claims of *Man and the Glacial Period*, then sent his hastily written paper to Chamberlin and Holmes, inviting them to "verify or correct" it. Verification, naturally, was what Upham preferred and briefly thought he had. Chamberlin and Holmes (and later Hrdlička) visited Lansing, and soon afterward Upham heard rumors that they had endorsed the site's great antiquity—rumors he vigorously fanned.

But the rumors were false. Unbeknownst to Upham, even before Chamberlin had left for Lansing he was already grousing about Upham's "fundamental untrustworthiness." Chamberlin's mood hardly improved at the site, where he concluded Upham—his former employee—had completely misread the stratigraphy and geology. Back in Chicago, Chamberlin blistered Upham in a string of letters, lecturing him on the proper character of loess, scientific ethics (like Wright, Upham had "gone public" with his claims about Lansing), and even accusing him of "direct falsification."

The battle lines were drawn once more: Upham, Winchell, and Wright fighting for a Pleistocene Age for the loess overlying the skeleton, with Chamberlin and Bohumil Shimek, the Midwest's leading loess specialist, dismissing the Lansing deposit as neither true loess nor Pleistocene in age. Holmes and Hrdlička joined forces with Chamberlin, chiming in that the Lansing skulls were no different than crania of historic Native Americans of the region, and hence surely no more than a few hundred or a thousand years old. To Abbott on the sidelines, it all recalled "the merry old days of earnest work ... [and] the controversial days that embittered me." And just like in the old days, neither side backed down.

Scarcely four years later and 120 miles farther up the Missouri River, the exercise was repeated. At the Gilder Mound, just outside Omaha, Nebraska, human crania—Neanderthal-like to some—were plucked from apparent Pleistocene "loess." In 1914, the scene shifted to the tar pits of Rancho La Brea, where a human skull was extracted from the ooze along with bones of an extinct (Pleistocene) condor. In two more years, it was Vero, Florida, where human remains rolled out of sand deposits yielding the bones of extinct mammoths and sloths. After that, the same story at Melbourne, Florida.

In each case, a swarm of archaeologists and geologists—Hrdlička usually leading the pack—descended on the site to inspect the skeletal remains and their geological context. In testimony to the sheer length of the dispute, there was now a second generation of participants. Literally, a second generation: Geologist Rollin Chamberlin visited Vero in place of his father, Thomas.

There were the habitual disagreements as to whether the human remains at each site were in primary context, or contemporary with the apparently ancient loess or extinct mammal-bearing deposits in which they were found. Hrdlička took a cue from Holmes: Since human beings bury their dead and because bone is so easily broken and moved in the earth, the odds were that any bone in ancient deposits came from later times. "Perhaps," paleontologist Oliver Hay tartly replied, "we get a clue here to the reason why civilized people nail up their dead in good strong boxes."

Besides, Hrdlička continued, even granting that human remains might be found in primary context, what assurance was that of great age? Geologists' opinions were utterly divided. The Lansing and Omaha specimens were either in true loess or not in true loess, and thus either Pleistocene or post-Pleistocene in age, while the Vero and Melbourne fauna were either Pleistocene or post-Pleistocene in age—all depending on which geologist was speaking. Hrdlička naturally followed the Chamberlins, but his true allegiance was to the bones. What did they have to say? Only if they spoke of an anatomically distinct pre-modern form could they be Pleistocene in age, never mind the geology.

Chamberlin was disappointed in Hrdlička's low opinion of geological testimony, but no more so than in many of his geologist colleagues. In fact, the irreconcilability of interpretations just about soured relations all around. Anthropologists bickered amongst themselves—but mostly with Hrdlička—over what a Pleistocene-aged human fossil should look like, then argued with paleontologists about the timing of mammalian extinctions. Paleontologists wrangled with geologists about where to draw the line between Pleistocene and post-Pleistocene formations. Geologists fought one another over the number, timing, and evidences of glacial history. Even linguists got in the act, clucking their disapproval at everyone's failure to provide them with sufficient time to account for the great diversity of native North American languages.

Once again the situation reached an angry impasse: Holmes snarled that the evidence from Vero was "dangerous to the cause of science;" journalist Robert Gilder, who found the Nebraska "Neanderthals," called Hrdlička a "liar."

Archaeologist Nels Nelson decided it would be best to "lie low for the present." Shrewd advice, and many followed it. Ironically, the key to resolving the dispute had, since 1908, lain quietly exposed in an arroyo in northeastern New Mexico.

IN THE BELLY OF THE BEAST

On August 27, 1908, torrential rains fell on a remote corner of New Mexico near the tiny town of Folsom, flooding the land and scouring deep channels in the earth. The foreman of the Crowfoot Ranch was checking fence lines and

In August 1908, George McJunkin (1851-1922), a former slave who was foreman of the Crowfoot Ranch near Folsom, New Mexico, was checking fence lines when he came across a deposit of fossil animal bones. The bones—those of prehistoric bison—were not excavated until after McJunkin's death.

flood damage when he spotted fossil animal bones poking out of a new and deeply exposed section of Wild Horse Arroyo. George McJunkin, born a slave in pre-Civil War Texas and educated on the High Plains of the American West, knew these were no cow bones. Bison, more likely, and bigger ones than any now living—possibly ancient ones. Whether McJunkin found artifacts with the bones has been long debated, but never resolved. Certainly, however, he spread the news of his discovery.

Even so, it was very much later—sadly, after McJunkin had died—that word of his discovery finally reached the Colorado Museum of Natural History. Museum Director Jesse Figgins needed fossils suitable for display, so he sent an excavation crew to Folsom in the summer of 1926, to recover "a mountable [bison] skeleton." In mid-July an artifact was found in the bone-bearing deposit; this was no "rude" paleolith, but a delicately made spear point with a distinctive central groove or flute.

Unfortunately, the artifact was out of the ground before it was spotted by the excavators. Both Figgins and Harold Cook, the Museum's paleontologist, quickly sized up the situation. If more artifacts were found in the deposit with what appeared to be Pleistocene-aged bison bones, then they must be left and inspected in place. Figgins warned the crew to "watch for human remains and then in no circumstances, remove them, but let me know at once." All summer he waited anxiously for the word. None came.

Nevertheless, that fall Figgins wrote a preliminary note on the excavations, reporting this apparent evidence of a Pleistocene human presence. It was, he

Jesse Figgins (1867-1944), director of the Colorado Museum of Natural History, and Raton, New Mexico, banker F.J. Howarth (right), pictured in 1926 enjoying a picnic lunch at the Folsom site. Later that summer, Figgins dispatched an excavation team to Folsom to recover the bones of a Pleistocene-aged bison. They found more than a bison, however; they also found projectile points—though none in place.

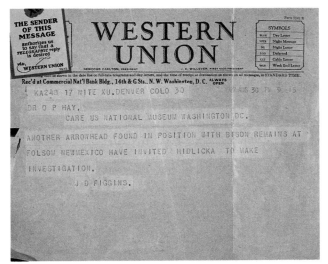

In August of 1927 the word went out of another find at Folsom, this time of a fluted point in place. It was this telegram, sent to the major museums in the country, that brought Brown, Kidder, and Roberts to Folsom to view the find.

confessed, "a deliberate attempt to arouse Dr. H. [Hrdlička] and stir up all the venom there is in him." As he explained, "Everyone seems to think Hrdlička will attack [and if he] tears a chunk of hide off my back ... there is nothing to prevent my removing three upper and two lower incisors, black one eye and gouge the other, after I have laid his hide across a barbed wire fence." Brave words, these, but when Figgins learned that a meeting with Hrdlička himself had been arranged in Washington, he allowed that perhaps Cook should go instead and "be the goat."

Still, Figgins recovered his faltering bravado and boarded a train for Washington. By the time he arrived at Hrdlička's Smithsonian office he was in a fearful lather. Yet, much to his astonishment (and relief), Hrdlička was courteous and "extremely pleased" to see the Folsom artifacts, and even offered Figgins some advice. If additional fluted points appear, Hrdlička told Figgins, leave them in place and immediately wire other museums and universities to send scientists to examine the finds on the spot.

Good advice, Figgins thought. What he didn't appreciate were Hrdlička's motives for offering it. Hrdlička didn't trust either Figgins or Cook, and in that he was not alone. Figgins and Cook had been brazenly proclaiming that three other North American archaeological sites they excavated were occupied upwards of half a million years ago. Were they right, all knowledge of the "spread of human culture" would have to be completely revised. But no one—

American Museum of Natural History paleontologist Barnum Brown (1873-1963), at right, and Carl Schwachheim, Figgins' excavator at the Folsom site, examine the first fluted point found in place with ancient bison bones.

Alfred V. Kidder (1885-1963) was at the Pecos site when news of the Folsom site find broke. As a member of the archaeological elite, his opinions were considered crucial. After investigation, he proclaimed that Folsom and its artifacts had indeed broken the Pleistocene barrier.

let alone Hrdlička—thought they were right, especially given the persistent rumors (later found to be true) that one of the sites was a hoax.

Having cried wolf three times already, Figgins and Cook naturally found a skeptical audience for their claims of Folsom's antiquity (which they actually thought was the youngest and weakest of their cases). Even so, Hrdlička and others straightaway saw that Folsom had more potential than any of the other three sites. But they weren't going to be satisfied by Figgins' and Cook's word on Folsom: Hrdlička wanted telegrams sent so the pros could come in and independently assess any discoveries.

Excavations resumed in the summer of 1927. More points were uncovered, this time in place, and the scientific community was duly alerted. Quickly responding were paleontologist Barnum Brown, from the American Museum of Natural History, and archaeologists Frank Roberts, a young colleague of Hrdlička's at the Smithsonian, and Alfred V. Kidder, of the Carnegie Institution of Washington. Roberts and Kidder were just a few hundred miles down the road, in Pecos, New Mexico.

Kidder, one of the archaeological elite, was then at the height of his considerable powers. His opinion on questions of artifacts, associations, context, and age mattered, and mattered very much. When he and Roberts, whom Hrdlička thought "very sensible," announced that the Folsom artifacts had entered the deposit at the same time as the ancient bison (its age verified by Brown), it carried tremendous weight within the scientific community.

What could Hrdlička do? From Washington, he mounted a few feeble probes to see whether there was any possibility the points were not in primary context. He did so more out of obligation than hope. Human hunters—Folsom

Paleoindians—had speared these great bison and the fluted points were embedded deep in their ribs. The association of animal and artifact was certain.

That certainty, however, gave way to uncertainty about the site's absolute age, since the taxonomy and timing of bison extinction was initially not altogether clear. Even so, within a matter of weeks Kidder proclaimed that Folsom had, at last, broken the Pleistocene barrier. Within the year, a new breed of USGS geologists had mapped the region, and concluded the Folsom deposits were at least late Pleistocene in age. Horatio had fallen.

HISTORICAL HOMILIES

So ended decades of intense dispute, a period when "no anthropologist, or for that matter geologist or paleontologist, desirous of a successful career would tempt the fate of ostracism by intimating that he had discovered indications of a respectable antiquity for the Indian." Or so Roberts later described it, with only slight exaggeration.

All those years of effort spent searching for Paleoliths or pre-*sapiens* fossils were now over, and strangely irrelevant. Folsom was indeed late Pleistocene in age, but looked nothing like everyone's expectation of a Pleistocene human occupation. That's a sobering lesson for those who today are so bold as to say what a pre-11,500 B.P. human presence ought to look like!

There are other lessons to be learned from this historical dispute, and indeed the old events are still mined nowadays by partisans on both sides of the debate, who regard them as object lessons for the current dispute. Naturally, the lessons they extract are not the same.

Proponents fondly recall both Holmes and Hrdlička getting their comeuppance at Folsom, and see in this history a vindication of their belief that critics (like Holmes and Hrdlička then, and University of Arizona archaeologist C. Vance Haynes now) hinder the recognition of bona fide early sites, and retard the progress of scientific investigation. That's a serious charge, but it needn't be taken too seriously. Historian of science David Hull observes that "the least productive scientists tend to behave the most admirably, while those who make the greatest contributions just as frequently behave the most deplorably." And sometimes Chamberlin, Holmes, and Hrdlička behaved deplorably: They were merciless in attack and engaged in no small amount of behind-the-scenes skullduggery.

Nevertheless, far from hamstringing inquiry, these critics actually sped it toward resolution. Asking the tough questions crystallized debate on stone-tool technology, the relationship between tool "grade" (form) and age, human evolution, glacial geology, dating techniques—critical issues all. Much was learned in 40 years or so of dispute, not least, what the solution to the human antiquity controversy had to look like. The swift acceptance of the Folsom evidence attests to that.

Besides, take a look over the sites that the critics rejected. In no instance, as archaeologist James B. Griffin and others point out, is there a locality Holmes,

Hrdlička, and Chamberlin insisted was postglacial, or recent in age, that has proven otherwise. Today, Trenton, Newcomerstown, Lansing, Gilder Mound, Vero, and all the other allegedly Pleistocene sites are significant because of the battles fought there, not because of the great age of their archaeological remains. None of them have lived up to the claims made for them.

Skepticism about a genuine Pleistocene human presence was not arbitrary, but forged in the face of repeated cases which failed to withstand scrutiny—cases often based, as proponents themselves admitted, upon unverified finds made under appalling field conditions by untrained farmers or collectors.

Nor was this skepticism simply a veil, hiding a refusal to accept any evidence for a human presence in America during the Pleistocene. It was not true, as one paleontologist teased, that Hrdlička would never be satisfied with Folsom's points embedded in bones unless he "fired the arrows himself." Still, after having battled long and hard, it is understandable that Hrdlička and Holmes chose to accept Folsom in their own way. Holmes, when queried, merely deferred to the prevailing judgment. Hrdlička shied away from the issue, but when confronted, found refuge in the fact there was still no pre-*sapiens* skeletal evidence in America. On that score he was (and remains) correct. Importantly, neither Holmes nor Hrdlička ever took the offensive against Folsom, and that, more than anything else, bespeaks their grudging acceptance.

Critics see quite another lesson in the history of this dispute. For them, site visits are paramount, and they look back to those halcyon days when the fate of a site (like Folsom) was decided quite simply by examining it on the spot. Could it possibly be that easy nowadays? Is the price of resolving the ongoing human antiquity dispute in America no more than the cost of the plane tickets to fly half a dozen skeptics to a corner of South America or the outskirts of Pittsburgh for an on-site evaluation?

Site visits to evaluate claims were common from the 1890s through 1927. Yet they were not always successful nor, for that matter, welcome. After everyone left Trenton in the late summer of 1897, Abbott griped he could not say that "looking back over the past four days ... I have enjoyed it. There is too much assumption of extra-carefulness, as they call it, which is simply a lot of childish twaddle."

Site visits were often confrontations in incompatibility, never achieving consensus and serving largely to highlight gaps in interpretation. At Trenton and Lansing, Gilder and Vero, proponents and critics all visited the various sites, looked at the very same physical evidence, but came away with radically different views of what it meant. The visit to Folsom, where everyone agreed on what they were seeing, was the exception rather than the rule.

More to the point, site visits were vital in those days when excavation techniques varied so widely; when there was such disagreement about ways of recognizing Pleistocene Age deposits; when so many discoveries were made under appalling conditions; and, most critical of all, when the age of a site could only

Aleš Hrdlička (*center*), on a site visit to
Nebraska, examined the pit that yielded
the "Neanderthal-like" human crania.
Robert Gilder (*left*), who discovered the
site, only later learned what Hrdlička
thought of the site. When he did, he was
not pleased and called Hrdlička a liar.

be determined in the field based on the stratigraphic position of the artifacts
and their associated fauna or deposits. Nowadays, careful attention to field
context, association, and stratigraphy is just as vital but, as Vance Haynes
stresses, in most cases "the only criterion for age is radiocarbon dating."

The effort to determine whether a site predates 11,500 years has become a
long and often tedious *laboratory* process. Most archaeologists, Haynes admits,
are too busy to visit a field site, so who has time to endure a six-month watch in
a radiocarbon laboratory to insure the dating samples are properly analyzed?
Fortunately, samples for dating can be split and sent to separate radiocarbon laboratories, and repetitive results nicely serve in the place of laboratory monitoring.

All this points up an asymmetry. Today, a site visit can reveal whether there
is something wrong with a claim of great antiquity, were it to show, for example,
that blunders had been made in interpreting the site stratigraphy, or that excavations failed to detect mixing of younger and older deposits and artifacts. Yet,
site visits cannot prove a claim: That must come from the laboratory as well.

Folsom was likely the first, and only, site in which a visit fully and without
ambiguity resolved a claim of great antiquity.

A MAMMOTH BARRIER

Folsom was a kill site. The projectile points were embedded between the bison
ribs, so there was no room to haggle over whether or not the points had tumbled
there accidentally. That made Folsom unlike virtually every other purportedly
ancient site found up till then, where it had been impossible to demonstrate that
the artifacts (or human skeletal remains) were deposited at the same time as the
Pleistocene-aged deposits or fauna with which they were found.

56

But if Folsom was unlike any other site previously found, it was very much like the dozens of sites found in the ensuing decades. This is hardly surprising. Having found Folsom, archaeologists learned what to look for. The strategy was simple: Search arroyo channels and ancient lake beds for the large (and easily spotted) bones of extinct Pleistocene mammals, then carefully search those deposits for associated human artifacts.

The strategy worked at a gravel pit just south of Clovis, New Mexico, where larger and less delicately made fluted points were found alongside mammoth bones. Those "generalized Folsoms"—later named Clovis points—occurred below a layer containing bison and "true Folsoms." Obviously, Clovis points were older. But just how much older in years would only be learned a couple of decades later, following the advent of Libby's radiocarbon dating.

Of course, the way archaeologists looked for Paleoindian sites predisposed what they found: lots of sites with artifacts and bones of extinct megafauna, and very few sites with artifacts but no bones. "Boneless" Paleoindian sites were—and still are—a lot harder to find. For instance, one of the most important recently discovered Paleoindian sites, the Aubrey Clovis site, was found by University of North Texas archaeologist Reid Ferring, while he was walking the outlet channel below an Army Corps of Engineers' dam outside Denton, Texas. No large bones called Ferring to the locality; just the chance to examine the Pleistocene-aged surface his geological canvass of the region had told him would be exposed there. On that surface, he found the tip of a fluted point, and beneath it an iceberg of a Clovis site. This kind of strategy will round out the biases in our Paleoindian archaeological record. It is all a matter of knowing the right place to look. (Ironically, after three years of meticulous excavations that resulted in an extraordinary archaeological record, the Aubrey site did finally yield one mammoth rib fragment.)

That so many Paleoindian sites were littered with large mammal bones seemed to speak of Paleoindians as super-predators, specializing in the killing of big game such as bison and mammoth. The inspiring vision of gutsy hunters, holding at bay a trumpeting and mortally wounded mammoth, would come to embody North American Paleoindians. It made for good copy, but the science was flawed—as we shall see later.

Meanwhile, what of the first Americans: Were they late Pleistocene Clovis Paleoindians? Or had they arrived earlier than the Clovis occupation? In the aftermath of the Clovis discovery, archaeologists began to search for traces of still older Americans. But by 1953, archaeologist Alex Krieger was already feeling the pinch. Archaeologists, he warned, having overthrown the Holmes-Hrdlička "dogma," were in danger of replacing it with another. The first Americans would now be permitted a late Pleistocene entry but, he feared, no earlier. Ten thousand years or so, Krieger worried, was fast becoming the new "allowed antiquity."

The **Malakoff heads**—named for the nearby Texas town—are huge sandstone boulders that were first excavated from a gravel quarry in the 1930s. Primitive "faces" have been carved into the surface of the boulders, but many believe the carving may have been the handiwork of practical jokers among the workers in the gravel quarry, and not by Pleistocene sculptors.

Still, in 1953 Krieger listed half a dozen sites he thought "may and probably do" break that barrier. A decade later, in 1964, he upped the total to 50 sites in North and South America that he believed pointed to a human presence predating the Clovis Paleoindians. Not all sites are created equal, and Krieger well appreciated that fact. But what impressed him most was how many sites actually looked old and, as he saw it, where there's smoke there's fire. The sites on his list included some with radiocarbon ages ranging from 21,000 B.P. in one case to more than 38,000 B.P. in another; many had bones of glacial-aged fauna that appeared split, burned, or broken by human hands; and then there were the Malakoff heads—giant sandstone boulders from deep in a Texas gravel quarry that had crude "faces" carved into them. Krieger even put on his list the sites of the American Paleolithic, Trenton included, for they demanded another look: They "cannot all be set aside as insignificant."

In fact, many of the sites on Krieger's list recalled the American Paleolithic. They contained crude, simple stone or bone artifacts, and lacked more "advanced" projectile points. Krieger insisted he was not equating artifact form with age, merely raising the possibility of a "pre-projectile (pre-Clovis) point stage." Perhaps. But few were eager to follow Krieger out on his speculative limb. And others were busy sawing it off behind him.

Why not? The idea that Clovis Paleoindians were the first Americans nicely fit the latest geological and radiocarbon evidence. The same year

Krieger published his pre-Clovis compendium, Haynes reported the first secure radiocarbon ages for the Clovis occupation. By then, Clovis artifacts were recorded throughout the coterminous United States, yet all the dated sites fell in a very narrow slice of time, between 11,500 and 11,000 years B.P. None were more than 12,000 years old and, as it happens, geologists had just declared that 12,000 years ago, for the first time in 15,000 years, warming climates had melted the great glaciers and there was again open passage between Alaska and the lower 48 states (nowadays, of course, we view the timing and nature of the passage differently).

It all made perfect sense. The land bridge connecting Siberia and Alaska only emerged during glacial cycles, but once migrants reached Alaska, glaciers blocked their path south. Either the first Americans came before the last major ice advance, in which case they had to contend with crossing open seas, or, they walked across the land bridge, then cooled their heels in Alaska waiting for the Canadian ice to retreat. The splendid correlation then existing between the disappearance of the ice and the appearance of Clovis occupations surely favored the latter hypothesis.

Alex Krieger's worst fears were coming to pass. The idea that Clovis was just one of the *older* occupations of North America was giving way to the idea that it was the *oldest* occupation in North America.

Still, in 1964 Haynes saw "good indications" there were people in America earlier than 11,500 years ago. He just didn't think they were related to Clovis groups. By 1969, he was less enamored of those "good indications." His conversion to skepticism was understandable. In the intervening years he had learned the hard way that sites that seemed too good to be true often were just that.

Tule Springs, located in the Las Vegas (Nevada) Valley, had everything going for it: genuine artifacts, bones of Pleistocene megafauna seemingly broken by human hands, and a radiocarbon date of 28,000 years ago. Anxious to learn more of this occupation, a team of archaeologists, paleoecologists, and geologists embarked on an ambitious excavation program, overseen by a blue-ribbon panel of scientists from those fields. Almost immediately Haynes, the site geologist, began to have doubts about the artifacts and hard questions about the stratigraphy. The "hearths" from Tule Springs proved to be just blackened deposits of plants. This was good news, solving as it did a long-standing puzzle: If these were hearths, why were they full of *unburned* snail shells? The curious fracturing of the megafaunal bones turned out to be restricted to remains found in the spring vents, and likely were the product of trampling by animals trapped in those quicksand-like sediments. The "burned" bones were merely stained by groundwater. All the *indisputable* artifacts were from deposits younger than 11,500 years ago.

Still, neither Haynes nor anyone else categorically denied the possibility of an older human presence. Just so, the seeds of skepticism were sown.

Prehistoric rock paintings, found on the back wall of the Pedra Furada rockshelter in southeastern Brazil in 1978, led to seven years of excavations and radiocarbon dates going back 48,000 years. A human presence at that great age is still being disputed, however.

4

FINDING THE TRACES

In 1964, Alex Krieger listed the sites he believed predated the Clovis horizon. In 1976, archaeologist Richard S. MacNeish—an equally enthusiastic proponent of a deep human antiquity in the Americas—did the very same thing. In 1988, so too did archaeologist Richard E. Morlan.

Their lists are almost completely different.

Krieger identified 50 apparently ancient localities across North and South America; for the same area MacNeish tallied 35; Morlan found just five with what he thought was "good evidence." Only four of Krieger's sites were on MacNeish's list, and none of Krieger's sites made it onto Morlan's list. From 1964 to 1988, Krieger's best hopes for the most ancient Americans were abandoned. What happened?

Supporters of deep human antiquity put a positive spin on such wholesale replacement: By 1976, MacNeish had at his disposal a gaggle of new and improved sites that had been unavailable to Krieger. Naturally, MacNeish would use these, his best weapons, in the battle over the antiquity of the first Americans. Maybe. But then, 31 of MacNeish's sites failed to make Morlan's 1988 list.

Critics read a different message, one about shelf-life. Claims for pre-11,500 B.P. sites last about a dozen years before fading into archaeological obscurity. If 90 percent of what was considered the best evidence in 1964 failed to survive until 1976, and if nearly the identical percentage of the best evidence from 1976 failed to make the 1988 list, why put much faith in the sites on the 1988 list? Or, for that matter, in any of the claims that seem to flower every summer field season?

There is one very good reason: Whether the first Americans came here before 11,500 B.P., and whether we have yet detected their traces, are wholly independent concerns. The mere fact that many sites have been proposed, but none accepted, tells us that all of those specific sites are unacceptable. It is also warrant for skepticism toward future claims of great antiquity. But it does not prove that humans were absent from the Americas prior to 11,500 B.P. It only proves that if their traces exist we have yet to detect them.

PASSING THE TEST

The problem is separating legitimate from illegitimate claims for great antiquity. The solution is to apply the criteria that Thomas Chamberlin raised in 1903 and that were finally met at Folsom. Any purportedly ancient site (nowadays, more than 11,500 years old) *must have undeniable traces of humans* (artifacts or skeletons), in *undisturbed geological deposits*, with *indisputable dates*. These are simple criteria. They are virtually identical to those used in Africa to identify the earliest (and often the most ambiguous) traces of human behavior found with pre-modern humans—traces which seem uncommonly uncontroversial.

Yet, as the wholesale changes between the lists of Krieger, MacNeish, and Morlan plainly show, the criteria have proven extraordinarily difficult to meet. So difficult, in fact, that proponents cry foul. The criteria, they charge, are excessively rigid, and were they generally applied to sites of all ages we would be left wondering whether, for example, anyone ever occupied Eastern North America after 11,500 B.P.

These are serious charges: Are the criteria so perversely narrow that they blind archaeologists from seeing legitimate evidence? A closer look is in order.

The first criterion (often the most troublesome) is the presence of genuine artifacts or actual human skeletal remains. So far, at least, human skeletal remains have not figured in the contemporary dispute, simply because few

Pleistocene human remains have been found in North or South America, and certainly none purportedly older than 11,500 B.P. Artifacts are another story.

Human artifacts come in a myriad of materials, but most commonly only those made of stone and, to a lesser degree, bone survive the rough passage of time. Almost certainly the earliest Americans fashioned artifacts of wood, antler, shell, and the like (ceramics and metals came later), but these substances decompose fairly quickly, and are seldom preserved or detected archaeologically.

An artifact is, by definition, any object made, modified, or otherwise used by humans. Oftentimes, fashioning an object for use renders it "unnatural" in form or appearance, making it easy to spot as the product of human hands: a chert cobble turned into a finely crafted spearpoint, or a piece of mammoth rib carved into a socketed wrench. These are easy to recognize as artifacts.

But at other times objects are hardly modified, and even after use show little sign of having been in human hands. A round river cobble may have been employed briefly to smash open a bone for marrow, but it may lack any trace or wear from that action. And just to complicate matters, nature's modification of stone or bone often mimics the action of human hands. Glacial ice and tumbling streams, for example, can fracture stone or bone to the degree that it begins to resemble crude artifacts such as rough-hewn choppers or scrapers. Here it becomes much harder to tell whether an object is an artifact.

Those cases require close scrutiny of *context*. Where was the object found and with what? A round river cobble found at a campsite high above the river, alongside charred and broken animal bones, a charcoal-laden hearth, and a dozen broken spear points, is safely inferred to be an artifact. Roll that cobble back into the river bed, amidst thousands just like it, and it would be indistinguishable. Worse, in that river bed would be naturally broken cobbles that looked more like artifacts than our round cobble. Where artifact look-alikes grade imperceptibly into broken cobbles bearing no resemblance to artifacts, and then into unbroken cobbles, the context bespeaks a natural origin for all. It seems straightforward enough.

TROUBLE IN THE HILLS

The Calico site is located in the hills high above Pleistocene pluvial Lake Manix, in what is now the Mojave Desert near Yermo, California. Scattered on the surface of those hills Ruth de Ette (Dee) Simpson found many stone artifacts, of varying ages. Some were obviously recent, while others looked "Paleolithic" (shades of Abbott and Wright!).

Louis Leakey, fresh from his triumphant discovery of two-million-year-old hominids at Olduvai Gorge, in Tanzania, visited Calico in May 1963. When he saw the site and what appeared to be artifacts in place deep in a commercial bulldozer pit, he was instantly convinced that this was a spot to find ancient Americans. "Dee, dig here," is what he said. "Here" turned out to be smack in the middle of a vast interglacial (pre-Wisconsin) alluvial fan, a mass of waterlaid

Located in the hills above California's Mojave Desert, the Calico site failed to fulfill early expectations as America's most ancient. The rocks jutting from the walls here in the excavation show why. Nature was responsible for breaking millions of rocks at Calico, so the small percentage that appear humanly modified are more likely just nature's imitations of genuine stone tools.

gravel, sand, and mud. Back then, its age was estimated at upwards of 100,000 years old, but it's now thought to be twice that old. Excavations plunged into the fan, and soon recovered "uniquely different" artifacts. Leakey returned in the spring of 1965, and in front of anxious excavation crews examined the haul. He judged at least 25 of the specimens to be humanly made. "Leakey's luck," it seemed, had struck again.

That was enough to entice the National Geographic Society to support more fieldwork at Calico, but with strings attached. The Society funded Vance Haynes and others to evaluate the site's artifacts and geology. When the visiting committee saw that the "artifacts" were being selectively plucked from hundreds of thousands of broken stones occurring naturally in the fan, they urged that all specimens be saved, whether identified as artifacts or not. They were.

Excavations continued at Calico into the 1980s. As the pile of rocks tossed aside as non-artifacts grew to cover several acres, so too did the number of Calico "artifacts" (now over 11,400 pieces). No surprise—millions of broken rocks will produce a proportion that look humanly fractured.

The Calico "artifacts" are simple flaked pieces, the kind nature routinely produces. Were they found in an otherwise indisputable archaeological context, they might be accepted as artifacts. But since they came from a giant, natural gravel crusher, Haynes supposed that none were humanly made. His criticisms sparked a lively discussion over the minutiae of flaked stone: Did the Calico pieces possess uniquely human attributes? In two studies, caliper-wielding critics measured edge angles on bona fide artifacts and naturally broken stones (the so-called Barnes test). When compared, the Calico specimens proved to be more like naturally fractured stones, not humanly fashioned ones.

Ruth "Dee" Simpson, left, and Louis Leakey examine Calico artifacts in 1968. But Dr. Leakey's "luck" as a discoverer of ancient archaeological evidence ran out in the California desert. Few now consider Calico to be an ancient site.

In a deep mass of gravel such as that in the alluvial fan at Calico, it is difficult to tell humanly fashioned artifacts from naturally broken stone. Calico produced many flaked pieces, but nature produces flaked pieces, too. Archaeologists measure the angles of the edges to try to determine whether such stones are genuine artifacts.

Proponents replied that other attributes of the stones bespoke their artificial origins. The problem was that they reached that conclusion after removing from their sample all the pieces not appearing humanly modified. Since the remainder were already supposed to be artificial, it is easy to see why they all looked alike, and all looked "artificial." The pattern reveals only their sorting criteria, and has no necessary bearing on whether these attributes mark human modification.

Archaeologist Nicholas Toth, who deals with Africa's (and thus humanity's) earliest stone tools, bemoans the absence of a "definitive 'litmus test' in ascertaining whether an assemblage of fractured lithic (stone) material is humanly manufactured or not." Without one, good context becomes indispensable.

Unfortunately, a site such as Calico represents "a worst scenario" (Toth's words) for documenting a human presence: Against the backdrop of all those naturally broken rocks, is there reason to suppose any are artificially fractured? Or if they were, could they be identified amidst the millions of naturally fractured stones?

In the end, Calico's best hope for an archaeological context vanished when a semi-circular "hearth," found deep in the excavations, proved not to be a hearth at all. It was a natural rock spread that, friend and foe admit, only looked hearth-like after the surrounding gravel was removed. Nowadays, very few archaeologists consider Calico an ancient archaeological site.

"Leakey's luck" ran out in the California desert, a couple of hours down the road from Las Vegas, where dreams are daily made, and lost, on luck.

STENO'S LEGACY

As archaeology moves into the 21st century, it carries with it a tool from a much earlier time. That tool is *stratigraphy*, the interpretation of layers of earth

Danish geologist and anatomist Niels Steensen (1638-1686), the forefather of the science of stratigraphy.

and their relative age. Niels Steensen, better known by his Latin pen-name, Nicolaus Steno, in 1669 formulated the first principle of stratigraphy: In an undisturbed deposit, layers of earth at the bottom are older than those at the top. That's pretty pedestrian stuff by modern standards, but still problems arise. The key word is "undisturbed."

In an ideal world (not this one), artifacts found in, say, Late Wisconsin age loess, would presumably be Late Wisconsin in age. Yet in the real world both natural processes (burrowing animals, shrinking and swelling of clays, erosion, among others) and human action—such as our tendency to bury our dead—disturb the deposits in which archaeological remains are found. Younger artifacts can easily intrude into older strata, falsely implying they are just as old.

Back in the pre-Folsom days, Holmes and Hrdlička guarded against that possibility by starting with the assumption that any artifact or human skeleton found in Pleistocene-aged deposits had arrived there much later. That's a bit extreme. Still, in the sometimes complex stratigraphy of ancient valleys, terraces, and especially caves, where claims of great antiquity hang in the balance, stratigraphic caution is honorable.

EARLY CHILD ON OLDMAN RIVER

On July 11, 1961, in a modern gully draining into the Oldman River of southwestern Alberta (near Taber), A. MacS. Stalker of Canada's Geological Survey came across the fragmentary skeleton of a four-month-old infant. Little could be told of the child's heartrending story, but perhaps the tiny presence was a story in itself. The remains were in a block of calcium carbonate cemented sands, apparently broken away from a layer of ancient stream deposits (alluvium) exposed on the gully floor.

The alluvium layer was deep below the surface of the prairie, itself no great sign of age. But more importantly, the alluvium was above one glacial till and beneath another. By Steno's law, the child predated the Late Wisconsin till; given how far beneath the till the skeleton was found, it might date well into the Middle Wisconsin.

A geologist by training, Stalker was aware of possible stratigraphic disturbance and intrusion, but in 1977 he expressly denied that such disturbance had happened at the Taber site. In his eyes there was no evidence for any erosion, older than the modern gully but younger than the alluvium, which might have carried the infant's remains down from the surface. No, the bones were old, he insisted, their age bracketed by the ages of the enclosing alluvium. Based on the age of that alluvium as radiocarbon dated from nearby sites, the bones were likely more than 18,000 years old, and perhaps in the range between 37,000 and 60,000 years old. Unfortunately, however, there was not enough bone to be directly dated using the radiocarbon techniques then available, and despite Stalker's almost annual visits to the site no more bone was found.

Stalker's confidence notwithstanding, few were completely satisfied with the antiquity of the Taber child. In 1978 and 1979, archaeologist Michael Wilson and others returned to the site to look for more remains and to clarify the stratigraphic sequence. They had no better luck finding skeletal remains than Stalker, but they did spot on the slopes of the Taber site patches of bone-bearing, redeposited Holocene sands.

Those recent sands possessed many features thought unique to the Middle Wisconsin alluvium, but careful inspection revealed the two sands were quite different in texture, color, and chemistry. Fortunately, the sand adhering to the remains of the Taber child had been saved and, when analyzed, proved to be like the Holocene sands, not the Middle Wisconsin sands. At some time in the recent past, the unfortunate child's bones were redeposited alongside, but not in, a layer of genuine antiquity.

Quite independently in the 1980s, a tiny piece of the Taber skeleton was dated by the newly developed technique of radiocarbon dating using an accelerator mass spectrometer (AMS dating, it's called). The results put the antiquity of the Taber child at 3550, plus or minus 500 years, B.P. That's a date Stalker rejects, because of possible contamination of the bone. Perhaps. But even if the date is off, the revised stratigraphy shows it is not off by much.

THE DATING GAME

Any purportedly early site must, of course, have secure radiometric dates testifying to its antiquity. Radiocarbon dating is the method of choice, for very good reason. It is based on the straightforward physical principle that every organism absorbs atmospheric isotopic carbon (^{14}C) and, that once the organism dies, the subsequent radioactive decay of ^{14}C occurs at a statistically known and measurable rate. The time it takes for half of the ^{14}C in a sample to decay—the radiocarbon half-life—is 5730, plus or minus 40 years. Estimating the remaining ^{14}C in a sample gives an age and its standard deviation (the accompanying ± figure, in years, represents a statistical best guess within which the true age falls). By convention, the "present" in radiocarbon years is set at 1950.

Over the decades since its development in the 1950s by Willard Libby, radiocarbon's underlying assumptions have been finely combed and its laboratory techniques refined to the point where even tiny samples in a potential age range upwards of 50,000 years old can be expected to produce valid ages.

Radiocarbon dating works on a range of organic materials, but not well in all instances. Because bone, ivory, and shell, unlike wood and charcoal, are unstable biochemically, and thus susceptible to organic and inorganic contamination, they can produce unreliable results. Still, advances in bone geochemistry insure that, when properly done, radiocarbon dates on bone yield accurate dates, though perhaps not as accurate as those on wood and charcoal. If anomalous ages do occur, enough is known to pinpoint their possible source of error and make corrections.

Radiocarbon dating transformed the science of archaeology and has become the method of choice in the dating of early sites. Its inventor, Dr. Willard F. Libby, is shown here in his University of Chicago laboratory in 1954.

Radiocarbon dating improved dramatically with the advent of AMS dating, wherein different carbon forms in a sample are separated at high speeds in a circular or oval particle accelerator. The isotopically heavier ^{14}C atoms fly off the racetrack and crash into a strategically placed mass spectrometer, which instantly counts them.

The conventional radiocarbon technique, by contrast, must wait for these ^{14}C atoms to decay back into nitrogen, specifically ^{14}N, and then catch the emitted electrons on a detector. Older samples with less ^{14}C obviously have fewer and more widely spaced emissions. Therefore, obtaining a statistically reliable count of them can take days, weeks, and sometimes even months. In fact, because ^{14}C is measured directly by the AMS dating technique, it also works on much smaller samples. All the better for dealing with rare traces of the first Americans.

But the handicap of radiocarbon dating, which will be especially felt if the first Americans prove to be far older than advertised, is that it does not provide reliable dates for samples more than about 50,000 years old. In theory it should, but for practical reasons it doesn't. So far, anyway. The major obstacle is that organic remains are rarely preserved from older sites. And if they are, the amount of surviving ^{14}C is so small and the contamination potential so high (even during sample preparation), that the results are easily skewed. Better sample preparation will help here, and may even get radiocarbon dating over the 50,000 B.P. hump.

Until then, waiting in the wings are dating methods offering ages within and beyond radiocarbon's limits. Most prominent among them are amino-acid racemization (AAR), which works off postmortem changes in the structure of amino acids, and uranium series dating, based on the radioactive decay of long-lived isotopes of uranium. But with AAR and many others as well, controversy re-enters the scene, for some are still experimental, and none (so far) are as tried and true as radiocarbon dating.

THESE OLD BONES

In 1973, a nearly complete female skeleton was excavated from the Sunnyvale drainage channel in the San Francisco Bay area. The skeleton had been interred in a well-defined grave, nearly 10 feet (3 meters) beneath the present surface. The grave was dug into—and thus by Steno's law was younger than—sediments containing Pleistocene megafauna and snail shells radiocarbon dated to approximately 10,000 B.P. Such burials were commonly dug along the shores of the Bay area in middle to late Holocene times. There was no reason to accord it any great antiquity. Until the AAR results.

Geochemist Jeffrey Bada, a pioneer in applying the AAR technique to bone (it was previously and successfully used on marine shell), announced in 1975 that the Sunnyvale skeleton had an AAR-determined age of 70,000 years. Not only would this be the oldest North American, it was then the oldest known

Willard Libby's process of radiocarbon dating is based on the decay of radioactive carbon 14 over time. The decay begins at the moment any organism dies and occurs at a known and measurable rate. The pathway of carbon 14 is shown in the chart at right.

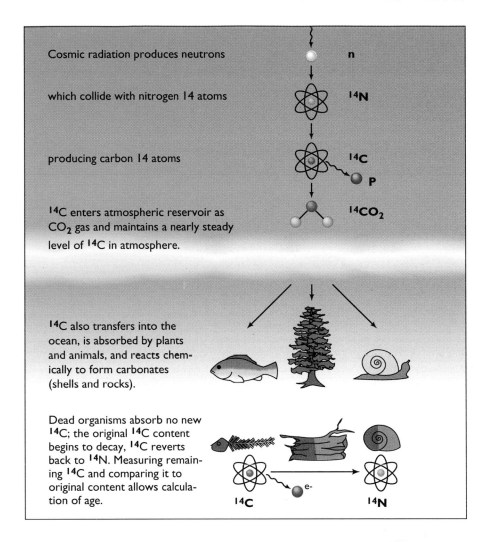

Cosmic radiation produces neutrons   n

which collide with nitrogen 14 atoms ^{14}N

producing carbon 14 atoms ^{14}C P

^{14}C enters atmospheric reservoir as CO_2 gas and maintains a nearly steady level of ^{14}C in atmosphere. $^{14}CO_2$

^{14}C also transfers into the ocean, is absorbed by plants and animals, and reacts chemically to form carbonates (shells and rocks).

Dead organisms absorb no new ^{14}C; the original ^{14}C content begins to decay, ^{14}C reverts back to ^{14}N. Measuring remaining ^{14}C and comparing it to original content allows calculation of age. ^{14}C e- ^{14}N

Homo sapiens sapiens in the world! More surprises: Half a dozen other human skeletons from southern California produced AAR ages that began at 23,000 and reached back over 50,000 years ago.

That was too much. Ancient Californians could be that old. Yet, these were the first dates from an experimental application which, certainly in the Sunnyvale case, thoroughly disagreed with known geological and archaeological evidence. Skeptics began sharpening their knives.

Uranium series dates slashed Sunnyvale's age from 70,000 to 9000 B.P. Now, at least, Steno could breathe easier. Then a series of AMS radiocarbon dates, directed by R.E. Taylor, shaved Sunnyvale's antiquity down to a modest (and archaeologically sensible) 3600 to 4850 B.P. Taylor's group ran AMS dates on all the ancient Californians. None was more than 5100 years old. The amino acid racemization dates had been off an order of magnitude.

When the University of Arizona's Accelerator Mass Spectrometer was installed in 1982, it was the first facility of its kind in North America. Shown here is the particle accelerator. Increasing in number, such facilities are revolutionizing radiocarbon dating, by making it possible to rapidly date minute samples that were previously undatable.

Amino acid racemization works well with marine shell. What went wrong in applying it to human skeletons? Lay part of the blame at radiocarbon's door: Racemization rates are calibrated against bones of known age. The calibration was based on a human skeleton from Laguna, California, radiocarbon dated to 17,150 ± 1470 B.P. Much later, AMS dating showed it was only 5100 ± 500 years old, but by then the damage had been done. The original radiocarbon date was used for the AAR calibration, which implied a slow racemization rate and produced AAR ages far too old.

Afterward, Bada showed that if he used Laguna's corrected (AMS) date to calibrate the racemization rate, the resulting amino acid racemization ages swung right into line with Taylor's AMS ages. But not perfectly, so amino acid racemization dating is not out of the woods yet. More must be, and is being, learned of racemization in bone, and of what other factors might skew AAR dates.

MANY CALL, FEW ARE CHOSEN

The problems at Calico, Taber, and Sunnyvale are matched in a roll call of sites from Old Crow in Canada's Yukon Territory, to Valsequillo in Mexico and Pikimachay in Peru. And so the lists of Krieger, MacNeish, and Morlan were winnowed of questionable artifacts, disturbed stratigraphy, flawed dates, or some combination of all three.

So many sites, so many problems. They all began with such promise, only to fade in the harsh light of critical scrutiny. The pattern is almost predictable.

The failure of so many sites does make one wonder: Are the criteria unfairly applied or unduly rigid?

Many proponents think they are, and complain that the criteria are not being applied to sites younger than 11,500 years old. But why should they be? We know people were here then. It is when we reach back before 11,500 years ago that our knowledge of prehistory crosses the boundary from the known to the unknown, and at that point the criteria become indispensable for evaluating claims of great antiquity.

Are the criteria too rigid? Hardly. These are the very same criteria met at Folsom in 1927. The fact that so many sites since then have not measured up speaks more of problems with the sites than with the criteria.

Of course, we must also admit that questionable artifacts, garbled stratigraphy, or bad dates can and do occur in sites younger than 11,500 B.P., but their effects are just not as devastating since our knowledge of prehistory helps fill in gaps and resolve ambiguity. So, too, there is no reason to think such problems are endemic in sites older than 11,500 B.P. Remember the decades before 1927: Archaeologists rejected scores of avowed Pleistocene-aged sites, but humans were here in the Pleistocene and ultimately their traces were found at Folsom. So we continue the search.

There are payoffs along the way. In the course of controversy new ideas, methods, and techniques are tried, and the field of archaeology advances as a result. William Irving, for example, found at Old Crow broken bones of Pleistocene megafauna in geological contexts upwards of 350,000 years old. He and colleagues showed experimentally that humans could create the fractures seen in the Old Crow bones. Fair enough. But then Irving laid down the gauntlet, insisting that *only* humans could make those fractures. It was "difficult to imagine," he said, nature breaking bones the same way.

His challenge was picked up by a crowd of researchers who showed how nature—carnivores gnawing, large animals trampling, rivers freezing and thawing, even volcanoes exploding—breaks bones in similar fashion. Few now believe the Old Crow bones were humanly modified, but nearly everyone agrees that in reaching that conclusion we learned a great deal more about the mechanics of bone breakage than we ever knew before.

Those invaluable lessons close critical gaps in our understanding of the archaeological record, and like other knowledge forged in this dispute, the lessons learned ripple out to benefit the archaeology of other times and places.

Its end carefully serrated, this caribou tibia bone tool, found in the Old Crow River drainage by Dr. William Irving, was initially radiocarbon dated to 27,000 B.P. No more bone tools were found, and when the specimen was later redated by AMS it proved to be only 1350 years old.

LOOKING FOR A FEW GOOD SITES

It all comes down to this: No matter how vigorously claims of great antiquity are promoted, and often they are promoted with great vigor, they will never prove convincing unless the artifacts, stratigraphy, and ages are unimpeachable. The claims must convince the community of archaeological skeptics. The fans already believe. Are there sites to convince the skeptics?

Meadowcroft Rockshelter is 30 miles (48 kilometers) west of Pittsburgh, Pennsylvania, along Cross Creek, a tributary of the Ohio River. Archaeologist James Adovasio and an interdisciplinary team of geologists, paleontologists, palynologists, and others began work in this large sandstone overhang in 1973. Over the next five years, meticulous excavations went through 16 feet (5 meters) of sediment, divisible into 11 natural strata, in which were artifacts, charcoal, and various features of human occupation, mostly from later (Woodland) occupations (marked by pottery sherds and early domesticated plants such as squash and corn). In the deeper levels of Stratum 11 was a rich record of Archaic hunter-gatherers and beneath that of Paleoindians.

The entire stratigraphic sequence is anchored by an extraordinary 52 radio-carbon dates (all on charcoal, save one), ranging in age from 31,400 B.P. up to the Historic period—the Declaration of Independence was signed just about the time the last fire at Meadowcroft went out. All but four dates are in proper stratigraphic order, and the ones out of order are minor flip-flops in Holocene-age levels. Steno would have been proud.

The action is down in middle Stratum 11a—bracketed between 11,300 and 12,800 years ago, which has produced an unfluted lanceolate projectile point—and lower Stratum 11a. (The underlying Stratum 1 lacks human traces.) Lower Stratum 11a has artifacts associated with six radiocarbon dates ranging from 12,800 B.P. to 16,175 B.P. These are genuine artifacts too and, while few in number (about 700), they include flake debris from stone tool making, long and narrow stone blades, unifacial (flaked on one side only) and bifacial knives, and pointed tools called gravers that possibly were used for bone or wood working. The stone for these artifacts came from distant sources in Ohio, West Virginia, and Pennsylvania.

The average of the dates associated with these artifacts is around 14,250 years B.P., considered to be the conservative interpretation for the first human presence at Meadowcroft. However, the date may be earlier still. Deeper in Stratum 11a, a small fragment of a plaited basket or mat was found and directly dated to 19,600 ± 2400 B.P.

But, skeptics say, consider the implications: 14,250 years ago the Laurentide ice sheet came within 50 miles (80 kilometers) of Meadowcroft. At that close range, Meadowcroft ought to have experienced near-glacial climatic and ecological conditions. Permafrost and tundra, perhaps, or short of that a boreal setting with cold-loving flora and fauna. Yet there is no evidence for either.

Present in the Pleistocene-age levels at Meadowcroft are wood and charcoal from deciduous trees (oak, hickory, and walnut), along with the bones of white-tailed deer, southern flying squirrel, and passenger pigeon. That speaks of a temperate environment, anomalous for such a time and place. Where are the bones of the extinct Pleistocene fauna, and the remains of displaced Arctic or boreal plant and animal groups? Certainly not in the lowest levels at

Painstakingly careful excavation was a hallmark of the work at Meadowcroft Rockshelter in Pennsylvania. The excavation sidewall is dotted with tags marking individual depositional events in the filling of the shelter by sediment and rockfall.

Meadowcroft, but then hardly any organic remains come from there. Nearly one million animal bones were recovered from the entire shelter excavations, but only 278 bones came from the lower reaches of Stratum IIa, and of those just II could be identified. Same story with the plants. Roughly 300,000 fragments of wood, charcoal, seeds, and fruits were recovered. The grand total from the glacial-age levels was a pitiful .4 ounces (11.9 grams).

That's a hopelessly inadequate basis on which to judge whether the anomaly is real, or a freak of sampling that netted only deciduous elements from the local complex boreal-deciduous forests. Adovasio's team sees no anomaly, attributing the absence of boreal species to Meadowcroft's low-lying and south-facing aspect. Still, without an adequate sample, the Meadowcroft paleo-environmental record cannot well support any interpretation.

Take the anomaly at face value, critics suggest: Might it imply the radiocarbon dates are wrong and that Stratum IIa is actually post-glacial in age? Meadowcroft is, after all, in western Pennsylvania coal country, and skeptics, Haynes foremost among them, wonder whether ancient coal, coming into the deposits as dust or through groundwater, contaminated the Meadowcroft radiocarbon samples inflating their actual ages.

Adovasio and colleagues counter that the closest coal to the rockshelter is 2625 feet (800 meters) distant, and neither coal particles nor coal-associated spores were found in microscope scans of the radiocarbon samples. Likewise, the coal-like wood on the floor of the shelter—the possible source of ground water contaminants—does not dissolve in water. Besides, if there had been contamination all 52 dates should have been affected. How could that have

happened, while still leaving them in near-perfect stratigraphic order? Maybe, Haynes responds, only samples from lower Stratum IIa sat in contaminated ground water and are proportionately older as a result.

Round and round it goes. So far, Meadowcroft has cheated archaeology's actuarial tables, with more written about it than any other potential early site, save Trenton itself. Most has been an ever-narrowing exchange over radiocarbon dates, and resolution now converges on a simple test: Will AMS dates on tiny plant remains from lower Stratum IIa confirm the site's great antiquity? We await those results, and the Meadowcroft summary volume. For with the complete publication of data, such as detailed descriptions of individual artifacts and precise information on their position relative to radiocarbon samples and the site stratigraphy, it should be possible at last to reach a consensus about Meadowcroft.

EARLY AMERICAN ART?

Toca do Boqueirão do Sítio da Pedra Furada is a shallow, 230-foot (70-meter) wide rockshelter located in the remote plateaus of northeast Brazil. In 1973 archaeologist Niède Guidon discovered prehistoric paintings on its back walls. Attracted by the possibility of dating the artwork, she began excavations in 1978 that continued until bedrock was reached in 1985. Her team dug through nearly 15 feet (5 meters)—and as many strata—of sediment that filled the shelter. They now have 42 radiocarbon dates tying down the age of the strata, the deepest of which is more than 48,000 years old.

Guidon recognizes two distinct archaeological occupations in the shelter. The earlier one, the Pedra Furada phase, extends from 14,300 to more than 48,000 years ago. The sediment in these levels is not conducive to preservation; it lacks bone, wood, or other organic remains. However, Guidon reports artifacts and fragments of rock art throughout those deposits, associated with numerous stone-lined hearths containing charcoal and heated pebbles.

The artifacts themselves are made entirely of local stone, quartz, and quartzite pebbles picked up from rock piles adjacent to the shelter. They are all simple blunt points, pebble chopping tools, knives, and flakes. Finished tools, Guidon's team believes, must have been taken off the site prehistorically, for they are few and the stone inventory is dominated by flaking debris.

Fragments of painted rock, fallen from the walls, occur in levels dated to approximately 32,000 B.P. But in Guidon's view, the best evidence for early art is a piece flaked from the wall on which are painted two red lines. It was found in a hearth dated to 17,000 ± 400 B.P., which would make it the oldest example by far of early American art, and among the oldest in the world.

Guidon describes the second and later occupation in the shelter, the Serra Talhada phase postdating 10,400 B.P., as having different hearths and artifacts than those in the older levels. These later assemblages include artifacts made more frequently of non-locally available flint, along with abundant ocher (a natural paint), and rock art. Such wholesale differences above and below

75

PREVIOUS PAGE: Archaeological evidence from the Meadowcroft Rockshelter, near the modern city of Pittsburgh, suggests that the Pennsylvania site may have provided a temporary home for humans as long ago as 14,000 years, when the mighty Laurentide ice sheet was beginning its retreat.

10,400 B.P. naturally attract the attention of skeptics who wonder whether the material down below is truly archaeological.

Given the scant published evidence, there is room for such skepticism. The site is cut into the base of a 330-foot (100-meter) sandstone cliff. Eroding from a conglomerate layer at the top of that rise are quartz and quartzite cobbles which, when dislodged by erosion, made that 330-foot free fall, or were otherwise carried down by what Guidon describes as "violent torrents of water." No wonder skeptics suspect there is a fuzzy and insecure line separating the crude specimens identified as humanly flaked from those discarded as naturally broken. Guidon's team apparently has made comparisons of stones flaked by natural free-fall and those modified by humans. Perhaps their results, when published with detailed descriptions of the specimens, will quiet this issue.

And the hearths? Critics suspect the burning in the earlier, less-defined hearths may have resulted from natural brush fires. Guidon regards the suggestion as "quite impossible" and a misinterpretation of the hearth structures themselves. Thermoluminescence analyses to measure whether the hearths were exposed to the high temperatures of a campfire were, at best, equivocal.

It is too soon to tell about Pedra Furada. Guidon unhappily complains about a "Cold War" in American archaeology, and calls for proponents and skeptics alike to seek out and evaluate together the necessary evidence. Fair enough. But science, like charity, begins at home, and so far only a handful of reports have been published on Pedra Furada. Under these circumstances, neither Guidon's claims nor those of her critics can well be accepted. The shrill accusation that American archaeologists are "biased" and breeding a "Kafkaesque" situation (Guidon's words) in which old sites are bad, can be put to the test simply and neatly by providing the detailed data necessary to evaluate the hearths, artifacts, and art from Pedra Furada.

BANKING ON CHINCHIHUAPI CREEK

Monte Verde, on the banks of Chinchihuapi Creek in southern Chile, 31 miles (50 kilometers) up the Rio Maullín from the Pacific Ocean, is the most extraordinary of all the candidates for great antiquity. What makes it so is a water-saturated peat bog that covered the sandy habitation surface soon after its late Pleistocene residents departed. In that oxygen-starved setting, normal decay processes stalled, preserving a stunning array of organic remains from wood, fruits, seeds, leaves (some chewed!), and stems, to marine algae, and even chunks of animal hide. That's not the usual fare at an archaeological site.

All the more surprising are the radiocarbon dates. Charcoal and bone, along with artifacts of wood and ivory from atop MV II, the habitation surface, have ages ranging from 11,790 ± 200 to 13,565 ± 250 years ago.

Excavations at Monte Verde were conducted from 1976 to 1985 by an interdisciplinary group directed by University of Kentucky archaeologist Tom D. Dillehay. The team members dug where the site was, and dug where it wasn't.

Cut into the 300-foot-high sandstone cliffs of the Serra Talhada, the Pedra Furada Rockshelter is thought to contain some of the oldest art and artifacts in the Americas. But the site's evidence has been disputed, prompting its excavator to accuse the critics of breeding a "Kafkaesque" situation. The accusation is overstated, at best.

Dillehay, with a sidelong glance toward Calico, ventured more than a mile up and down the creek to examine naturally deposited, non-artifact bearing sediments. That preemptive shoveling deflects inevitable questions about whether the site formed naturally, by highlighting differences between natural deposits and suspected archaeological ones.

The differences are impressive. Unlike the natural deposits, the MV II surface is rich in plant remains, a number of which came from the Pacific coast, from high Andean settings, or from faraway arid grasslands. Those plants were carried to the site and, coincidence or not, many of them have economic or medicinal value. The remains of mastodons, Pleistocene llamas, smaller mammals, fish, and shellfish also appeared on MV II.

The MV II surface is adorned with two large hearths and more than two dozen smaller ones, many of which are lined with imported clays. Next to one hearth was a most "unnatural" item: a human footprint in the clay. All these hearths are among the remains of 12 rectangular huts, roughly 10 x 11.5 feet (3 x 3.5 meters) in size, defined by split and planed logs and branches, held in position by stakes and ties made of different plants. Some logs have bits of animal skin clinging to them, possibly the remains of hide that once draped the shelters.

Just 100 feet (30 meters) downstream—but on the MV II surface—was a wishbone-shaped mound about 13 x 10 feet (3.9 x 3 meters) composed of compacted sand and gravel, hardened with animal fat, and lined with stubs of wooden posts. It was fronted by a cache of salt (brought from the coast), a hearth, a scatter of mastodon skin and bones, plant remains, chewed boldo leaves (a medicinal tea), and artifacts.

Most of the artifacts on MV II are wooden—digging sticks, mortars, a lance—while others are bone, and still others (some 715 specimens) are stone. Not all the stone pieces, not even the majority, are indisputably artifacts. Many are unmodified stones from the stream bed or distant coastal beaches, which, because they were found on sandy sediments and show an unnaturally narrow range of shapes, are tentatively accorded human authorship. Still, this is no Calico. There are bona fide artifacts, including a polished basalt perforator, bifaces, flake tools, choppers, bola stones and grinding stones, along with two nearly identical bifacial points, one from the hut area and the other from near the wishbone-shaped mound. Most of the stone was locally derived, but about 80 specimens come from distant sources. So too did the bitumen, a natural tar from the coast, flakes of which still mark specimens once attached to wooden or bone handles.

Dillehay and others see Monte Verde's testimony partly corroborated at Taima-Taima, Venezuela. The points from the two sites resemble each other, and at Taima-Taima they were closely associated with the skeleton of a young mastodon dated to approximately 13,000 B.P. Skeptics question the Taima-Taima association, wondering whether the points sank through overlying wet sediment, ultimately to come to rest next to the bones. If so, nature is wonderfully mischievous. One of the points rests snugly in the cavity of the mastodon's right pelvic bone. The jury is still out on Taima-Taima.

Same story with Monte Verde, though it is far more of a challenge to find flaws with its evidence. Cornell University archaeologist Thomas Lynch has tried. In a critique handicapped by the incomplete nature of the published data on Monte Verde, he suggested there were few artifacts at the site, and those that were found likely came from later (Archaic) occupations in the area. To which Dillehay responded, there are no later deposits in the area.

After learning that the Monte Verde points also were associated with mastodon bones, Lynch re-interpreted Monte Verde as "early" Paleoindian. By doing so, presumably, MV II becomes just another Paleoindian occupation and the Clovis-age barrier remains intact. Will the radiocarbon dates allow that?

The oldest of the MV II dates is 13,565 ± 250 B.P. It was run on charcoal which was found sealed and preserved in a clay-lined feature. Dillehay thinks this sample best represents the age of the occupation. Maybe, but with eight other dates from MV II ranging over 1700 years, he knows there are alternative interpretations, and he offers some. That's not enough for University of Massachusetts archaeologist Dena Dincauze, who chides Dillehay for "enthusiastic, uncritical use" of the radiocarbon ages.

Monte Verde, located in southern Chile, because of its rare and extraordinary preservation, yielded half-chewed leaves, seeds, the remains of fruit, and chunks of animal hide, as well as the wood, shown here, that framed the huts of this ancient settlement.

Found near one of the many clay-lined hearths at the habitation surface of Monte Verde was this human footprint preserved in clay. Artifacts found at this stratum have dates of over 12,000 B.P.

The proper approach, Dincauze explains, is simply to drop the oldest date. After doing so, the remaining dates center around 12,300 B.P. As it happens, this was an alternative Dillehay considered. But he saw more justifiable ones: excluding bone and ivory dates because of their biochemical instability, for instance, and including only those on charcoal or wooden artifacts. That approach puts the MV II occupation between 12,500 and 13,500 B.P.

Given the scatter of MV II radiocarbon ages, it is easy enough to pick ones that make the occupation younger (or older). The trick is doing so whilst being true to the archaeological context and violating the fewest canons of radiocarbon dating. The scatter of dates is understandable given the materials dated and the different laboratories involved, but it can and should be tightened. While MV II may get younger, it will not be by much. The youngest date is still nearly 12,000 years old.

Much more is to come on Monte Verde. The first of the published volumes concentrated on the site geology, chronology, and paleoenvironment. Soon the second volume on the artifacts and architecture will appear, and it will provide skeptics a detailed presentation of the artifacts, especially those radiocarbon dated, and the structures, footprint, and hearths.

Then too, perhaps, we will learn if Monte Verde is, in fact, far more than 12,000 to 13,000 years old. About 5 feet (1.5 meters) below the MV II level, but 80 meters away from the main site area, is another sandy unit, MV I, in which excavations turned up 26 stone specimens (three unequivocally artifacts), and three small, shallow, circular hearth-like basins, each containing charcoal dated to more than 33,000 years old. Unfortunately, MV I hasn't the spectacular preservation of MV II. For now, MV I remains an enigma.

Lynch and Dincauze, meanwhile, valiantly try to squeeze MV II into a Clovis Paleoindian age. Even granting their success, Monte Verde may not go away that easily. At 12,300 years old, it would be older than any Paleoindian site in North or South America and still have considerable implications for the antiquity of the first Americans.

Hunter-gatherers can travel quite quickly within familiar environments in which they know where (or how) to find water; which plants are edible and when; how animal prey behaves; where rock outcrops are available to replenish their stone supplies; and so forth. Such knowledge is hard won over lifetimes and generations, but it pays off handsomely. In vast and ecologically homogeneous niches, groups such as the caribou-hunting Nunamuit Eskimo, Southern Methodist University archaeologist Lewis Binford reports, use about 8,500 square miles (22,000 square kilometers) during the course of a lifetime.

Yet, to the first Americans this was new and exotic land, which became ever more alien to their Beringian experience as they encountered different habitats on their journey south (those differences would have been vastly greater on an inland route, as opposed to a coastal one). With every ecological boundary they crossed, and there were many, the process of finding water, food, and critical materials began anew. That took time—lots of time. This was not the Monte Verde Land Rush, with a known destination, a timetable to meet, and wagons bulging with homesteading provisions.

Of course, there is no particular reason to think these groups would hurry if they could hurry. Imagining the first Americans as bold explorers impatient to see over the next hill is appealing, tapping as it does romantic currents in our own history. Still, the reality may have been far different. Unlike Portuguese seafarers and French fur trappers and traders, whose business it was to explore new land, the first Americans were there to set up homesteads. They might migrate quickly across unsuitable regions, but once a better habitat was found, would easily lose that incentive. When populations grew too large, or some calamity occurred, migration would become necessary. But for obvious reasons it likely involved a move to similar habitats wherever possible, and not so far that kinship links with the original population were broken. The migration process has slow rhythms, not too far and not too fast.

Under these circumstances, if people were at Monte Verde as late as 12,300 years ago, they must have left Beringia many thousands of years earlier. Just how many thousands depends—on their adaptive strategies, obstacles they may have encountered (such as the great ice sheets), and whether their route took them through more homogeneous environments (such as down the coast). Suppose these groups took an inland route, and the ice sheets were an obstacle between 20,000 and 14,000 years ago. If the early Monte Verdeans were there by 12,300 B.P., then either they came through the ice-free corridor just after it reopened, and in just 1,700 years traversed 7500 miles (12,000 kilometers) of complex and unfamiliar environments to reach the subantarctic, or—likelier under the circumstances—they migrated south before the corridor closed 20,000 years ago.

WHERE WILL WE FIND THE FIRST AMERICANS?

Seen in those terms, Monte Verde in South America raises hard questions about the initial entry to North America. If people were down there before 11,500 B.P., why haven't much older traces of their presence been found up north? Could it be that North American archaeologists haven't looked in the right places or in the right way for possibly ancient sites?

There is a curious fact about the archaeology of rockshelters and caves in North America: Paleoindian traces are rarely found in them (Meadowcroft is an obvious exception). Yet around the world, from Arago, France, to Zhoukoudian, China, caves were used beginning at least 250,000 years ago. Various hypotheses are contrived to explain why Paleoindians failed to inhabit North American caves, notably that they never found them. University of Texas archaeologist Michael Collins has another idea: North American archaeologists only excavate the younger (generally Holocene) deposits in caves, and routinely fail to peer beneath massive roof spalls—like Adovasio did at Meadowcroft—to see what lies in older, Pleistocene sediments. It may only seem as if Paleoindians did not live in caves.

In fact, we know there are many areas yet to be searched systematically for the traces of the first Americans: deeply buried late Pleistocene surfaces, bogs and coastlines, wetlands, forests (particularly in the tropics), even the 37-mile-wide (60-kilometer-wide) bottleneck connecting North and South America, through which the earliest South Americans must have traveled. Searching those settings will require more than the usual archaeological field techniques. Geological and geophysical remote sensing techniques will become increasingly in demand.

Only when those gaps in the archaeological record are filled can an absence of evidence for the first Americans be taken as evidence of their absence. Until then, Clovis-age traces remain the oldest agreed-upon presence in this hemisphere, but the betting money is on MV II at Monte Verde to break the 11,500 B.P. barrier.

Meadowcroft and Pedra Furada may clear the hurdle too, but if they do, it will be without Monte Verde's help. The antiquity of the one has no effect on the antiquity of the others. After all, the discovery at Folsom broke the Holmes-Hrdličkian logjam, but Abbott's paleoliths became no older as a result. If sites on Krieger's, MacNeish's, and Morlan's lists were not old archaeological sites before Monte Verde, they will not become old archaeological sites because of Monte Verde.

Teeth help tell the tale of the first Americans. Research traces signature dental traits from prehistoric Native Americans and modern Asians t

determine genetic relationship.

5

WHO WERE THE FIRST AMERICANS?

"The hour has at last arrived," linguist Pliny Earle Goddard crowed in the spring of 1927, "for an extensive reorganization of our conception of the peopling of America." And about time, too. Goddard had just read Harold Cook's proclamation that Texas' Lone Wolf Creek site, with its artifacts and extinct bison, proved beyond "reasonable doubt" that humans were in America in the Pleistocene. (Along with Folsom, Lone Wolf Creek was one of the sites Figgins and Cook were championing.)

Goddard had known it all along. But he was delighted to hear the news from Cook, for it meant that Holmes and Hrdlička, whom he despised (the feeling was mutual), were wrong. Goddard scolded them for refusing to admit a deep human antiquity on this continent. People so inclined to be critical, he sneered, should have doubted that humans were recent, not the other way around. How else could one explain the great number of languages spoken by Native Americans?

Assuming the first Americans spoke one language "as pure biology would require," it was logical to conclude that they must have arrived "many millenniums" ago for their single language to evolve into the hundreds now spoken in native America. Goddard guessed 100,000 years or more was about right. Not a bad number, Cook supposed. Lone Wolf Creek, as he figured it, was easily 100,000 years old.

But Holmes and Hrdlička weren't buying. Cook's paper was just "another head of the Hydra," which they moved swiftly to sever. Goddard's many languages were easily explained by successive migrations from Asia of different-speaking peoples, they said. Besides, Hrdlička argued on his own preeminent authority, Native Americans and Asians were so similar physically that they could not be long separated.

Archaeologists, physical anthropologists, and linguists still haven't stopped bickering over the origins of the first Americans. However, for a few years now peace has been threatening to break out.

Quarry Bank on Lone Wolf Creek, Texas, was the site of an early archaeological dispute over the relative antiquity of the first Americans.

SPEAKING OF THE FIRST AMERICANS

In 1983, University of Arizona geneticist Stephen Zegura listened attentively as Stanford University linguist Joseph Greenberg offered his radical claim that all Native American languages could be clustered into just three linguistic families, each one the descendant of three independent groups that had migrated separately to America.

Zegura was astonished. He had heard the punch line before from his colleague at Arizona State University, Christy Turner, except that it hadn't been based on languages at all. Turner studies teeth. Zegura took another look at the genetics of Native Americans: With just a bit of prodding, genetic evidence could also be made to fit a model of three migrations to America. This was no coincidence. The evidence from languages, teeth, and genes was rapidly converging on a single story of the number, relative order, and antiquity of migrations to the Americas. And if all that weren't enough, the whole seemed to fit neatly with archaeological and geological data. It's quite a story.

At the time of European arrival, Native Americans spoke a bewildering number of languages. Just how many, no one knows. Over the centuries since, hundreds have disappeared. Today, linguists recognize more than 1000, of which 600 are still spoken (the number is plummeting as elderly speakers pass on).

Linguists seek to classify those languages, and not just to bring order to Babel. Languages evolve. Old ones change, new ones appear. Yet those sharing an ancestor retain vestiges of their common inheritance, evident in word and grammatical similarities among them. Classifying like languages is a vital first step in recognizing their shared ancestry.

In 1891, the Bureau of American Ethnology's John Wesley Powell sorted North American languages into 58 families (a group of languages with similar features). From there, linguists progressively lumped languages and families together until, by the 1920s, Edward Sapir had the 58 families down to six, each presumably sharing a common ancestor.

Explorer, geologist, and anthropologist John Wesley Powell, photographed with the Paiute chief Tau-Gu. In 1891, while working for the Bureau of American Ethnology, Powell sorted North American languages into 58 families.

Sapir did so against the formidable opposition of his own mentor, Franz Boas, the father of American anthropology. Boas chided Sapir for assuming that similar languages had to be related. After all, Boas reminded him, languages can be alike for many other reasons, borrowing and chance chief among them. Worse, different elements of languages—words, sounds, meanings, inflection, syntax, semantics, and grammar—might be similar in different languages for different reasons.

Sapir understood all that, but he possessed remarkable linguistic intuition, and the courage to voice it. He was playing a hunch with his scheme, sensing that the similarities among these many languages resulted from relatedness and no other cause. And as even his critics admit, Sapir's hunches were better than most others' proofs.

Still, Sapir expected amendments to his classification, friendly or otherwise, and he got them. One camp, the post-Sapir majority, splintered his groups into 150 or so separate language families, believing no fewer were justified on evidence so far obtained.

The other camp, led by Joseph Greenberg, out-Sapired Sapir himself. Using a technique called *mass comparison*, Greenberg reduced Sapir's six North American language families to just three for all the Americas: Eskimo-Aleut, Na-Dene, and one vast family called Amerind. As he said, it was "a very bold thesis indeed." Could it also be right?

Similar languages can be grouped from the bottom up by painstakingly comparing a few languages at a time, then building larger and larger families. Or they can be clustered from the top down, simultaneously comparing as many as possible. The latter—mass comparison—sacrifices details, but

Greenberg thinks the cost is worth it. With so many languages to compare, doing so by twos or threes takes a lifetime. Besides, two distantly related languages may look different when compared only with each other, but similar when compared against many others.

Take English and Hindi. Their words for "tooth" are only vaguely similar. Yet, the term in Hindi is close to the word in Kashmiri and Sindhi, which is similar in turn to the word for tooth in Italian and Spanish. Thence, it is an easy step to "tooth" in German and Dutch, and from there to English. The successive links thus form a linguistic chain joining Hindi and English.

Of course, just because many languages have a similar word for tooth does not a shared ancestry make. Any single match can easily result from borrowing or chance. To show common origin, Greenberg argues, it is necessary to play the odds: Compare a list of words. The longer the list of shared words across the greater the number of languages, the theory goes, the more likely it is that similarity results from common ancestry rather than another cause. Naturally, the more similar the languages, the closer their historical relationship. Family trees, even linguistic family trees, are like that. Hindi and English share an Indo-European ancestor, but perch on distant branches of the tree of Indo-European descendants.

Greenberg's mass comparison, applied in his *Language in the Americas* (1987), involved a list of approximately 300 words and, latterly, grammatical markers, scanned across as many Native American languages as possible. He didn't look randomly at words, but focused on long-lived pronouns and body parts, words not readily lost from a language.

There are some 10 languages in the Eskimo-Aleut family, including Aleut, spoken on the Aleutian Islands; Yupik, or western Eskimo, spoken on the Siberian and Alaskan coasts; and eastern Eskimo, Inuit-Inupiaq, spoken in the northern Arctic from Alaska to Greenland. Eskimo-Aleut languages are striking in their homogeneity, Inuit-Inupiaq especially so. European travelers learning an Inuit dialect at one end of the range were able, albeit with increasing difficulty, to converse with speakers of other Inuit-Inupiaq dialects across thousands of miles of territory.

The 38 Na-Dene or Athabaskan languages are spoken today by three widely separated peoples. Northern Athabaskans (such as Koyukon, Dogrib, Chipewyan, or Sarcee) are the majority, and inhabit a large area of interior subarctic Alaska and Canada; Pacific Coast Athabaskans live in the major river valleys of British Columbia, Oregon, and northern California; Apachean speakers, who include the Navajo, live in the Southwestern United States. Apachean apparently separated from the Northern Athabaskan complex in the last millennium.

Amerind embraces the more than 900 other indigenous languages of the New World, spoken from Hudson Bay to Tierra del Fuego. Amerind brings together different languages spoken across vast terrain by groups surely separated by thousands of years of prehistory. Yet by Greenberg's tally they share some 281 words, and a few distinctive grammatical forms—notably the use of first-person pronoun *n* and second person *m* (in many Indo-European languages, first person is *m* [me or moi], second person *t* [thou or tu]). So widespread and uniquely American is the *n/m* pattern, that Greenberg believes it should lead any "historically minded" linguist to conclude that there was shared ancestry.

Profound differences between Eskimo-Aleut, Na-Dene, and Amerind convince Greenberg that these were distinct families before they migrated to America, and that they arrived at different times. But in what order? The greater the differentiation within a language family, and the greater its geographic extent, Sapir argued, the older the family. And the older the family, Greenberg added, the fewer the links to Old World languages, and the farther south its location.

By this reasoning Amerind must be the oldest. The most differentiated and widespread, it lacks all but the slightest affinities with Old World languages. The fact that Amerinds inhabit nearly the entire hemisphere, far from Beringia, must mean that their ancestors arrived when no other humans were here to impede their movement. To ancestral Amerinds, this was truly a New World.

That was not the case for the Na-Dene and Eskimo-Aleut, who today occupy lands north of the Amerinds, and whose southward progress was presumably blocked. Ancestral Na-Dene speakers, whose language family is less internally differentiated (relative to Amerind) and still preserves slight links to Old World languages (such as Sino-Tibetan), must have followed the ancestral Amerinds. Only afterward came the ancestral Eskimo-Aleuts, whose languages today are the least differentiated and maintain the most conspicuous ties to Siberian and Old World languages.

Understanding their relative order, however, is not the same as knowing precisely when the migrations occurred. Linguistics, Greenberg admits, is terribly weak at gauging absolute antiquity, but that is no surprise. Languages exist in the present, and give few direct clues to their age. Bridges must be built to other lines of evidence.

TALES FROM TEETH

In the 1920s, as Sapir was reducing all Native American languages to six families, Hrdlička was pursuing physical traits common to all Native Americans. One of the most significant proved to be a distinctive "shovel shape" on the upper incisors (where extra ridges on the tongue side give the crowns of the teeth a shovel look). This trait, inherited genetically, satisfied Hrdlička that the Native Americans were all descendants of one historically related population. That was important to him, because the physical unity of Native Americans meant they hadn't been here long enough for evolutionary diver-

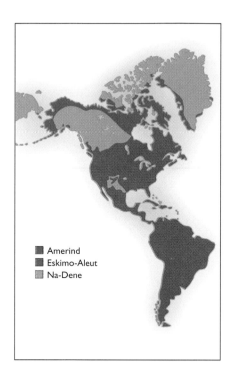

According to linguist Joseph Greenberg, these were the three main language families in the New World. He believes they were distinct groups before their migration and that they arrived in the New World at different times.

- Amerind
- Eskimo-Aleut
- Na-Dene

The migration routes of the first Americans are tracked here on the basis of dental evidence. Since tooth anatomy is genetically inherited and since the structure of teeth changes very slowly across space and time, it is possible to trace lineages through the different characteristics of teeth. Based on this evidence, anthropologist Christy Turner believes the Amerinds reached North America first, followed by the Eskimo-Aleuts, and Na-Dene very much later.

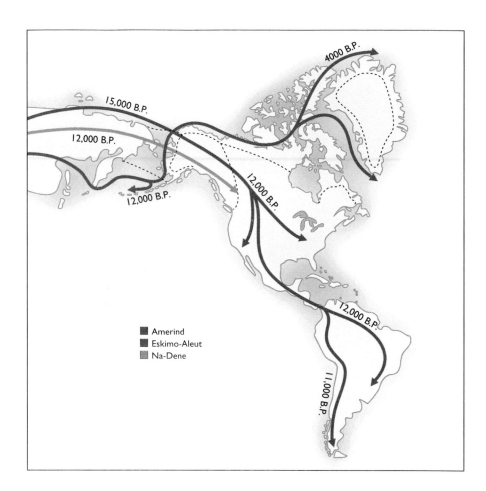

gence to occur, proof that his staunch opposition to Pleistocene Americans was justified.

Still, Hrdlička admitted to contrasts between American Indian, Athabaskan, and Eskimo populations. The subtypes represented different migrations—the "dolichocephalic" (long-headed) and "brachycephalic" (round-headed) American Indians arrived first, followed by Athabaskans ("a virile brachycephalic type"), then Eskimos.

Of course, even if Hrdlička had an axe to grind, his subtypes (ignoring their antique physical descriptions) may be correct. At least Christy Turner of Arizona State University thinks so, based on far more extensive analyses of Native American teeth.

Why teeth? There are many reasons. They preserve extraordinarily well, invariably outlasting the body's soft parts, and usually the bones, too. And while all humans share the same general dental traits (32 adult teeth, comprised of incisors, canines, premolars, and molars), we differ in some secondary dental traits. More importantly, Turner points out, tooth anatomy is genetically inherited, and is little modified by environment, use, health, or diet. If two groups have these same secondary dental traits, he argues, they are almost certainly related. Even better, because tooth structure changes slowly, it becomes possible to trace a dental lineage across space and through time. Best of all from our vantage, teeth can be dated. We may never know what language prehistoric Americans spoke, but we can know what their teeth looked like.

Turner knows, because he has seen plenty of them: 200,000 teeth taken from 9000 individuals in various prehistoric sites throughout the New World. For comparison, he has also looked at thousands of teeth from Siberia, Asia, Africa, and Europe. In studying these teeth, Turner examines some two dozen of the secondary dental attributes. Along the upper jaw he notes incisor shoveling, winging of the central incisors, the number of roots on the first premolar, and the presence of a feature called Carabelli's trait on the first molar and hypocone on the second molar. On the lower jaw, he tallies the number of roots on the first molar, the cusp pattern on the first and second molars, and the grooves on the second molar. No one of these features is ubiquitous in any one population and absent in all others. Rather, all groups possess each trait in different frequencies, as the examples in the table attest. In the absence of a single diagnostic criterion, a group's dental pattern is defined statistically based on similar values for the constellation of traits.

PERCENT OF INDIVIDUALS WITHIN THE GROUP POSSESSING

Group	U incisor shoveling	U molar Carabelli	U molar Hypocone	3 rooted L molar	Y groove L molar
Europe	<1	58	76	1	19
SE Asia	24	44	92	11	18
Eskimo	68	16	72	27	20
Athabaskan	75	23	68	10	10
South America	92	42	90	6	8

(U=upper, L=lower; data from C. Turner, "The first Americans: the dental evidences," *National Geographic Research*, 1986, Table 1)

Such statistical analyses straightaway distinguish Asian teeth from those of Africa and Europe, then broadly divide the Asian sample into two groups, Sundadont and Sinodont. The Sundadont pattern, ubiquitous in Southeast Asia, is the older of the two (appearing sometime between 30,000 and 17,000 B.P.), and is the stock from which Sinodonty, characteristic of northern Asian and *all* American populations, later evolved. These two differ in many ways, not the least of which is the higher incidence in Sinodonts of winging, shoveling, double shoveling, and especially three-rooted lower first molars.

Sinodonty occurs in crania from the upper levels of the famous cave site of Zhoukoudian in Northern China (home also to much earlier *Homo erectus* skeletons). Their dating has shifted over the years, but they are possibly 20,000 years old. On the opposite side of the Pacific, the Sinodont pattern appears in the Cerro Sota and Palli Aike caves of southernmost Chile 10,000 years later—or so it seems.

Sinodonts in America, as expected, differ from their Asian ancestors in a number of ways, notably in slightly greater frequencies of Carabelli's trait, protostylid (a ridging on the cheek-side surface of the lower molars), shoveling, and double shoveling, and lower frequencies of three-rooted lower first molars and Y groove patterns. Nor are all American Sinodonts alike. Turner subdivides American Sinodonty into three groups: Eskimo-Aleut, Greater Northwest Coast (which includes Southwest Athabaskan speakers), and all other American Indians.

Eskimo-Aleut and American Indian are least like each other, the former having a lower incidence of shoveling and Carabelli's trait but a higher frequency of three-rooted molars (among other traits). Awkwardly perched between these well-defined extremes is the Greater Northwest Coast cluster, its dental traits betwixt the other two, yet showing less internal differentiation than either. This tells Turner that the ancestors of this group were already present in Siberia, and were not hybridized between Eskimo-Aleuts and American Indians more recently.

After 1986, Turner linked his dental clusters with Greenberg's languages, but the change was in name only. Turner's dental groups were already partly defined on the basis of "common culture and closely related languages." Like Greenberg, Turner sees his three groups as the result of three separate migrations from the Old World.

Although all three are traceable to the same 20,000-year-old northern Chinese, late Pleistocene, Sinodont ancestors, Turner thinks they went their separate ways in Siberia, arriving in the New World at different times via different routes. Ancestral Amerinds drifted initially to the west then north, he thinks, through the Lena River basin, then along the Arctic shelf across Northern Beringia. The Eskimo-Aleuts went east and north, then down the Amur River to its mouth, then sidled over to Hokkaido, up the Sea of Okhotsk, thence across the Aleutian Islands. The first Na-Dene traveled the gap between the two.

Christy Turner believes the Amerinds were the first to reach America, but by his dental evidence the Eskimo-Aleuts came second, and the Na-Dene arrived a distant last. His sequence differs, of course, from the one that is based on languages.

As to the absolute antiquity of the migrations, Turner uses dentochronology, a technique based on the assumption that dental attributes change at a genetically paced constant rate, and thus the dental difference (or, as he puts it, the mean measures of divergence, or MMD) between two populations becomes a measure of time elapsed since they diverged from one another.

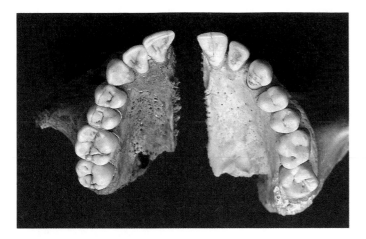

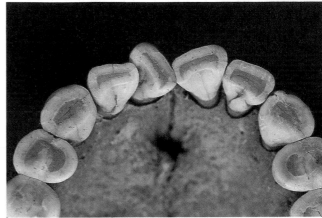

Modern Asian examples *(top left)* show shovel-shaped upper incisors. The specimen on the left exhibits pronounced shoveling of the upper central and upper lateral incisors, while the specimen on the right has spatulate incisors with no evidence of shoveling. In late prehistoric Native American teeth found in Texas *(top right),* there is winging on upper central incisors as well as shoveling of both central and lateral incisors. A 17th-century Native American example from the Mitchell Ridge site in Texas *(bottom left)* exhibits Carabelli's trait (cusp) on upper first molar. Also significant is the large depression on the left side of tooth adjacent to the second premolar. Clusters of these traits help trace population and geographical roots.

Averaging MMD between samples of roughly known ages from around the world, Turner arrives at a world dental microevolution rate of 0.01003 ± .004 MMD per 1000 years.

Multiplying that rate by the MMD between average Amerind and Northern Asian populations results in an age of approximately 13,500 years. Performing the same exercise with Eskimo and Northern Asian populations yields an estimated age at splitting of around 11,500 B.P. The numbers for Na-Dene are more elusive, but nearly all postdate the Eskimo divergence. Altogether, not too bad a fit with the archaeological evidence, Turner will tell you. But does it fit with other physical evidence?

GENES THAT TICK

In 1732, Alexander Pope wrote that hope springs eternal. But more than his words have come down through the centuries. His genes have, too. Naturally, the specific combination of genes (genotype) expressed as Pope (phenotype) has long vanished. But certain individual genes the poet once carried likely survive today. Hope *and* genes spring eternal.

Indeed, observes Luigi Cavalli-Sforza, a geneticist at Stanford University, every human group contains practically all the extant human genes. The trick to mapping the differences among them, as it was with teeth, is measuring the frequency with which certain genes and mutations occur in the various populations.

The study of genetic distance between human populations began with serological markers—blood group antigens (A,B,O and Rh blood groups), serum proteins, immunoglobulins (antibody molecules), and various enzymes. To those 100 or so inherited traits (the "classical genetic markers"), geneticists recently have added studies of DNA in the cell nucleus. These are largely neutral traits, which change by mutation rather than the forces of natural selection. Similarities among them mark shared ancestry, not common adaptation;

the more similar the traits of two (or more) groups, the closer in time their shared ancestor.

Together, the classical and nuclear DNA evidence nicely sort the world's major populations, with the greatest genetic distance occurring between African and non-African populations. This suggests, simply, that Africa is the origin of *all* members of our species, *Homo sapiens sapiens*. Populations radiating from Africa reached Asia, and from there departed for the New World.

Not all New World populations are genetically alike. Some see differences between Amerind and Eskimo-Aleut, especially in the diseases that Pennsylvania State University physical anthropologist Kenneth Weiss labels the "New World Syndrome," or NWS. The Amerinds are much more susceptible to adult-onset diabetes, gall bladder cancer, cholesterol gallstones, and obesity than the Eskimo-Aleut, so much so that Weiss believes the genes behind these linked metabolic diseases must reach back to distinct ancestral populations. (In fact, the genes are older than the diseases. The genes control metabolic processes that help hunter-gatherers cope with food shortages in an unpredictable world. Unfortunately for the hunter-gatherers living in our modern world of plenty, the genes and the response they trigger produce the NWS diseases instead.)

But beyond this point, the differences between Native American groups become hazy—and disputed. Zegura admits that comparing genes within New World populations gives a picture of "discordant variation." Classical markers and nuclear DNA are stubbornly irresolute on whether there are genetic groups within Amerind. The Na-Dene seesaw back and forth between Amerind and Eskimo-Aleut.

Zegura attributes the haze to thousands of years of gene exchange, random flutters in gene frequencies, and inbreeding, all of which conspired with natural selection to obscure what may have once been discernible genealogies. Unraveling millennia of history from 20th-century genetics becomes, he admits, a "challenging and highly speculative enterprise."

But times are changing. In the early 1980s, Allan Wilson, a geneticist at the University of California at Berkeley, and others began looking at DNA in mitochondria (organelles responsible for energy metabolism), which occurs in a circular molecule divisible into 16,569 base pairs, the sequence of which varies among individuals. Mitochondrial DNA (or mtDNA) and nuclear DNA differ fundamentally: Both occur in males and females, but when an egg is fertilized, the mtDNA from the sperm is discarded. The fetus carries only maternal mtDNA. The bane of human genetics—the combination and recombination of genes in mating—does not occur in the almost exclusive passage of mtDNA down the maternal line.

Better still from a genealogical perspective, mtDNA accumulates mutations five to ten times faster than nuclear DNA. Even if a group has separated only recently from a genetically identical parent population, mutations will have

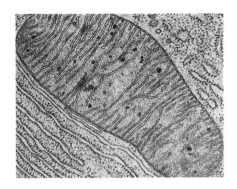

This mitochondrion resembles a footprint inside its cell. Every living cell contains mitochondrial DNA (mtDNA), and distinctions between population groups are measured by the frequency with which certain genes and mutations occur. Unlike nuclear DNA, mtDNA passes almost exclusively down the maternal line, and accumulates mutations five to ten times faster than its nuclear cousin. Further studies involving mtDNA eventually may help pinpoint the moment the first Americans left Siberian shores.

accumulated within each group and between the two. The difference in the mtDNA between two (or more) groups becomes a measure of the years since their separation.

The rate at which mtDNA differences arise is calibrated by using cases where one knows the mtDNA distance between two groups and the point in time when they split from a common ancestor. The rate is now put at 2 to 4 percent per million years (2 to 4 nucleotide bases per 100 will mutate every million years), in part based on a date of 12,000 B.P. for Native American mtDNA divergence from Asian ancestors.

How reliable is the mtDNA clock? Geneticists haggle over the details, but many are confident the true rate falls somewhere in the 2 to 4 percent range. Others reject it outright. Pitfalls lurk in conflicts over how fast mutations occur, whether mutations occur uniformly over time (for clock purposes, it is assumed they do), and the potentially fatal effects of mtDNA lineage extinction (loss of a mtDNA lineage would lead to an underestimate of the total mtDNA diversity and, in turn, to age estimates that were too young).

Leaving aside those prickly issues, what exactly is measured by the ticking of the mtDNA clock? It is the time elapsed since two or more mtDNA molecules, once genetically identical, began to diverge. This molecular-level split may take place *within* a population, so mtDNA differences may not represent splits of a population where, say, a daughter population leaves a parent population. The daughter population could carry off a number of already distinct mtDNA lineages. Still, the molecular-level and population-level mtDNA divergence could coincide, and may have coincided, in the peopling of the Americas.

In the mid-1980s, Emory University biochemist Douglas Wallace began looking at mtDNA in Native Americans, specifically Arizona's Pima peoples. Their genes bespoke an ancestry of only a few mtDNA lineages. Later, casting the sampling net wider on the chance that the small number of lineages was a Pima-specific pattern, Wallace and his team examined mtDNA from the Yucatan Maya and South American Ticuna. This time, all three showed high frequencies (but not the same high frequencies) of identical genetic variants, again bespeaking common ancestry.

And there was something else. The ancestral population of these widely separate groups had to have been very small—a population *bottleneck*, geneticists call it—and must have left Asia with only a tiny fraction of the genetic variability present in the parent population (the geneticists' *founder effect*). That explains why they share a high frequency of genetic forms that originated, but are relatively rare, in Asian populations. For that matter, it explains why Amerinds (and only Amerinds) share the New World Syndrome diseases.

Best of all, this evidence clearly implies that the mtDNA clock started ticking when the first Amerinds left Siberian shores—precisely the moment we seek. The genetic differences within and between their descendants mark their time in the New World. But there is a twist. By the mtDNA, ancestral

Amerinds left Siberia between 21,000 and 42,000 years ago. Far longer, of course, than generally accepted Paleoindian ages, but consistent with older claims from places like Monte Verde. So long as the clock and the archaeology are both correct.

Since the Pima, Maya, and Ticuna are members of Joseph Greenberg's Amerind family, support for the three-migration model has to come from additional studies of non-Amerind groups, studies now underway. In January, 1992 Wallace's team published a comparison of mtDNA in Amerind and Na-Dene populations. Their results confirm the genetic integrity of the Na-Dene, although they leave their affinity to Eskimo-Aleut unresolved. The results also suggest that Amerinds have been around longer, and even raise the possibility of a separate migratory pulse between Amerind and Na-Dene, with the earlier Amerind arriving about the time Monte Verde was first occupied (MV 1 times) and the later—but still pre-Na-Dene—pulse arriving about the time of Clovis *Paleoindians* (ancestral Amerinds).

There is much more to come from mtDNA studies. Still, one fact already stands clear: Amerinds may all be descendants of a single migrating population, just as Joseph Greenberg and Christy Turner claimed.

GETTING TO BERINGIA ON TIME

Language, teeth, and genes point to three migrations, but archaeology must provide the direct physical evidence of those events. In the Far North, Greenberg, Turner, and Zegura believe, archaeology does just that.

Starting with the youngest of the migrations, the earliest Eskimo-Aleut appeared, archaeologist Don Dumond of the University of Oregon reports, sometime after 4500 B.P., but their archaeological traces are ambiguous, and the story is not a simple one. Some came from Northeast Asia—the Aldan drainage of Siberia and the Sea of Okhotsk region—to merge with extant Alaskan and Eastern Aleutian populations. Archaeologically, they are manifest in many artifact complexes: the Norton, Arctic Small Tool, and Ocean Bay traditions.

Preceding them were the ancestral Na-Dene, marked by the distinctive stone blades, microblades, and wedge-shaped cores of the *Paleoarctic* Tradition, which appears soon after 10,700 B.P. from Kamchatka to Fairbanks. In the millennia that follow, Paleoarctic sites muster in a time-transgressive line down the Northwest Coast, the oldest near Juneau, Alaska, successively younger ones in British Columbia (around 9700 B.P.), the Queen Charlotte Islands (about 7000 B.P.), and the Strait of Georgia (around 5000 B.P.). Sites occur inland, too, in the boreal forests of Alaska and Western Canada (but no farther east than Canada's MacKenzie River).

The Paleoarctic has ties to Diuktai culture sites in the Aldan River valley of Eastern Siberia. The age of Diuktai sites is controversial, but none appears to be earlier than 20,000 B.P., and most may fall around 14,000 B.P.—leaving plenty of time to get to Kamchatka by 10,700 B.P.

Paleoarctic groups were not the first Americans. Paleoindians were in the New World long before Paleoarctic groups reached Washington state. But the Paleoindian path has proven exceedingly difficult to follow.

Clovis fluted points, by which Greenberg, Turner, and Zegura mark the arrival of ancestral Amerinds, are rare in Alaska and the Pacific Northwest, and nonexistent in Siberia. More perplexing, the few, poorly dated Alaskan Clovis points appear to be younger than those farther south. Not much help here.

However, there are sites in central Alaska that William Powers and John Hoffecker lump together as the Nenana Complex. These appear around 11,300 B.P., and contain lanceolate projectile points (unfluted), bifacial and unifacial knives, and scrapers. None possesses typical Paleoarctic microblades and microcores. Nenana artifacts look Paleoindian, without the Clovis points. Perhaps they were left by the same (Amerind) migrating population, who would only later, and farther south, invent Clovis fluted points.

But if these are ancestral Amerinds, where did they come from, and when? Earlier in time, and off to the west, the trail grows cold and complicated. The Lena basin, where dental evidence led Turner to suppose that the Amerinds originated, contains not a hint of ancestral Paleoindians. A few sites around Beringia, which together date to around 14,000 B.P., are promising leads. Stemmed bifacial points, not wedge-shaped microcores, dominate these assemblages (though microblades are present in 15,000-year-old deposits in Bluefish Caves in Alaska). Promising, too, are artifacts from sites in the maritime region of Northeast Asia.

Then there are the Siberian Diuktai sites. Again. While many link Diuktai with the Paleoarctic, others, emphasizing its bifacial tools, see similarities between Diuktai and Paleoindian assemblages. Both might be right. Diuktai is so broadly defined it includes sites of different ages and artifacts that may not be related to one another. Time, and a great deal more archaeology in Siberia, will tell.

There's the nub of the problem: Before we can speak of the peopling of Siberia, Siberia will have to be peopled by more archaeologists. Until then, in Siberia—the place of departure for all groups heading east to America—there is no hint of a human presence earlier than 20,000 years ago, and perhaps none earlier than 14,000 years ago. What a difference those 6000 years would make.

ONE IF BY LAND, TWO IF BY SEA

Leaving Siberia at 20,000 B.P., the first Americans would have Beringia before them, a cold, dry grassland (Guthrie's Mammoth Steppe) broken by dunes and loess. It was a stable landscape and, for northern peoples and animals, easily crossed. Going south from there was another matter. At that moment, the North American ice sheets were fully extended, creating a biological (if not physical) barrier to human passage. There were two options: Move into Alaska, then wait a few thousand years for the interior route to open, or bypass the interior altogether and skirt down the coast on foot or by boat. After all, as coastal advocates are quick to say, it worked in Australia.

More than 40,000 years ago the first Australians rafted some 56 miles (90 kilometers) of open ocean to reach the island continent, then clung to its edges to work their way south. The first Americans, were their subsistence tuned to coastal resources, could have journeyed from Kamchatka to Panama without ever setting foot in the hinterlands. Imagine how easy it would have been if they had had boats. Perhaps that explains, advocates say, why the oldest New World sites are in *South* America.

But comparisons with Australia are misleading. The first raft crossing to Australia was almost surely accidental; regular voyaging around the South Pacific began only 3500 years ago. The North and South Pacific are very different waters, especially during glacial episodes. No early Australian on a raft had to contend with a northern winter's dark skies and frozen seas, the treacherous ice floes and squalls of summer, and year round severe climates.

Indeed, safely reaching Alaskan shores would have been the easy part. The route south through the inland waterway—still used today for safe passage—was then nearly jammed with glacial ice. Along much of the Alaskan and Canadian shore heavily crevassed Cordilleran outlet glaciers, 12 to 30 miles (20 to 50 kilometers) across, flowed onto the continental shelf. Small, ice-free pockets between them would provide welcome landfall to storm-tossed rafts, but these ice-locked refuges would hardly provide vital food resources.

Under those circumstances, rafting or walking down the coast would have been impossible—*at that time* in glacial history. Earlier or later, perhaps, a coastal route may have been open, but if any people did travel that way, their traces were long ago drowned beneath rising postglacial seas.

No matter. A coastal route would have been unnecessary if the first Americans did not move east from Siberia until 14,000 B.P. By that time Beringia, though breached by rising seas, was still frozen and passable in winter. And by then, no Alaskan layover was necessary. The space between the ice sheets had become habitable.

ALL ROADS LEAD TO CLOVIS

Here, then, are how the lines seemingly converge: There were three, not one, migratory pulses to America by ancestral Amerind, Na-Dene, and Eskimo-Aleut groups. Judging by their teeth (Sinodonts all) and shared genetic markers, these groups had a common Asian ancestor 20,000 years ago (as measured by dentochronology), but had already begun to diverge from one another before leaving Siberia. Their descendants remain distinct, at least by language and teeth. It is too soon to tell about their genes.

Amerinds were the bow wave of migration, followed by the Na-Dene, then the Eskimo-Aleut. Unless the linguistic and archaeological evidence is wrong,

Excavations such as the **Walker Road site** in the Nenana Valley in the north-central foothills of the Alaska Range produced a range of artifacts including small gravers and end scrapers on blades and bi-facial points, both triangular and tear-shaped. ^{14}C dates range from approximately 11,000 to 11,820 B.P., the bulk falling around 11,300 B.P.

and the dental evidence correct, in which case Eskimo-Aleuts came second and the Na-Dene third.

The haggling may go on about second place, but evidence from across the sciences is closing fast on the first Americans. They were a small band of ancestral Amerinds, homogeneous in language, teeth, and genes, who split from their Asian forebears between 21,000 (mtDNA) and 13,500 (dentochronology) years ago. Their artifacts appear in Eastern Siberia after 20,000 B.P. (if Diuktai links are allowable), and in Beringia by 14,000 years ago. By then the land bridge was largely intact, but the lower parts were under water, so their crossing may have been in winter.

Once across, they moved into central Alaska where, by 11,300 B.P., they developed the prototypic Paleoindian artifact assemblage (seen in the Nenana Complex sites), minus the distinctive fluted point. With those artifacts in hand, they left central Alaska through the now-open interior route, inventing fluted points on the journey south. They moved quickly, reaching Clovis, New Mexico, in just a few hundred years, and Cerro Sota and Palli Aike in southern Chile by 11,000 B.P. Over the next 10,000 years, as their descendants swelled in number and grew apart, their language, teeth, and genes diverged, but not so much that traces of their common inheritance were altogether obscured.

OR DO THEY? GRIDLOCK AT THE INTERSECTION OF SCIENCE
The convergence of the linguistic, dental, genetic, archaeological, and geological evidence on the number and timing of migrations to the New World is impressive and unprecedented. It may also be badly wrong.

At least, those rallied in opposition say so. If it were all so clear, they argue, why the discrepancy between the dental and linguistic migration sequences? Why are the migration traces so complex and poorly evident in the archaeological record? Why are genetic markers pointing to the presence of groups undetected by either the language or dental studies? Why does the latest archaeological and genetic data indicate a human presence far earlier than dentochronology allows (for the moment, it is difficult to say which is in error, but it is helpful to bear in mind that archaeological data calibrate both dentochronology and molecular clocks). There is no perfect correlation between artifacts, language, teeth, and genes, Louisiana State University linguist Lyle Campbell argues. People can easily learn a new language or adopt new artifacts, but they cannot learn new genes or teeth.

Unlike years gone by, when disputes mostly raged between disciplines—recall the sniping between Hrdlička, Goddard, and Cook—today strong opposition also comes from within.

TALKING TROUBLE

In the last few decades Sapir-inspired lumping of languages fell from grace in American linguistics, and hard-nosed linguists began busily dismantling language families they believed had been sloppily pasted together. Greenberg's *Languages in the Americas* was bucking the trend, and he knew it, predicting certain quarters would receive his ideas with "something akin to outrage." He was right. The book was detrimental to linguistics, Lyle Campbell charged, and ought to be condemned. Strong words, but Greenberg himself estimates that 80 to 90 percent of linguists agree with Campbell.

Greenberg's many critics do not dispute his goals; theirs are the same. They even believe most of the 150 or so American Indian language families currently accepted may prove to be historically related. But they think Greenberg went too far, too fast, on bad evidence. They are particularly unhappy with his Amerind family.

Cynics might dismiss the dispute as just another academic turf-war, and it's not hard to see why. Greenberg is an authority on African, not American, languages. In truth, he has mishandled the American data, as experts in those languages are quick to show. The number of errors in Greenberg's word lists, one critic grumbled, probably exceeds the number of correct forms.

Yet in tackling all the languages of the Americas, Greenberg freely admitted there would be mistakes: "It would be miraculous," he said, if there weren't. Still, he and his supporters believe that his success with mass-comparison in Africa warrants applying the method to America. There again he and his critics part company.

To them, mass comparison means trouble. Greenberg, they say, relies overmuch on word similarities, paying inadequate attention to grammar, sound, and meaning. Greenberg replies that grammatical forms played a key role,

At the height of the last glaciation in the Late Pleistocene, an open passageway from Siberia to Alaska was exposed. The barriers to migration were removed for tens of thousands of years, allowing for multiple migrations over a long period.

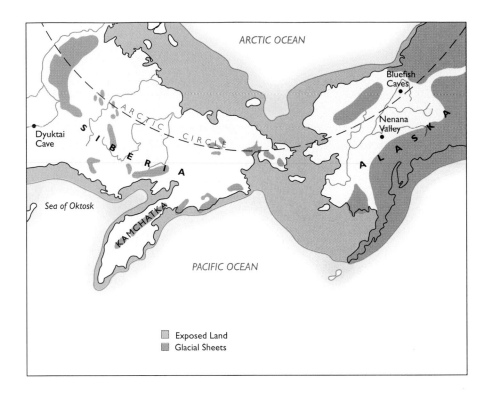

pointing to the *n/m* pronouns. Campbell and others are unconvinced. The frequency of *n/m*'s in America, they argue, is "grossly overstated." Worse, *n/m* occurs outside America, while Greenberg's non-American pronoun pattern (*m/t*) is indeed abundant in America. (Oddly, neither Greenberg nor his critics tally just how often *n/m* and *m/t* occur or fail to occur in both American and non-American languages, making it impossible to judge whether there are statistically significant differences in the frequency of the *n/m* pronoun here as opposed to elsewhere.)

Nor are Greenberg's critics happy with his criteria for spotting word similarities between separate languages. He sometimes uses long word-association strings, and at other times no more than a single matching consonant. The result, critics claim, is that mass-comparison is incapable of distinguishing Amerind from other languages of the world. Worst of all, they believe Greenberg ignores the possibility that the similarity results from borrowing or chance. And, of course, he does just that—believing mass-comparison, correctly applied, precludes these processes.

Greenberg wants *Languages in the Americas* judged as a whole. His critics declare they have done so, but ultimately reject the claim that those 900 native North and South American languages are part of a single, related language family. Greenberg seeks refuge from his critics behind the dental and mtDNA support for his model, but these are no longer safe havens.

Christy Turner groups teeth based on their similar attributes. The resulting groups should be distinct and internally homogeneous. But they aren't.

Aleut teeth are statistically more similar to those of Na-Dene than to Eskimo (with whom they belong). Na-Dene teeth from the Gulf of Alaska are closer dentally to Eskimo-Aleuts than they are to Athabaskans, who, of course, are also Na-Dene. And Paleoindian teeth, all ostensibly Amerind, are more similar to Eskimo-Aleut, Na-Dene, and Amerind as a group than they are to Amerind itself, which strongly hints of subgroups within Amerind. Physical anthropologist Emöke Szathmary of the University of Western Ontario wonders whether Turner is merely interpreting his analytical results in light of a pre-existing hypothesis he assumes to be true—that three, and only three, dental groups exist.

That charge highlights a fundamental quandary. Prehistoric teeth say nothing of the language they once spoke. How can they be assigned an appropriate language family? Turner makes the connection according to where the teeth are found. For instance, a sample of like teeth from prehistoric sites in regions now occupied by Eskimo-Aleuts are Eskimo-Aleut. It can be as simple as that, and cause trouble just as easily.

Turner has to make what Margaret Conkey of the University of California at Berkeley calls the Goldilocks Assumption: Each group, like the Three Bears, has its own—and only its own—territory, which is plainly marked by language, artifacts, and (in this case) teeth. They all overlap completely and exactly, and over time the territory does not change hands (or teeth).

Goldilocks stays out of trouble some of the time. Teeth and artifacts from a 900-year-old site on the north shore of Hudson Bay are likely ancestral Eskimo. There is good reason to think no one else has been there since. Still, go back just another 500 years in the same place and the archaeological record looks very different. Whose teeth are those? Goldilocks grows unreliable as the sites grow older.

Nearly all the teeth in Turner's sample are only a couple of thousand years old, and their young age, tied to the hope that territories haven't changed much in the last 2000 years, makes us want to believe in the Goldilocks Assumption. But the previously mentioned anomalies in the groupings have burst that bubble.

Goldilocks also gets into trouble in places that have long trafficked in human beings—Alaska, for instance, the corridor for all American migrations, however many there were. Not surprisingly, teeth from this area do not fall neatly into corresponding language groups.

The dilemma is obvious: The places and times in which we might hope to catch a dental record of migration to the Americas are the very places and times in which we have the least chance of figuring out *who* those people were. Of course, if Turner found three dental groups in Alaska, one dated to 12,000 B.P., the other never occurring before 10,700 B.P., and the third always postdating 4500 B.P., it would be powerful evidence of three migrations, regardless of who owned the teeth. But only a dozen individuals in Turner's sample of 9000 date to the late Pleistocene, and many of those may not be Paleoindian in age. Even the Cerro Sota and Palli Aike teeth, anchoring the Amerind series in far South America at 11,000 B.P., may be much younger. None have been dated—yet—and by Turner's own dentochronology they are no more than 3400 to 7800 years old.

So goes the dental evidence, neither a direct record of migration nor tightly linked to identifiable groups, nor (so far at least) producing internally homogeneous groups.

BROKEN BOTTLENECKS

Studies of mtDNA of Native Americans are yet in their infancy. Nevertheless, Wallace's results point straight to the conclusion that there were but a few mtDNA lineages in all Amerind populations, and, minimally, that there had been a dramatic bottleneck at their ancestral migration. Naturally, all other Amerind groups should show the same pattern. Unfortunately, the very few studies done so far show just the opposite.

Biochemists Ryk Ward and Svante Pääbo, of the universities of Utah and Munich, respectively, and others have analyzed mtDNA in 63 individuals of the Nuu-Chah-Nulth (Nootka) Amerind group, now inhabiting Vancouver Island, British Columbia, and Washington's Olympic Peninsula. The Nuu-Chah-Nulth number no more than 2400, and yet display startling high mtDNA diversity—at least 28 separate lineages in four reasonably well-defined clusters. Such high genetic diversity, to put the number in perspective, would be expected in a population of more than 22,000 individuals, not a mere 2400.

Why so much diversity in a single group? One possibility, of course, is that the Nuu-Chah-Nulth have been in America for a long time. But it would have had to be a very long time, for the genetic distance between the four Nuu-Chah-Nulth clusters implies they began to split from one another 41,000 to 78,000 years ago. And that's only the time needed to account for the divergence of the four Nuu-Chah-Nulth clusters. What if there are other distantly related mtDNA lineages and clusters in other Amerind groups? Either way, that's much more time than all but the most ardent proponents of an early entry to the New World are willing to concede.

Alternatively—and this interpretation Ward's group favors—the great genetic diversity among the Nuu-Chah-Nulth did not develop here, but originated in Asia before their ancestors entered the New World. This means, of course, that the founding first Americans did not experience a genetic bottleneck or founder effect. Their populations were heterogeneous at the outset. If there were three migrations, Ward argues, they were not genetically homogeneous peoples. That is *if* there were, in fact, three migrations. For now, that question remains very much open.

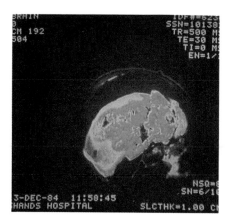

A color-enhanced, magnetic-resonance image showing preserved brain tissue from one of the 168 crania found at the Windover site. Such well-preserved tissue—the burial site is 8000 years old—gives geneticists the opportunity to study the mtDNA of these early Americans.

Scattered skeletal material was found during the first year's work at Windover, Florida—a "wet" site. Later excavations at the site in 1985 and 1986 turned up articulated skeletal material.

Ward's evidence also means that the mtDNA clock did not start ticking at the moment of departure for America, but much earlier. If so, Douglas Wallace's age estimates (42,000 to 21,000 B.P.) may have no bearing on when the first Americans arrived, save that it must have been after these lineages were formed.

Are Ward and Pääbo's results dependable? Geneticist William Hauswirth, studying mtDNA from spectacularly preserved human tissues of scores of individuals in an 8000-year-old underwater burial site at Windover, Florida, has also been finding substantial mtDNA variation.

Wallace believes the great diversity found by Ward and others might somehow fit within the four broad mtDNA lineages his group defined. Perhaps. But as yet their results are not comparable, since each group used different techniques and studied different nucleotide sites in the mtDNA molecule.

Two other explanations also come to mind. As Ward suggests, the initial migrating group had a number of genetically distinct individuals, or there were multiple, genetically distinct groups who made the initial trek to the Americas and whose descendants together comprise "Amerinds."

MULTIPLE MIGRATIONS?

Archaeologists have long assumed that migrations to the Americas were few, each of a small number of people, closely related to one another and very different from those who came before or after. That assumption seemed reasonable, given what linguists and physical anthropologists had to say. But now there are hints that these migrations may have been far more complex. Are there reasons to think there were only three (or some limited number) of migrations?

None so far as we know. Throughout the late Pleistocene there were no longstanding barriers to passage across Beringia or south from Alaska. Coming to North America was not restricted to circumscribed routes within narrow time windows. Beringia was an open passageway over which Siberian populations could have traveled to Alaska (and back again), over tens of thousands of years. And well they may have. Instead of conceiving of early migration as a single pulse by a small group of Amerinds, think of it as Hrdlička did: a "dribbling over from northeastern Asia, extending probably over a long stretch of time."

How early and how often? It depends on when people reached Siberia and western Beringia. That's now 20,000 B.P., but the possibility that they were there earlier is very much alive. Also, it depends on the size of the parent population(s), and the environmental, climatic, and social catalysts that might have spurred out-migration. All these variables are unknown.

Hrdlička (and Sapir too), suspected those dribbles may have been from unrelated groups. That, of course, would produce the great genetic diversity seen by Ward and Hauswirth, and the linguistic diversity Greenberg's critics argue exists within Amerind. What would not appear in the genes and languages would be any trace of migratory dribbles that were unsuccessful.

Not all migrations are successful. Small, isolated founding populations in a new land could easily disappear without a trace for want of ability to cope with events in their environment. It happened to the Norse, who made it to northern Newfoundland 1000 years ago, but just barely. They were driven off shortly thereafter by native "Skraelings" (perhaps ancestral Beothuk Indians).

Languages, teeth, and genes of Native Americans today hold the best promise of understanding who their earliest ancestors were. But 12,000 years or more after the fact, millennia over which populations mixed and moved, the lines originally separating a stream of small and unrelated groups are easily blurred. Perhaps only in their mtDNA will those original lines come back into focus.

Those migrations that may have disappeared without issue will never be seen through their language or genes. Their story, if there is one to tell, will come only from archaeology and, perhaps, from teeth. Even so, there is a far more compelling story—of the group(s) who came together as Clovis and other Paleoindians.

In their efforts to validate artifacts, modern archaeologists move into the lab. Here, the Smithsonian's Dennis Stanford attempts to ascertain bone fragments) has been broken by humans by comparing it with the lighter bone, an elephant radius broken under human-applied stresses.

whether a mammoth radius (the darker of the two

NORTH AMERICAN PALEOINDIANS

Edgar B. Howard, of Philadelphia's Academy of Natural Sciences, had been ambushed before, so this time he moved fast. He caught a westbound train on November 12, 1932, alerted to the news that a road crew, mining gravel from an old pond on eastern New Mexico's High Plains, had struck bones. Lots of them, apparently, and big ones, too: mammoth and bison. That summer, Howard had seen scraps of the bones and fluted points that ranchers had been finding in wind-cut "blowouts" in these old ponds. The road crew seemed to have hit the mother lode. Howard knew the stakes. Earlier, his cordial relationship with paleontologist Barnum Brown had soured when Brown took credit for a fluted point found in Pleistocene bone-bearing sediments in Burnet Cave near Carlsbad, New Mexico. Howard, who had made the find while Brown was in Montana, was not amused. Nor was he pleased to learn that his idea for a national committee to investigate potential late Pleistocene archaeological sites had been scooped, and the committee formed without him. In the years following the discovery at Folsom, everyone, Howard most of all, wanted in on the action at early sites.

It was a long trip from Philadelphia. But on November 16, 1932, Howard flashed a telegram to the academy: "Extensive bone deposit at new site. Mostly bison, also horse & mammoth. Some evidence of hearths along edges. Will tie up permissions for future work & spend a few more days investigating."

But only a few more days. Back in Philadelphia the very next week, he announced in the journal *Science* the finding of humans "at a very remote period," and staked the academy's claim to what became the Clovis site.

The following summer Howard discovered spearpoints, larger and less-refined than those in the Folsom bison, embedded in mammoth skeletons at Clovis, New Mexico. Pleased by this testimony of human antiquity, but anxious to find earlier sites closer to Asia, Howard turned Clovis over to a young graduate student, then began planning fieldwork in the ice-free corridor region and, ultimately, Siberia.

Howard's plans flopped. But back at Clovis, archaeologists glimpsed a culture that, within a decade, they would trace across North America. Clovis groups had, it seemed, moved far and moved fast to colonize the continent. Their hallmarks were everywhere. It would take another 50 years to realize that there was less here than met the eye. But that's getting ahead of the story.

CLOVIS HALLMARKS

Paleoindian sites found on the Great Plains and Southwest in the aftermath of discoveries at Folsom and Clovis also had artifacts alongside the remains of large mammals. On that evidence, it appeared Paleoindians were predators, specializing in mammoth in Clovis times and bison in later Folsom times, supposedly changing prey because mammoth became extinct and changing points because bison could be killed with smaller caliber shot.

Unlike Folsom Paleoindians, who had kept mainly to the Great Plains, Clovis Paleoindians traveled great distances. Their fluted points, along with a monotonously similar toolkit (mostly bifaces, knives, end and side scrapers, drills, gravers), were soon reported coast to coast. That covered a lot of habitats: southern and northern forests, grasslands, tundra parkland, semi-arid desert, and alpine meadow.

Environmentally unstable habitats, too. Paleoindians were there for the final throes of the Pleistocene, when North America posed great and novel adaptive

Edgar B. Howard, of Philadelphia's Academy of Natural Sciences, was first on the scene of what was to become known as the Clovis site in eastern New Mexico. He and John Cotter, right, examine the artifacts from the site—fluted points, stone knives, and scrapers—the first tangible evidence of the Clovis people, whose archaeological traces would eventually be found throughout North America, and who remain the earliest undisputed inhabitants of the continent.

challenges to those groups who were determined to inhabit the entire continent. Yet Paleoindians seemed prepared for them all. So little apparent regard did they have for ecological and climatic barriers that they spread throughout North America at an astonishing rate. Or so it appears by the remarkable likeness in their fluted points east and west.

No subsequent North American occupation would ever reach so widely across the continent. The key to Clovis Paleoindian success, it's been argued, must have been a uniform adaptation, which, with only one toolkit, enabled them to cope, whatever the nature of the habitat. If western Clovis sites were any guide, that adaptation was "big-game" hunting: mammoths, or, where those were rare—as they were in the eastern forests, for example—mastodons. Unfortunately, no mastodon kills were ever found in the early decades of searching. Instead, thousands of fluted points were uncovered in regions heavy with mastodon fossils. Still, it seemed only a matter of time before the fluted points would be found between mastodon ribs.

Latching onto large mammals, which were adept at overriding ecological boundaries, must have enabled Clovis groups to do likewise, with little alteration to their artifacts or adaptation. After all, a mammoth was a mammoth, no matter where it lived, and if it happened to be a mastodon, horse, or camel instead, Clovis hunting strategies required only a few adjustments. So the argument went.

The Paleoindians trailing this wide-ranging big game must have been highly mobile, too. Just how mobile was revealed in their fondness for superior quality chert, jasper, chalcedony, and other fine-grained types of stone, all durable, easy to chip to a desired form, and sharp-edged. Since such stone is often distinctive in its color, the fossils it may contain, or its elemental composition, we can usually pinpoint where the material was quarried. The distances between where stone was quarried and where it was abandoned are an odometer of Paleoindian travels. Sometimes those distances were great. Pieces of agatized dolomite from the Texas Panhandle were fashioned into Clovis points left in the Drake cache in northeastern Colorado, 300 miles (480 kilometers) away. Distances of 200 miles (320 kilometers) are common. Such figures only record the stretch between two fixed points, and take no account of side excursions, return trips, or any other archaeologically invisible travel. Actual Clovis mileage may vary.

IGNOBLE HUNTERS?

Our image of Clovis Paleoindians as highly mobile hunters pursuing big game across the entire continent does more than explain the fast spread of the Clovis point and the standard-issue toolkit. It also makes Clovis Paleoindians a prime suspect in a centuries-old unsolved murder mystery—the extinction of the Pleistocene megafauna.

Most of the 35 genera of mammals that became extinct had estimated adult body weights of at least 110 pounds (50 kilograms) and, in the elephant-sized animals, perhaps as much as 4.5 tons (4 tonnes). So much meat on the hoof, University of Arizona paleoecologist Paul Martin says, was irresistible to Clovis hunters, who liked megafauna so much that they hunted them to extinction.

As Martin envisions it, Pleistocene overkill began when a band of 100 highly skilled Clovis hunters exited the ice-free corridor onto the northern Great Plains 11,500 years ago. They found themselves alone in a vast territory teeming with game that had never before peered down the shaft of a spear, and lacked the hard-won defensive behaviors of their wily Old World relatives (the model, of course, cannot well tolerate humans in America before 11,500 B.P.).

Killing this naive prey was easy, he figures. If just one hunter in four was successful each week, it would devastate local animal populations. Slow breeders, like most of the Pleistocene megafauna, cannot reproduce fast enough to survive even if only a third of their population is killed outright. Clovis hunters were spurred south by the prospect of abundant food, and left dead and dying animals behind. By Martin's estimate, they made good time: 10 miles (16 kilometers) a year. Not bad for a population doubling every 20 years—a 3.4 percent annual growth rate.

In Martin's theory, the hunters moved in an expanding wave front, a continental-sized dragnet from which no animal could hide. Within 350 years the Clovis population numbered 600,000 and had reached the Gulf of Mexico; 1000 years after entering North America they were at Tierra del Fuego 10,000 miles (16,000 kilometers) away. In their wake were tens of thousands of fluted points (the smoking guns in this murder mystery), carcasses of some 150 million herbivores, and carnivore populations that boomed with the sudden increase in scavengeable carcasses, then went bust when the supply ran out.

NOT LIKE ANY HUNTER-GATHERERS WE KNOW

A chilling scenario, this overkill. And it is unrealistic, too. Armies, not hunter-gatherers, come in waves, and few hunter-gatherers reproduce at the high rate overkill demands (Martin's 3.4 percent annual growth rate is taken from that of H.M.S. *Bounty* mutineers on Pitcairn Island, who apparently shed their inhibitions along with their ship). Hunter-gatherers can and do move between habitats, but theirs is not a scorched-earth policy.

Rather, as the Marginal Value Theorem from evolutionary ecology suggests, they leave a habitat when food supplies dip below what is available elsewhere (hunter-gatherers constantly monitor other habitats). That's usually long *before* animals and plants in the habitat are used up, as the University of Washington's Eric Smith argues, so long as there are alternate habitats offering good returns. This must surely have been the case for Paleoindians who, the very first Americans or not, obviously had their choice of productive habitats in which to hunt and gather.

If they resembled most foragers, Paleoindians were only occasional big-game hunters, targeting a few well-known prey species. But just a few. Indiscriminate hunting of nearly three dozen genera of megafauna continent-wide demands a comprehensive knowledge of places and animal behavior few hunters could possess. Besides, archaeologist George Frison of the University of Wyoming argues, no one hunting strategy would work on all mammoths, let alone all megafauna.

Armed with stone-tipped spears, Paleoindians could take big game. Still, there was no reason to make a habit of it. Hunting big game had more than its share of risks, such as coming home empty-handed—or not coming home at all. If their modern, highly intelligent, unpredictable, and vengeful relatives are any indication, hunting mammoths or mastodons was riskiest of all. Elephants, Africa's Hadza hunters say, do not behave like animals, they behave like enemies. Where elephants are hunted, it is at a distance with high-powered rifles or up close with metal broadswords, both far superior killing weapons than hand-held, stone-tipped Paleoindian spears.

Under the circumstances, one wag suggested, each Clovis generation probably killed one mammoth, then spent the rest of their lives talking about it.

WHEN SCARCITY OF EVIDENCE BECOMES EVIDENCE OF SCARCITY

Of course, if the Paleoindians killed more than one mammoth a generation, the archaeological record should show it. Take the missing moas. Soon after humans colonized New Zealand some 1000 years ago, this flightless and nearly defenseless bird was hunted to extinction. We know this because there are so many moa kill sites. The widespread slaughter envisioned in American overkill should have left equally unmistakable traces.

The Clovis toolkit was marked by its distinctive fluted points, unifacial *(extreme right)* and bifacial *(extreme left)* stone tools, and occasionally stone blades, and by specimens of bone or ivory. The bone shaft wrench *(center)* was likely used to straighten spear shafts. The bone foreshaft *(beside it on the right)* may have been used to attach Clovis points *(second and third items from left)* to spears.

Yet, more than 60 years after the Folsom and Clovis discoveries, megafauna kill sites are still rare outside the Great Plains and Southwest. Why? It might be poor preservation; in areas such as Eastern North America, where high rainfall and heavy vegetation conspire to increase soil acidity, bone is quickly destroyed.

It might also be for want of looking in the right places. Pleistocene-aged surfaces are buried now, deeply in some places—nearly 30 feet deep, as Reid Ferring discovered at the Aubrey Clovis site in north Texas. Large mammal carcasses shot full of Clovis points lying on those surfaces are often beyond notice or reach and are usually encountered only by chance.

Or perhaps big-game kill sites *should* be rare. Paul Martin thinks overkill happened so quickly—just a few centuries in any one area—that the odds are against any kill sites being preserved in the geological record. After all, adds Gary Haynes, a University of Nevada archaeologist who has studied elephants in the wild, African elephants have been hunted for centuries, yet kill sites with their bones are quite rare.

But remember the moas. They were killed in far greater numbers than African elephants, and in just as narrow a time slice as the Pleistocene megafauna allegedly were. Nevertheless, there are lots of moa kill sites. With all the Pleistocene megafauna ostensibly involved, kill sites should be the rule, not the exception. And there's no hiding behind poor preservation, even in Eastern North America. There and elsewhere thousands of megafauna fossils have been found, yet only a few have associated artifacts. Kill sites *are* genuinely scarce.

And those kill sites we have identified are very much alike in the prey they contain. Only mammoth and mastodon remains are found. There are no Paleoindian horse kills, no sloth kills, no camel kills, no tapir kills, nor kills of any of the other 30-odd genera of megafauna that went extinct. Isn't it odd, then, all these animals vanished at the same time. Or did they?

TIMING WAS EVERYTHING

Overkill helped Martin solve a vexing problem: What could cause so many very different animal genera living in very different habitats to disappear *simultaneously*? Only human hunters, he thought, moving rapidly cross-country. Changes in climate and environment, he rightly supposed, vary too much in timing, area, and severity to kill off so many animals so quickly.

However, after years of radiocarbon dating their fossils, we now know these animals did *not* become extinct at the same time. All were gone by roughly 10,800 B.P., but only eight of the 35 megafauna genera lasted until 12,000 B.P. The others disappeared earlier. If this pattern holds, which archaeologist Donald Grayson of the University of Washington shows is statistically likely, it means that only a fraction of the megafauna shared the landscape with Paleoindians, for no more than about 400 years in some areas, and not at all in others. Paleoindians arriving in Northeastern North America around 10,600 B.P. could hardly be responsible for extinctions occurring there hundreds or thousands of years earlier.

It means, too, that the extinction of the other 27 genera may have been smeared over time. If so, complex climatic and environmental changes become more attractive causes, and paleoecologists are busy exploring how these changes affected the lives of different animals in different places at different times.

Already, there are suspects—chiefly, changes from equable to seasonal climates, increasing temperature and decreasing rainfall (especially in the West), and changes in growing-season length (it got much shorter in the Far North). Those look more extreme at the Pleistocene-Holocene boundary than across previous glacial-interglacial divides, and the reshuffling of biotic communities in their wake fatally upset the delicate balance of animal and plant life—which is the key to why animals such as the sloth and the horse became extinct, though the plants they ate did not. The plants were part of larger habitats that did disappear.

Much more will come from these studies. Paleoindians, at least, are cleared of the charges against them. But if they weren't overkilling megafauna, what were they doing?

WHEN HUNTERS GATHER

Not all Paleoindians are alike, we now realize, and not all Paleoindians are Clovis. Clovis groups lived on the High Plains and Southwest and, so far as we can establish, were the oldest of the Paleoindians. Nowadays, the age of their occupation has been revised slightly upward to between 11,200 and 10,900 B.P. To the east and west, Paleoindians inhabited very different environments, lived at different times, and practiced very different adaptations. Strategies for exploiting plants and animals on western grasslands would not have been terribly effective in the mixed boreal/deciduous woodlands of Eastern North America or other distinctive habitats.

What, then, is the Clovis adaptation on the Great Plains and Southwest? If mammoths were hunted only occasionally and at great risk, how were they taken and why were they taken only in this particular region? What were the adaptations of Paleoindian groups in other areas? Or, even on the Plains but later in time? And what of the Clovis hallmarks, thought to be so widespread across space and through time? Good questions, but only recently have we begun to provide good answers.

BACK TO CLOVIS

At the time of its initial occupation just over 11,000 years ago, Clovis was a spring-fed pond, located just north of and feeding into Blackwater Draw. The springs attracted plants, animals, and people for many thousands of years, beginning in Clovis times. (To which the University of Arizona's Vance Haynes is wont to add, the springs attracted plants and animals but no people in the millennia before Clovis, which seems to him especially good evidence that people had yet to arrive in America.)

Those springs may have been especially valuable in Clovis times. Across the American West, just about then, Haynes sees evidence of a brief but severe drought (many artifacts, including three Clovis points, were found in the spring conduits, placed there, Haynes believes, as offerings). Such conditions would force animals, especially large ones like mammoths, to gravitate toward places where water, if not ponded on the surface, was within digging reach.

The Clovis pond and springs would have been such a magnet, and the late Pleistocene deposits contain, among others, bones of bison, horses, camels, peccaries, ground sloths, an extinct antelope, a couple of large carnivores, turtles, and mammoths. Lots of mammoths: 15 skeletons were excavated, but quite a few more passed unnoticed through gravel quarry machinery. (Unfortunately, the quarrying that had led Howard to the Clovis site didn't cease, and as the quarry's giant scoops dug out the gravel, they ravaged overlying layers of artifact and bone.)

Of the known mammoths, more than half a dozen were stuck with Clovis points or artifacts. Those animals died at different times, some on the pond's margins, others in its center. Their skeletons were nearly complete and *articulated* (the bones lay in proper anatomical position). Obviously, animals had been butchered where they fell, but only partially. Flesh was stripped from the upper skeleton, skulls were smashed to obtain brains, but otherwise carcasses were left to rot.

This pattern of partially butchered mammoth bones in pond or stream settings recurs in Clovis sites. So much so, that it looks purposeful. It looks as though Clovis hunters drove mammoths into shallow water, or waited in ambush until the animals slowed down or got stuck in the mud and became easy targets.

Perhaps. Yet once mired, animals that large are difficult to butcher and near impossible to extract, as the articulated skeletons clearly attest. For that matter, healthy animals (especially full-grown adults) are not easily bogged down in shallow water or mud. Besides, George Frison argues, good hunters would take mammoths elsewhere and on their terms. They might quietly isolate a juvenile mammoth (less risky!) from the herd's protection and away from bogs, wound it, then patiently wait for it to become disabled or die. And all the while hoping or insuring that the animal did not stagger to a water hole to collapse and die.

OPPORTUNITIES FOUND

If that's so, why are most of the Clovis-stabbed mammoths at water holes? Over his many seasons spent studying African elephants, Gary Haynes saw a disproportionate number of younger elephants frequenting water holes when ill (water helps cool rising body temperature) or during drought. Often they died there. He thinks it no coincidence that most mammoths in Clovis sites died young too. Hard hit by drought and teetering on the brink of extinction, many sick and enfeebled animals became mired in ponds, where they presented risk-free targets for passing—or patiently waiting—hunter-gatherers who took what meat they could, then moved on.

Archaeologist James Judge of Ft. Lewis College calls this sort of strategy *opportunistic scavenging*, and thinks it—more so than deliberate big-game hunting—is characteristic of Clovis. That certainly would explain all those partially butchered animals stuck in the mud, and why so many Clovis mammoth "kills" look like animals who died naturally, but with a few Clovis points in their bodies.

Opportunistic or not, Clovis groups were occasionally quite adept at snaring big game. In the San Pedro Valley of southern Arizona, bones of 13 mammoths, mostly calves or young adults, were excavated by archaeologist Emil Haury—and later by Vance Haynes—on the Lehner Ranch. Scattered amongst mammoth ribs, hindquarters, and jaws were 13 Clovis points made of locally available chert, chalcedony, and (in three cases), quartz, along with stone scrapers, knives, and a chopper. The Lehner mammoths died serially, in the century around 10,930 B.P.

The San Pedro Valley was a ripe field. At Murray Springs, 12 miles (20 kilometers) north of Lehner and slightly later in time (around 10,900 B.P.), a mammoth and, nearby, 11 bison, were killed (bison, in fact, were also exploited at the Clovis, Aubrey, and Agate Basin sites). Haynes recovered Clovis points,

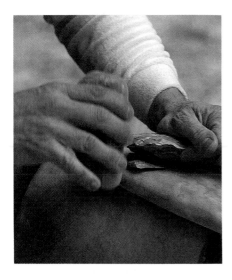

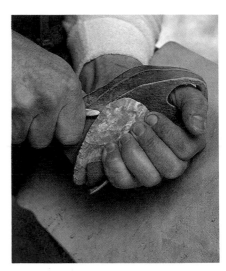

Errett Callahan, an expert in stone tool-making, knaps a Clovis spearpoint from a fine-grained stone. In the hands of the Paleoindian hunters who lived on the High Plains some 10,500 years ago, these distinctive points were capable of bringing down mammoth, bison, and other large game, but were also versatile enough to be used as knives, scrapers, and general all-purpose tools. Callahan uses a variety of tools made of stone and moose antler to reduce a grapefruit-sized piece of Texas chert to a finished point ready to be attached to a wooden shaft.

tools, and thousands of tiny stone flakes littering the bone beds, evidence of the constant resharpening of tools that dulled easily when butchering animal flesh. The dead animal may have had other visitors, too: Haynes found mammoth tracks leading up to the skeleton. Perhaps, like elephants, mammoths examined the carcasses of their kin.

The Clovis groups camped near the kill, hauling in mammoth and bison filets, and repairing broken weaponry. Curiously, Clovis points used against bison were far the worse for wear. Many had *impact fractures*, flakes driven backward off the point tip. These fractures occur when stone hits bone at high velocity, and may distinguish a spear thrust in a lumbering (or mired) mammoth from one thrown at a hard-charging bison. One fact is certain: Impact fractures are exceedingly rare on Clovis points, yet common on points in bison kills of all ages.

THE BIG ONES THAT GOT AWAY

At Clovis, Lehner, and Murray Springs, there were opportunities found. But there were opportunities lost, too. Just down the San Pedro from Lehner and Murray Springs was the Naco mammoth, found eroding out of the sidewalls of Greenbush Creek. Most of the skeleton was there, save the hindquarters which had washed away. Eight Clovis projectile points, remarkably variable in size, were found with this one animal. One lay at the base of the skull, another near the left scapula, two were wedged between ribs, and one against the surface of the atlas vertebra. Yet, no butchering tools were found, nor did any bones show signs of filleting. The Naco mammoth had escaped, to die quietly of its wounds with hide intact. But escaped from whom? The stone from which the Naco points were fashioned was used by the same hunters who stabbed the Lehner and Murray Springs mammoths.

Nearly 11,000 years ago, at a place now called Murray Springs in southern Arizona, hunters killed a mammoth and 11 bison. Archaeologists recovered Clovis points and other tools from among the litter of bones. Archaeologist Vance Haynes also found mammoth tracks—visible in the photograph at right—leading up to the mammoth skeleton, suggesting that the carcass may have been examined by the animal's surviving kin.

Nor is Naco alone. The Manis mastodon in Washington, and the Domebo mammoth (pronounced like Disney's big-eared elephant, but found in Oklahoma), got away too. So did the San Pedro Valley's Escapule mammoth—evidently another escapee of the Lehner and Murray Springs carnage. In all cases, paleocoroners ruled the deaths natural, unrelated to the stone and bone points the animals carried to their graves.

WHEN THE BIG-GAME WAS OVER

Pleistocene extinctions had a profound impact on Plains Paleoindians, but had nothing to do with depriving them of their favorite foods, and much to do with providing an alternative food source. In the warmer and drier millennia of the latest Pleistocene, the Plains grassland became less diverse and increasingly dominated by warm-season grasses (which have maximum growth during the summer months, and furnish high-quality forage into the fall and winter), and by one of the few large animals that could tolerate their anti-herbivore toxins: the bison.

Huge bison herds grazed the Plains throughout the Holocene, and Paleoindian hunters often organized mass kills. About 8500 years ago, nearly 200 bison were ambushed and driven into an arroyo, or dry gulley, at the Olsen-Chubbuck site in southeastern Colorado, and then slaughtered. In 1957, wind erosion exposed the skeletal remains.

In Late Prehistoric times, huge bison herds grazed the Plains, and human hunters orchestrated mass kills, taking hundreds of animals in early fall, drying the meat, and smashing and boiling the bones for marrow and grease to make energy-rich pemmican, all stored for use over winter and into the following year. (Yet another reason to doubt overkill. Bison were hunted on the Plains throughout the Holocene and the hunting was often highly wasteful—of the nearly 200 bison driven into the arroyo at the Olsen-Chubbuck [Colorado] site, for instance, fully 25 percent of the animals at the bottom of the pile were left to rot unbutchered or only partially butchered. After 10,000 years of this, bison were still around when the Spanish arrived, and despite being threatened with extinction in the late 19th century, are still here today. It is telling that an animal relentlessly hunted for 10,000 years failed to go extinct, while 35 genera of animals which were not hunted at all or very little did.)

Paleoindians were much more modest. Folsom kills, Colorado State University archaeologist Larry Todd reports, typically involved less than 30 bison (about 100 in later Paleoindian times). Judged by patterns of tooth eruption and wear, most kills occurred in winter when nutritionally vital bison fat reserves were low and it was too late to dry meat. Partially butchered animals are common; bones rendered for fat or marrow, rare. This was gourmet butchering, Todd says. Choice cuts of beef were selected, then frozen to keep them edible until warm weather arrived. On occasion, the hunters wintered over on the spot.

At the Agate Basin site in eastern Wyoming, for example, Folsom groups some 10,780 years ago camped on the floodplain of an arroyo, near where they had trapped and butchered at least eight bison. Hide-covered structures (with one "tent peg," a bison rib, still stuck in the ground) and the large surrounding area were densely littered with the debris of point manufacture, along with end and side scrapers, cutting tools, gravers, knives and choppers, a crystal-studded abrader (for hide softening), bone and antler artifacts (including eyed needles), and the slab used to pulverize the red ocher that covered the bones and artifacts.

Features like the arroyo trap at Agate Basin recur in Folsom and later Paleoindian sites. They were careful, these hunters, for bison in those days, *Bison antiquus*, were several hundred pounds larger and carried horns each about 12 inches (30 centimeters) longer than those on today's *Bison bison*. In fact, cows then were the same size as bulls now—which average roughly 1800 pounds (800 kilograms) and stand about 5.5 feet (1.65 meters) at the shoulder. Almost certainly, bison were then as fast, nimble, and unpredictable as they are now, and quite a challenge to pedestrian hunters.

Bison hunters used different risk-reduction features, Frison argues, but mostly the plan was to restrain the animals long enough for the hunters to act. At the Folsom site, the bison were maneuvered into a steep-sided arroyo from which they could not easily escape, then speared. At Bonfire Shelter in Texas,

The **Folsom** camp at Agate Basin, seen over 10,000 years later. Visible at the site were the traces of a hide-covered structure (shown in purple), within which was a hearth, and tools and flakes (shown as red dots), some from the manufacture of projectile points. Bone was rare within the structure, but outside it were the remains of antelope, canids, rabbits, and especially bison.

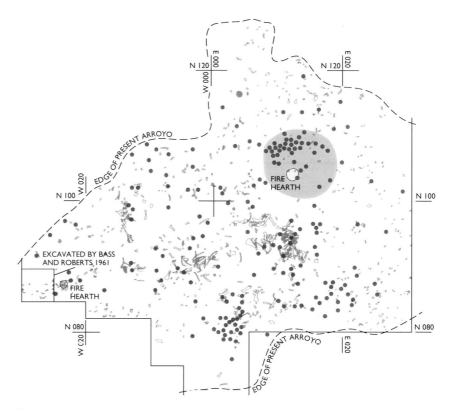

A crystal-studded abrader, most likely used for softening animal hides, was found among other artifacts at the Agate Basin site in eastern Wyoming. Here, some 10,780 years ago, a group of hunters trapped and butchered at least eight bison.

animals were run off a steep bluff and fell to their deaths. Yet such bison jumps, requiring large, fast-moving, and close-packed herds, were less common early on. In time, elaborate corrals, drive lines, and various artificial features would enhance the use of arroyos, bluffs, and other natural traps.

EAST MEETS WEST?

Mammoth altogether eluded the fluted spearpoints of Eastern Paleoindians, and for the most part, the forest-dwelling mastodon were nearly as successful (possibly for reasons tied to the timing of their extinction). Except at Kimmswick.

Since 1839, many mastodon skeletons have been mined from the Kimmswick bone beds, south of St. Louis, Missouri. There was talk early on that ancient human remains were there as well. William Henry Holmes himself excavated there in 1901 and 1902 to lay that chatter to rest. It didn't work. In the 1980s, a team directed by the paleontologist Russell Graham reopened Kimmswick, and in ancient pond settings reminiscent of sites farther west, found fluted points in association with mastodon bone (yet undated), along with butchering tools and thousands of tiny manufacturing and resharpening flakes.

Other eastern Paleoindian sites offer hints that mastodon had once been taken there, but the indications are strong only at western New York's Hiscock

University of Texas archaeologists set up a vertical profile of the Bonfire Shelter in southern Texas where bone fragments from Paleoindian kills of big game have been found. The shelter lies below a precipitous limestone bluff where Paleoindians and later peoples stampeded bison over the edge to their deaths.

site. Curiously, at Hiscock the fluted point lay closer to elk, than to mastodon, bones. That in itself is no proof the elk was the main target. But other members of the deer family, especially caribou (reindeer), are known prey at a few Northeastern Paleoindian sites, and suspected prey at many others, from Nova Scotia to the Great Lakes (all occurring in the centuries around 10,600 B.P.).

Today, caribou move in great herds, wintering in the forest and summering on the tundra. In Paleoindian times, however, the tundra was less expansive, and both the range and size of caribou herds were probably reduced and in the process of adjusting to postglacial changes. Even on a smaller scale, however, their migratory habits and herd instincts made them a prime resource in northern forests and parklands.

An annual one, too. In successive seasons some 10,500 years ago at Maine's Vail site, caribou were intercepted at what R. Michael Gramly, the site's excava-

An aerial view of the Vail site in Maine where, some 10,000 years ago, hunters killed and processed a number of caribou. The animals were killed on a sandy patch on one side of the river—identified by the discovery of 10 broken fluted points—then butchered for hides, meat, and marrow at a camp on the other side marked by tools, flakes, and the bottom halves of points broken at the kill.

Migrating caribou swim across the Kobuk River in Kobuk Valley National Park, Alaska. Even in Paleoindian times when their range and size were smaller than today, the caribou's migratory habits and herd instincts made them an important resource in Northern North America.

tor, calls the killing ground. This was a sandy patch, marked by 10 fluted points, but nothing else. There animals were processed for hide, meat, and marrow, 800 feet (250 meters) away across a river from a camp marked by tools and flakes.

In camp, the caribou hunters repaired their weaponry. Many of their points suffered the same impact damage seen in western bison kills (and probably for the same reason). The camp and kill areas were literally joined at the base. Broken point tips lost at the killing ground fit onto broken bases back at the camp where hunters had re-armed their spears. After a string of good years, Vail was abandoned, Gramly believes, when the caribou chose another valley on their annual trek. They can be fickle.

Archaeologists have long suspected that white-tailed deer were targeted by Paleoindians farther south in the eastern woodlands—as they were by virtually all subsequent hunter-gatherers of the region. The evidence is meager, though deer bones are abundant just across the academic border separating Paleoindian and later *Archaic* groups. The Archaic is marked by the disappearance of fluted points, which happens about 10,500 B.P. across much of the Southeast. Yet, aside from a change in point style, the remainder of the toolkit stays virtually the same. One suspects that the adaptive strategies were retained as well. That being the case, deer were on the Paleoindian menu, as well as elk, an occasional bison, many species of fish, turtles, rabbit, squirrel, raccoon, beaver, muskra , and turkey, with hickory nuts, walnuts, acorns, hackberry, and persimmon.

ROUNDING OUT THE PALEOINDIAN DIET
What else Paleoindians may have eaten is coming into view, sometimes in unexpected places—such as big-game "kill" sites. In addition to mammoths,

Lehner yielded charred and roasted rabbit bones. Folsom hunters killed bison at Agate Basin, but also pronghorn antelope (there are antelope blood stains on Folsom artifacts at the Mitchell site, which lies on the outskirts of the Clovis site). At the Hanson Folsom site in Wyoming, mountain sheep, deer, marmot, and cottontail rabbit were also foods.

Back east, the Clovis levels at Kimmswick produced 23 species of mammals; of those, deer, snakes, rodents, and turtles were as abundant as mastodons, and as much a part of the meal plan. Along with caribou in a couple of the northeastern sites were burned scraps of beaver, birds, and fish.

TURTLES ON THE HALF SHELL

Prey animals obviously varied by habitat, but one occurs in many Paleoindian sites, whether in the woodlands, as at Kimmswick, or on the Plains, as at the Aubrey and Lewisville Clovis sites in north-central Texas.

Sometimes large, and always slow-moving, Pleistocene turtles—many subsequently gone extinct—were the best kind of game. They were obviously no threat to human life or limb. Clovis groups seem to have pursued them (leisurely, of course) and eaten many. At the original Clovis site a turtle-roasting pit was found. Six or seven turtles were stacked one atop the other and cooked in their shells. Turtle remains also dominated the Little Salt Spring site in Florida, together with the giant extinct land tortoise, *Geochelone crassicutata*, and the wood spear that had skewered it as the centerpiece. (The spear was radiocarbon dated to 12,030 ± 200 B.P., making the site's age an anomaly. It is older than any Paleoindian site in Eastern, let alone Western, North America. A date on the tortoise bone of 13,450 ± 190 B.P. is even less trustworthy, given the material dated. No stone tools, fluted or otherwise, were found with the tortoise.)

Ultimately, we may discover that turtles were one of the Paleoindian staples, more important in the diet of these early Americans than faster, bigger game. And why not? At sizes of 37 inches (94 centimeters) in length, 30 inches (75 centimeters) in width, and with a shell height of 23 inches (59 centimeters)—the estimated dimensions of the Little Salt Spring *Geochelone*—that's a lot of meat under the hood.

FRUIT AND FIBER

Still, only humans who occupy arctic environments live by meat alone, and there it's not by choice, but by necessity. Archaeologist Lewis Binford of Southern Methodist University has shown that hunter-gatherers in more temperate regions depend on plant foods for upwards of 70 percent of their diet. Oddly, some insist that plant foods were "neither a provable nor logical part" of Paleoindian diets. Big-game hunting myths die hard. True, the degree of plant use among Paleoindians remains *unproven*, but it is both provable and, as Binford and others demonstrate, eminently logical.

PRECEDING PAGE: Large, slow-moving
Pleistocene turtles were a favorite item
on the Paleoindian menu. Turtle-roasting
pits have been uncovered at a number
of Clovis sites, including the original one
in New Mexico, and at Little Salt Spring
on the Gulf Coast of Florida.

Certainly the few surviving Paleoindian teeth were worn down from a diet that included plants, as physical anthropologist Gentry Steele has shown. One day, studies of bone chemistry, which can gauge the relative use of plants and animals by Paleoindians, will reveal just how important each was. Until then, better recovery techniques will help immensely, for seeds, berries, and other traces of plant (or even small animal) foods are not easily detected, even if they are preserved. A little luck helps, too.

Better technique and good fortune came together at Shawnee-Minisink, in eastern Pennsylvania. During the excavations in the mid-1970s, directed by Charles McNett, 10 percent of all the excavated sediment was poured into large, water-filled washtubs; minute pieces of organic materials (bone, wood, charcoal, seeds) floated to the surface and were collected, while the remainder of the sediment was passed through fine mesh. This flotation captured aca-lypha, hackberry, blackberry, chenopod, hawthorn, plum, and grape seeds—even tiny fish bones—from meals prepared 10,600 years ago.

Shawnee-Minisink, however, is an exception. Other Paleoindian sites, mostly excavated before flotation became customary, lack plant remains, but not necessarily the artifacts used to process plant foods. Although far more abundant in later times, grinding stones are present in a number of Paleoindian sites, not the least of which is Clovis itself. So, too, stone knives with a "sheen" or polish produced by repeated harvesting of plants, especially grasses, are found along with fluted points in northeastern sites. That's a pretty meager record of recognizable plant processing tools from Paleoindian sites. Still, archaeologists are comforted by the fact that only a fraction of such implements recorded historically among the Iroquois are found in their archaeological sites. The rest are biodegradable.

The fluted points themselves, like prehistoric Swiss Army knives, were useful for various tasks—skinning rabbits, prying open turtle shells, or digging out stubborn roots. While very few have impact fractures, a great many show the wear of all-purpose knives.

Perhaps this use of fluted points explains why thousands of them litter the landscape, often isolated from other stone tools or bone. They were used for more activities more often in more places than any other tool in their toolkit.

In recent years, archaeologists have taken to mapping the distribution of these isolated fluted points and, on the Great Plains and in the Great Basin, a clear pattern has emerged. Points are clustered along the edges of now-dry Pleistocene pluvial lakes, marshes, and springs. A similar pattern is evident in Florida, which was also dry in latest Pleistocene times. There, fluted points cluster around sinkholes or in low spots where freshwater emerged from an underground source.

Whatever these Clovis and other Paleoindians were doing, Donald Grayson points out, they were doing it near shallow water. If sites in the same place, but slightly later in time, can bear witness, what they were doing was exploiting small mammals, birds, fish, and mollusks.

122

MADE IN AMERICA

In 1935, Edgar B. Howard went to Russia to search for ancestral fluted points. He failed to find any, and that told him something: Fluting was an American invention. Knowing where the practice originated, and how it spread, are vital to tracking Paleoindian movements in America.

The obvious place to search for fluting's origins is between central Alaska and the Northern Plains, and archaeologists have done just that. What turns up, however, are fluted points *younger* (10,500 to 9500 years old) than they are farther south. So we know that fluting was invented south of the Canadian border. The Great Plains are a possibility; the oldest fluted points known occur there.

Another possibility is Eastern North America. Since a greater variety of fluted points occur there than anywhere else, Lawrence University archaeologist Ronald Mason argues, then that's where they must have originated (the principle that diversity reflects age is the same that Joseph Greenberg applied to fix the relative antiquity of his three language families). Finding eastern fluted points that predated those out west would settle the issue. In the meantime, it has been noticed that the unfluted lanceolate from Stratum IIa at Meadowcroft would make a fine fluted-point precursor.

Once invented, fluting spread over the Paleoindian world, even reaching into Northern South America. But how? Were fluted points carried by migrating Paleoindians, or was fluting a technique passed among neighboring Paleoindian populations? The jury is hung, and may stay that way, until we learn whether there were earlier "fluteless" Paleoindians.

Nevertheless, it's hard to understand why fluting proved to be so popular. Fluting a projectile point is one of the last manufacturing steps, and by far the most difficult. Failure rates were high, and the mistakes costly. And for what? Fluting served no pressing function. The idea that flutes were bayonet-style grooves to intensify the mammoth's bleeding fell from grace when archaeologists realized the flutes were sandwiched between foreshafts of bone, wood, or ivory, or embedded in sockets that attached, or hafted, the point to the spear. Nor does it appear that fluting enhanced the hafting. Unfluted points can be just as firmly anchored to a spear shaft.

Maybe, Frison and others argue, the reason we cannot show how fluting directly enhanced the performance of the point, is that it didn't. At least not in ways visible 10,000 years later. Fluting may have been a Paleoindian art form, or possessed ritual significance—and in that context, as we know, the costs of possible failure don't matter.

Whatever significance fluting possessed, a great many Paleoindians used it. Fluting appears across America. Still, not all fluted points are alike, except in a most general sense. All share a lanceolate shape, are ground along the lower edges and base (which insured that the edges did not cut the sinew binding or socket haft), and have flutes that extend from the base partially up one or,

Stone points seem to have been the Swiss Army knives of Paleoindian times. Archaeologists believe they were hafted to shafts for use as spears, but also that they were used for skinning animals, opening the shells of turtles and clams, and even for digging up roots. However, there was more than one standard manufacture. Clovis *(left)* and Folsom *(right)* points have decidedly different shapes, but both have fluting on the face. This fluting appears to have been invented in North America.

The 11,000-year-old Thunderbird site in Virginia was used as a stone quarry by Paleoindians. It has yielded artifact-rich clusters of stone flakes that have helped archaeologists to understand how Paleoindian groups fashioned their points and tools.

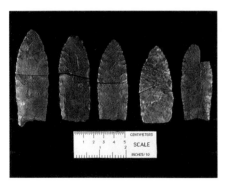

Among the Clovis points left behind at Thunderbird were specimens that broke in the very last stages of manufacture, instantly became useless, and had to be scrapped. Occasionally, the broken bases are found in the site many feet away from the broken tips, indicating a healthy pitch followed the fatal break.

more commonly, both faces of the point. On a "classic" Clovis, the sides are parallel, the flutes travel less than halfway up the point, and the points are relatively long and thick (though deliberately fashioned Clovis miniatures are known—children's toys, some call them). A freshly minted Clovis point would be slightly more than 4 inches (10 centimeters) in length, just over an inch (3 centimeters) in width and less than one-third of an inch (7.5 millimeters) in thickness.

Beyond that, the points vary considerably in size, shape, length, and depth of the flutes, the number of flutes (three per face is about the limit), the kind of chipping used to fashion the point, how the point's edges were finished, and a host of other minutiae that delight archaeologists. Broadly speaking, there are a few instantly recognizable types—Folsom points, for example.

Other fluted point types are not so readily defined, though archaeologists are beginning to make headway, especially in Eastern North America. Teased out of the plethora of fluted points are types traveling under such names as Gainey, Barnes, Crowfield, Debert, Cumberland, Suwannee, Quad, Redstone, and Hardaway-Dalton. These types appear to be geographically restricted: Gainey, Barnes, and Crowfield, for example, to the Great Lakes regions, and Debert to the east in New England and the Canadian Maritimes. That may be the key (here's Goldilocks sneaking in again) to identifying separate Paleoindian populations.

Paleoindian toolkits (not just the points) also vary across America. In some areas, however, variation is expressed more in the frequency of certain tools—end scrapers, for example—or in the kind of stone used, than in the types of tools. That sort of pattern tells us more about what was done with the tools than who did it.

How Paleoindian groups fashioned their points and tools is revealed in a number of sites, especially those situated close to stone sources. Debris gathered in these sites reveals the steps in artifact manufacturing, including the failures experienced along the way. Often present at these sites are the areas where lone knappers sat and flaked stone. At the Thunderbird site in the Shenandoah Valley of Virginia, excavation teams under William Gardner's direction uncovered exquisite artifact-rich clusters of flakes that silhouetted in stone the knapper's crossed legs (the silhouette was created as flakes rained down on either side of the knapper's legs).

Archaeologists rarely find bone and ivory artifacts made by Paleoindians, but those we do discover are striking. A mammoth bone wrench, possibly for straightening ivory or bone spear foreshafts, was found at Murray Springs. No bone foreshafts accompanied it, but examples have been recovered in half a dozen other sites scattered in the West, and from underwater sites in Florida. Bone spear points, awls, beads, and even bone needles (a sure sign of tailored clothing), complete the repertoire.

Ivory artifacts are scarcer still. Among the few, the most striking is a cylindrical ivory point or foreshaft from the Clovis levels at the Agate Basin site. The Clovis site itself produced a half-chopped section of mammoth tusk, which at the time it was lost or abandoned was on its way to being further reduced and fashioned into ivory artifacts.

Overall, the spotty distribution of bone and ivory artifacts says little about whether and how these materials were used by Paleoindians, since they were almost certainly used more frequently and in more ways than we have evidence. The spotty distribution, however, does say a great deal about how poorly bone and ivory are preserved in the archaeological record.

HOME IS WHERE THE HEARTHS ARE

Although not engaged in headlong pursuit of big game, the Paleoindians were mobile all the same. Mobility in their case, as with all hunter-gatherers, brings security, since nature's bounty is unevenly distributed. Game-rich areas may lack edible plants; plants may not be edible at all times of the year; animals, especially larger ones, can wander away from a habitat, or change their range altogether. It's a volatile market for hunter-gatherers, and they monitor it by moving. But not constantly. Depending on the richness of the resources in the habitat and elsewhere, the season of the year, and a host of other factors, groups will settle in one place for shorter or longer periods before traveling on.

Paleoindian structures are not well known, since none were made of stone but of less permanent materials, such as wood or skin, which quickly degrade and disappear. Nor are the structures easily spotted in the archaeological record. Often their traces are no more than slight circular stains in the soil

The first Americans fashioned tools of great efficacy and simplicity. Archaeologists believe this wrench-like tool was made from mammoth bone and probably was used to straighten spear shafts. It was discovered at the Murray Springs site in Arizona. Such finds are rare, however.

(postmolds), marking where wooden posts were once planted. One such structure was reported at Thunderbird—a line of postmolds forming a rough oval 30 by 40 feet (9 by 12 meters) in size.

At other times, evidence of structures can be as subtle as slightly hardened earth, or the presence of artifacts concentrated around burned or charcoal spotted areas (as at Agate Basin). At Hanson, for example, Frison detected vaguely circular, hard-packed, sandy floors, less than an inch thick, as well as burned bone, rock, and soil, but neither charcoal nor postmolds.

Although such clues reveal little of the habitations once standing there, they do hint at the use of the site, and the scale of the occupation. In Northeastern North America, for example, Paleoindian sites typically are composed of a number of discrete artifact concentrations, less than a dozen on average, each yielding the same range of tools. That suggests the domestic activities of individual households.

Occasionally, broken artifacts from different clusters fit together, which—along with the layout of the clusters—might be evidence that different households (or whatever they may have been) were on the site simultaneously. In other instances, the concentrations are less discrete, sometimes overlapping (*palimpsests*, we call them), which would indicate successive occupations.

For the most part, Paleoindian sites were occupied for short periods, and only a few times, before being dropped from the settlement round. No surprise there. With a continent to themselves, the Paleoindians' only incentive to return to the same spot was a prized resource, such as stone (as at Thunderbird) or, while it lasted, a migratory game trail (as at Vail), or an especially rich grove of nut-bearing trees. But with a continent to themselves, there was also great incentive for separate families to gather seasonally or annually to socialize, exchange items and crucial information, maintain old kin ties, and establish new ones through marriage.

CACHE AND CARRY

Even while temporarily settled, hunting or foraging parties took forays away from the main site to keep an eye on what was available elsewhere. Security, a Nunamuit Eskimo caribou hunter explained to Binford, means knowing where to find food when the time comes to leave the spot you're in.

We calculate Paleoindian mobility by the straight-line distance from quarry to site. It's a blunt measure, saying nothing of the number and timing of their moves, nor the area covered. But by it, we know they were highly mobile, particularly in the Great Plains (in Clovis and later times) and Far Northeast, where resources were locally clumped but widely separated. They were less mobile in the eastern forests, where food-rich environments kept them moving, but not in such large forays.

As Paleoindian (and other) hunter-gatherers looped around the landscape, straying far from strategic supply points (like favored stone quarries), they carefully maintained their equipment. Fluted points, for example, that dulled or broke, were carefully resharpened, which helps explain the Paleoindian preference for high-quality, longer-lasting stone. Ultimately the resharpened points became too small for use as such, and they were then recycled into other tools, such as scrapers and wedges.

Being a highly mobile Paleoindian with a preference for quality stone from a few favored quarries did create logistical problems. Your settlement round brought you past quarries only occasionally, and you could only carry from the quarry limited amounts of stone on any one trip. And yet you spent the stone all over your territory, sometimes exhausting your supplies far from the quarry itself. The solution—their solution—was to cache supplies of stone in convenient places around the landscape. When tools broke, wore down through resharpening, or were lost, as all inevitably were, resupply at a cache could save a long trip back to the quarry.

Some Paleoindian caches contain scores of large biface preforms ready and still waiting to be fashioned into one or more finished tools, as well as exquisitely made and inordinately large fluted points—some up to 8 inches (21 centimeters in length)—and, occasionally, bone foreshafts, and pieces of antler and ivory. Often these artifacts were sprinkled with red ocher (hematite), a natural mineral paint.

At the Anzick, Montana, and Crowfield, Ontario, sites, artifact caches may have accompanied burials. Here, at least, the artifacts may not have been intended for later recovery and use.

In the northern latitudes Paleoindians cached meat as a precaution against difficult times. They stashed mammoth meat at the Colby, Wyoming, site 11,200 years ago—two large piles of it, still on the bone and stacked 110 feet (33 meters) apart. The first bone pile held the remains of three immature mammoths as well as a few tools. The second also yielded the remains of three mammoths, mostly articulated ribs and shoulder bones, and a pelvic bone, the whole thing topped by a skull. Directly underneath the innominate, the large flaring pelvic bone, was a fluted point (an offering, perhaps?). George Frison, who excavated Colby, believes that both of these piles accumulated over several kill episodes, and that the first cache was reopened and the meat used, but not the second.

Caribou meat was cached, Michael Gramly believes, at Vail and, perhaps a season earlier, at the nearby Adkins site. There, more than half a dozen boulders, weighing 220 pounds (100 kilograms) or more apiece, were arranged around a pit, creating a storage chamber about twice the size of an average household refrigerator—and in Maine, at the end of the Pleistocene, easily just as cold.

But that was the end of the Pleistocene, and very soon the end of the Paleoindian era. The descendants of North American Paleoindians further diverged from one another as they traversed the long haul of American prehistory.

The quarter-mile-long Great Serpent Mound, near Cincinnati, Ohio, is a vestige of the Adena people. The structure, still five feet high, was built some 2500 years ago; its associated burial mound was found to contain a rich cache of grave goods.

7

THE LAST 10,000 YEARS

I n the late summer of 1927, archaeologists Frank
Roberts and A.V. Kidder were in Pecos, New Mexico,
when the telegrams flashed from the tiny bungalow at
Folsom, a few hundred miles to the north. Kidder was set
to leave for Los Angeles, but he couldn't resist the detour
up the Folsom road—and back 10,000 years.

The Folsom site lured Kidder, but for more than just
the usual reasons. Like everyone else, Kidder cheered the
opening of a new era in the study of the first Americans.

Yet unlike Roberts, Edgar Howard, and others, who glimpsed the untapped riches of Paleoindian studies, then dove headlong into them, Kidder happily watched from the sidelines. He was more interested in the Paleoindians' descendants: He excavated late prehistoric Pueblo and Maya ruins before Folsom, and did the same after Folsom. All he ever wanted from Folsom was the assurance that the first Americans had arrived by the late Pleistocene. But he wanted that very, very badly.

Kidder was "100-percent American" when it came to the origin of New World prehistoric civilizations, believing that the Maya, Inca, and the rest had developed independently of any Old World stimulus. His wasn't a trendy position. Few supposed that the trappings of complex cultures—agriculture, pottery, metal-working, pyramid-building—were separately invented around the world. Most looked to Old World cultures, especially the Nile Valley civilization, as the wellspring from which, via diffusion, the "idea" of cultural complexity spread across the globe.

However much Kidder believed that New World civilization arose independently of any inspiration from the Old—and he believed it passionately—Kidder failed to win many converts in pre-Folsom days. Back then, there just was not enough time allotted to American prehistory for the natives to have developed civilization on their own. How could a band of hunter-gatherers lately arrived in America, diffusionists asked, build great cities within the space of a few thousand years? They insisted it was impossible. Prehistoric Americans must have had outside help. Until North American prehistory was able to go deeper, Kidder was stymied.

But when it did go deeper, at Folsom, Kidder at last had the chronological elbowroom (his words) for an independent run up to New World civilizations. That, he confessed, was a great relief. It made him wonder, though. If the archaeologically familiar southwestern Pueblos and eastern Moundbuilders were less than 1500 years old, and yet the first Americans arrived 15,000 years ago (Kidder's 1927 estimate), what was going on during the millennia in between?

SNAPSHOTS

Plenty. And that goes for the last 1500 years, too. The descendants of North American Paleoindians weathered severe drought on the Great Plains; bartered Wyoming obsidian for Great Lakes copper and Gulf Coast shells in Midwest commodities exchanges; teased wild plants until they bore seeds and fruits fit to eat, drink, or smoke; dug miles of canals across arid scrubland and made desert gardens bloom; settled down from their ancestor's mobile ways, and built towns of stone, earth, and wood.

And they accomplished much, much more. More, certainly, than can be treated in a single chapter; whole books are written about this sort of thing. Yet, snapshots of the last 10,000 years, however fleeting, help bridge the gap between the settling in of the first Americans, and the utter disruption of the

During the time of the Altithermal drought, which lasted some 2500 years, the burnt summer grasses on the Great Plains were not enough to sustain a grazer as large as *Bison antiquus*, shown in the illustration below. The large animal slowly shrank in size until it stabilized at the size of today's *Bison bison* (right in the illustration, and on the hoof at bottom).

lives and cultures of their descendants in the centuries after 1492. So snapshots they will be here, starting early on the Plains, then moving through time west, south, east, and north.

WHEN THE BUFFALO DON'T ROAM

The lessons about bison hunting learned on the Plains in Folsom times were put into practice in the early millennia of the Holocene, and bison kills—often spectacular—dominate the archaeological record. That was true, too, of the most recent millennia of the Holocene, when sophisticated corrals and hunting tactics, the advent of the bow and arrow and, ultimately, the reappearance of the horse (brought by Spanish explorers), made bison hunting a fine art. In the last few centuries of prehistory surplus bison meat was exchanged for corn and other crops grown by farmers west and east of the Plains.

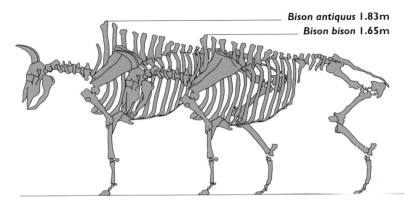

Bison antiquus 1.83m
Bison bison 1.65m

But in Middle Holocene times (approximately 7500 to 5000 B.P.) the Plains were very different. The land was in the grip of a long dry spell geologist Ernst Antevs called the *Altithermal*. Antevs thought the Altithermal drought reached across the west, but we now know it was severe in some places, the Plains, for instance, and barely noticeable in others.

Just how severe can be measured against the 1930s Dust Bowl, seared into history by John Steinbeck's novel, *The Grapes of Wrath*, and the photographs of Dorothea Lange and Arthur Rothstein. For however harsh, and however profoundly the Dust Bowl changed America, it was climatically trivial. Lasting less than a decade, the Dust Bowl scarcely registers in the geological record. We would look largely in vain for traces, for example, of the 350 million tons of soil that blew off parched fields in May of 1934 and blotted out the sun.

But the Altithermal left its mark. This was a drought that laid waste the Plains not for 10 years, but for 2500. Rainfall-fed ponds dried and deflated, creating sand sheets and dunes that began marching across the landscape. Even trusty springs dried, as underground aquifers pumped without refill.

Drought is certain on the Plains, and most plants and animals easily coped. But not the bison. There was too little to drink and not enough to eat. Summer droughts (as the Altithermal may have been), burn up the warm season grasses the bison love. No wonder in these few thousand years *Bison antiquus* shrank to *Bison bison*; this animal was under intense ecological stress.

Hard times for bison meant hard times for bison hunters. Not so hard that, as earlier thought, the Plains were completely abandoned by Altithermal groups, fleeing—like the Joad family of Steinbeck's novel—for better points west. The times were hard enough though, with food and water dangerously unreliable.

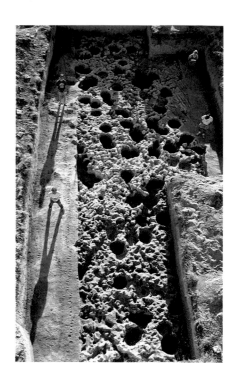

An exposed wellfield at Mustang Springs, Texas, shows a cluster of circular wells. More than 60 were found at the site. All were dug during the Altithermal.

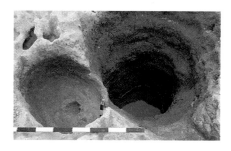

Two of the wells were exposed by archaeologists during a year when the water table was up. The deeper of the two wells, on the right, filled with water during the period of the excavations, giving a demonstration of how it must have looked when it was first dug.

Altithermal peoples solved the water shortage by digging wells with fire-hardened sticks, as deep as 10 feet (3 meters) into the floor of dry lakes. At Mustang Springs in Texas, more than 60 wells were found in an 860-square-foot (80-square-meter) area, dug early in the Altithermal about 6900 to 6800 B.P., but not all at once—different wells caught the falling water table at different levels. After a few hundred years these groups dug no more, perhaps because the water table fell beyond reach or because water was more easily obtained elsewhere. The wells filled with wind-blown silts, and the site remained unoccupied until the rains returned and the pond refilled a few thousand years later.

The existence of such wells provides a tidy answer to the question of how humans obtained water on an otherwise dry Altithermal landscape, but what did they eat? Few organic remains have been preserved in the Altithermal sites investigated so far; only terribly worn and fragmented stone tools, mostly scrapers and grinding stones, occur. It seems likely that the drop in bison numbers led hunter-gatherers to subsist on hardy grasses and cacti instead, along with drought-resistant ground- and brush-dwelling birds, turtles, snakes and lizards, rodents, jack rabbits, and pronghorn antelope.

Wells made water predictable, but Altithermal groups could not stay in one place long. Slow to fill and quick to foul, the wells had a limited life. Since surrounding plants and animals were rapidly depleted by hunting and gathering, Altithermal hunter-gatherers decamped frequently, and for long distances—at least 100 miles (160 kilometers) as measured by the source of their stone—tethering their movements to other well sites. Few other well sites have been found, but that's no surprise. The best places to dig wells, low, well-protected, and often deeply buried locations, are the last places archaeologists usually see.

DEEP CAVES, SHALLOW WATERS
The Great Basin, sandwiched between the Rocky Mountains and the Sierra Nevada, is a vast (approximately 165,000 square miles or 427,357 square kilometers) internally draining desert, punctuated by steeply rising mountains and deep valleys. Historically, it was thinly populated by scattered, mobile hunter-gatherers who ate gathered foods (especially piñon nuts), which proved most reliable in these uncertain environments. In the most general sense, adaptations were similar in prehistory, even during the Altithermal, which here looks no worse than any historic drought—in the main.

In the eastern Great Basin deep, lakeside caves record long occupations largely—not entirely—uninterrupted by drought. At Hogup Cave on the northwest edge of Utah's Great Salt Lake, for example, more than 13 feet (4 meters) of dry deposits span 7000 years of human life, beginning around 8350 B.P. Early on, the occupants used Hogup Cave as a base camp while they foraged along the edge of a dwindling marsh, threshing pickleweed seeds collected from its salty edges. There, they also gathered cattails, bulrushes, and dozens of other plants

Hogup Cave, right, is located on the northwest edge of Utah's Great Salt Lake. Archaeologists have uncovered evidence of human activity spanning more than 7000 years. The earliest remains date to about 8350 B.P.

Among the artifacts found at the Hogup Cave site are these fiber and bone figurines. Only 2 ½ to 3 inches (6 to 7 centimeters) high, the figurines are about 1500 years old, bear magical horns, and may represent the sickness that shamans professed to suck from the bodies of their patients.

for food, fuel, and raw material for baskets and mats. Waterfowl, shore birds, and small mammals such as rabbits and rodents were hunted as, occasionally, were pronghorn antelope, mule deer, mountain sheep, and bison.

Equipment reflected lifestyle. Seeds were collected in baskets and ground on large milling stones. Rabbits, small mammals, and birds were snared in nets or small traps. Bigger game was speared with large stone points. The very same artifacts for exploiting lakeshore plants and animals were used in non-lakeshore settings. There were no specialized toolkits here, unlike elsewhere in the Great Basin.

Change came to Hogup Cave around 3200 B.P., when the Great Salt Lake rose and drowned the nearby marsh. Waterfowl disappeared from the cave deposits, as did the seeds and stones marking the use of wild plants. Overall, the number of artifacts dropped dramatically, as Hogup Cave became a hunters' hotel for groups who entered the area pursuing the antelope and bison that still grazed the region. It wasn't until more than 1000 years later that horticulturalists would redouble the residency at Hogup Cave, whilst foraging and tending their small-scale gardens.

As Hogup's excavator, Melvin Aikens of the University of Oregon, points out, here and in other caves of the *eastern* Great Basin, the Altithermal went unnoticed, and when change did arrrive it was driven by local changes in hydrology. Things were different on the other side of the Great Basin.

There are traces of a human presence reaching back to 7100 B.P. in the one-time basin of Pleistocene pluvial Lake Lahontan, but these are sparse, and followed by millennia without firm occupational evidence. Only around 4600 B.P.

133

Exploring Lovelock Cave in northwestern Nevada in 1924, archaeologist L. Loud of the University of California at Berkeley found a basket of 2000-year-old duck decoys. The decoys were probably used on nearby Pyramid Lake, all that is left today of an enormous inland sea known as Lake Lahontan. Before the advent of the Altithermal, Lahontan and its Great Basin neighbor, Lake Bonneville, were 1220 feet deep and covered an area of 20,000 square miles.

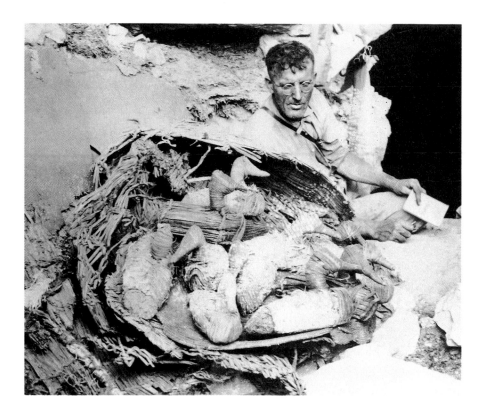

is there a steep rise in human use of the western Great Basin which is tied, some argue, to the post-Altithermal recharge of lakes and rivers.

The lakes were certainly important, judging by the artifacts discovered in caves used then more as storage centers than camps. Lovelock and nearby Humboldt Caves in Nevada yielded stunningly realistic duck decoys, fashioned of tule reed bundles, painted, and wearing actual skin and feathers; trotlines with the fishhooks still attached; nets for both fishing and catching those water birds that skim low over the water rather than flying straight up when startled; and a complement of hunting weapons (snares, arrows, and spears). Also found were tools to gather and process plants (digging sticks, sickles, and grinding stones) and artifacts of everyday life—wooden bowls, shell beads, basketry, and woven sandals.

The artifacts, bone, and plant parts, and especially the dried human feces (coprolites) in the caves, reveal a diet dominated by fish and fowl (minnows to chub, ducks to herons), and staples of rushes and grasses, in addition to small mammals and a few large ones. Nearly all of the foods were acquired locally, evidence to some investigators that these groups lived by the lakes year round. That's a bit extreme, Great Basin archaeologist David Hurst Thomas thinks. More likely, groups wintered near the lakes, then dispersed in spring to forage, coming together in the fall to harvest piñon nuts and lay in winter stores.

THE STAFF OF LIFE

The corn in Hogup Cave was a descendant of a plant that was domesticated in Mesoamerica and came north through the Southwestern United States. But the road over which corn—and its traveling companions, beans and squash—made it north was not an easy one. These tropical domesticates are poorly suited to the dry Southwest. In higher elevations it is wet enough to grow corn, but there are usually not enough frost-free days to bring in the crop. The summers are longer in lower elevations, but there the climates are too dry. The puzzle of how these tropical crops managed to take root, and where, has recently become clearer, but only after a false start, then a course correction, at Bat Cave in the uplands of west-central New Mexico.

Bat Cave overlooks a dry lakebed, and when archaeologist Herbert Dick excavated there in the late 1940s, its deposits yielded a range of wild plants, large mammals and, most importantly, small, primitive-looking corncobs. Back in those pre-AMS days, the corn kernels could not be directly dated, but nearby charcoal could, and it gave an age of 6000 B.P. That was far earlier than anyone expected, and certainly earlier than any place in the Southwest. The Bat Cave evidence, the University of Arizona's Emil Haury thought, testified that Mesoamerican crops had moved north via mountain chains, were cultivated initially in wetter uplands of the Southwest, and stayed there for thousands of years before descending across the southwestern lowlands.

Yet, in the ensuing decades radiocarbon dates on corn from other southwestern sites all fell in an age range between 3000 and 2500 B.P. Were the 6000-year-old charcoal and corn from Bat Cave from the same strata? Excavations in the 1980s by Wirt Wills of the University of New Mexico and others, and AMS dates on the corn kernels themselves, have now brought Bat Cave into line. The earliest corn there dates to just 3120 B.P.

In fact, Wills believes the radiocarbon record at Bat Cave and other sites indicates not only a later appearance for the first southwestern corn than hitherto supposed, but a more widespread one. The first corn was not restricted to the uplands, but also occurred in desert lowlands. Squash and beans, with early dates at 2900 and 2470 B.P. respectively, came close on corn's heels, indicating to Wills that they were cultivated together nearly from the outset, which he puts at around 3500 B.P. Perhaps no coincidence, this was in a period (4000 to 2000 B.P.) of above-average rainfall, which made it possible to nurture plants in lowland settings where the whole experiment wasn't so likely to fail from an early frost.

Why cultivate plants? Perhaps wild resources in the area became unpredictable or had grown scarce. Or perhaps access to such resources became restricted in the face of an ever more populated landscape. Whatever the cause, one consequence was clear: Mobility was more limited. A gardener's presence was required, minimally, at least in spring and fall for planting and harvesting.

But which came first, cultivation or a reduction in mobility? Bat Cave holds a clue. The deeper layers, Wills found, displayed evidence of only ephemeral

Duck decoys from the Lovelock Cave region were made from buoyant tule reeds gathered from the water's edge. The lifelike decoys often were covered with feathered birdskins to increase their effectiveness.

In the late 1940s, archaeologist Herbert Dick excavated at Bat Cave in the uplands of west-central New Mexico. Initial dating of charcoal near a find of small corncobs suggested the specimens were from 6000 B.P.

Excavations at Bat Cave in the 1980s brought the age of discoveries at the site into line: AMS dates on the corn kernels themselves go back to just 3120 B.P.

occupations, while the first appearance of cultivated plants coincided with a sharp buildup of habitation debris—thick living surfaces, pockmarked by large storage pits, lots of rubbish, and an abundance of baskets, wooden tools, and grinding stones. This is a pattern repeated and amplified at other sites, including nearby Tularosa Cave. These are signs, Wills believes, that the hunter-gatherers settled down, biannually, to the business of gardening, while moving around during the intervening months in order to collect wild foods. But they likely never strayed so far that they were unable to keep an eye on their gardens. And they always returned.

These were not full-time farmers living in permanent villages. Nor were they cultivating gardens in such upland locations because these were ideal spots to grow corn, beans, and squash. They weren't. Instead, Wills argues, hunter-gatherers gardened near Bat and Tularosa Caves because that's also where desirable wild foods such as piñon nuts and wild game could be found. People were there then to monitor, and perhaps even lay claim to, wild resources. Thus, the risk of relying on wild foods was reduced, while the harvest of domesticates boosted the diet.

BRINGING WATER TO THE DESERT

The first tropical domesticates took root in the Southwest by 2500 B.P. The next wave, which included cotton and more varieties of beans and squash, came some 850 years later (around A.D. 300). At the same time, southwestern hunter-gatherers were settling in to a more sedentary lifestyle. Their early villages were unassuming: shallow pithouses, walled and roofed by thatch or mud, clustered around an open area and strewn with the debris of a recent invention—pottery. Mobile peoples cannot easily transport bulky and rigid clay vessels;

their containers are more commonly fashioned of animal skins, grasses, or wood. But once groups settle in villages, clay pots become a more efficient, versatile, and practical container for storage, cooking, and a myriad of other purposes.

By A.D. 750, villagers began to move above ground across the Southwest, their pithouses replaced by buildings, often multi-roomed, of stone or adobe. By then, domesticates outpaced gathered foods in dietary importance, but wild foods were never abandoned in this region where environmental uncertainty could foil the best farmers.

The prehistoric Hohokam of southern Arizona knew that well, for they were superb farmers in an area badly suited to farming—the Sonoran Desert, amidst the Gila and Salt Rivers. Rainfall was low, and temperatures (and evaporation) high. Still, if one can solve the problem of water shortage, the growing season is more than 200 days long, plenty of time for any crop.

The Hohokam solved their water problem by digging irrigation canals, beginning around A.D. 700 and continuing for many centuries. The results are impressive. At least 360 miles (579 kilometers) of canals are known from the present-day Phoenix area alone. The canals tapped rivers and carried water to fields, where it was let onto farm plots by a network of ditches controlled by headgates of stone or earth. The labor invested in these canals was substantial. And it didn't end when the digging was done; that's just when the cleaning and repairs started.

On their fields, University of New Mexico archaeologist Patricia Crown notes, the Hohokam grew corn, beans, squash, amaranth, bottle gourd, cotton, agave, little barley grass, tobacco, sunflower, and other plants. Yet, they also gathered mesquite, yucca, cholla, groundcherry, saguaro, other native cacti and grasses, and hunted rabbit and deer. Why bother with wild foods after investing all that effort in irrigation farming?

Back to risks. The Salt and Gila are fed by biannual rains in the mountains of east-central Arizona that raise water levels in late spring and late summer. But in this arid land, rainfall often fails to materialize, and when that happened irrigation canals went dry and the Hohokam shifted their attention to native plants and animals. Wild resources were a supplement in good times, and insurance in bad times.

Hohokam irrigation was most extensive between the Salt and Gila rivers, less so beyond the major rivers where gathering and non-irrigation farming was the rule. The most spectacular Hohokam sites are also found in the area between the rivers. Snaketown (Arizona), excavated by Emil Haury, is one of the largest, comprising hundreds of houses spread over .3 square mile (1 square kilometer). Like many other Hohokam sites, it reached maximum size in the centuries around A.D. 1000, though it is estimated that no more than 300 people lived there at one time.

Snaketown sat amidst the Hohokam exchange network, which exported pottery and shell ornaments, imported turquoise from New Mexico and seashells from the California Gulf, and reached deep into Mesoamerica to acquire

As artisans, the Hohokam were skilled and innovative. Seashells, such as this one, possibly a frog or horned toad effigy, were decorated with turquoise mosaics. Effigies often were made of tiles of blue turquoise and red mollusk shell or the red mineral argillite, glued to bittersweet clamshells gathered from the beaches of the Gulf of California. They were worn on necklaces by men of high status in a number of southwestern cultures.

Snaketown, seen here from the air, was excavated by archaeologist Emil Haury in the 1930s and 1960s, and was the principal site of the prehistoric Hohokam people of southern Arizona. Although they lived in an area ill-suited to agriculture—the Sonoran Desert—the Hohokam were superb farmers, bringing water to the land by digging hundreds of miles of irrigation canals. Snaketown reached its maximum size around A.D. 1000, and sat in the middle of a trading network. Three hundred years later, Snaketown and other Hohokam centers were in severe decline. Evacuated twice and covered over, Snaketown now lies again beneath the desert floor.

These Snaketown clay animal figurines may be representations of female deer, and might have played a role in Hohokam fertility rites.

macaws and parrots, then copper bells, iron pyrite mirrors, ceramic vessels, and even a few ideas. In many Hohokam towns, Mesoamerican-like clay-capped and walled platform mounds and oval ballcourts—more than 200 of them—were built. Because they only occur in the larger sites, these may have served as community centers to integrate smaller, scattered Hohokam farmsteads.

By A.D. 1100 Hohokam exchange was in decline, and 200 years later construction of ballcourts and platform mounds had ceased. Within another century the Hohokam region was largely abandoned. No one knows why, but Patricia Crown suspects that conflict (possibly from bickering over water rights), salt-ruined fields, decades of low water, or even a flood in A.D. 1358 which may have irreparably damaged the canals, all contributed to the decline.

GREAT HOUSES BUT NOT GREAT HOMES

Cycles of occupation and abandonment are hardly uncommon, but in few places were they more spectacular than New Mexico's San Juan Basin. The boom began soon after A.D. 900, but the cycle itself lasted for just two centuries. Hundreds of buildings went up, though the crown jewels were a dozen great houses built along the floor and adjacent uplands of a 10-mile (16-kilometer) stretch of Chaco Canyon, beside an ephemeral stream in a desert of hot summers and cold winters.

The great houses were extraordinarily large, averaging more than 200 rooms; the largest, Pueblo Bonito, had nearly 700, stacked five high in the rear. Each had dozens of kivas and one or two great kivas (kivas are usually round subterranean rooms, generally thought to have been devoted to religious and social activities, as they are in modern pueblos). One great house, archaeologist Stephen Lekson and others estimate, was constructed with 50 million pieces of stone for walls and 215,000 trees for ceilings, floors, roof supports, windows and doors. The stone was local, but not the trees: Felled in forests 25 to 47 miles (40 to 75 kilometers) away, they show no sign of being dragged or rolled. Instead, beams averaging slightly over 600 pounds (275 kilograms) were *carried* to Chaco Canyon.

The great houses were engineered in an extraordinary fashion. Rooms were planned and built in grid-like patterns forming D- or E-shaped clusters around an open plaza, and carefully stair-stepped from plaza to rear wall. Doorways, windows, and air vents were set at regular intervals along walls and story to story, with an occasional corner window tucked in to mark solstices. Kivas had regularly spaced and sized wall niches. Stone and mortar were laid in tidy courses, according to the style of the time.

The great houses yielded stunning artifacts: Turquoise from 100 miles (160 kilometers) away; Pacific Coast shell beads, bracelets, and pendants; effigy ceramics; pottery stamps and seals; conch-shell trumpets; decorated wood; ornamental copper bells, parrots, and macaws from Mexico; and stone and clay from sources up to 90 miles distant.

All this activity, and yet Lekson and others say that the great houses were idle much of the year, and that only a fraction of the rooms were used as residences (housing around 100 people). The rest of the rooms, they think, were non-habitation suites with adjoining storage, or small rooms facing out from outer walls and inaccessible from within. Nearby middens of trash seem to have accumulated episodically, as though great houses were seasonal hotels.

Chaco Canyon had permanent residents living in nearby smaller villages of a dozen or so one-story room blocks and a few kivas. None of these displayed the care or planning that went into great houses and have yielded fewer luxury items. Were these Chaco's rural poor? Or were they different clans? Caretakers for the great houses? If so, who was checking in, and from where? Chacoan roads may point to the answer.

These exit the canyon in all directions via stairways, ramps, or gaps, then travel hundreds of miles (often in straight lines) across desert scrub to outlier sites, of which 150 are known, and 20 of which are great houses like those in the canyon. Along the roads were way stations and hills atop which signal fires had burned. The roads were carefully engineered Lekson and colleagues add. The Great North Road follows a bearing close to true North for almost 30 miles (50 kilometers). On-the-ground mapping and aerial surveys of more than 200 miles (320 kilometers) of the surviving Chacoan roads by the National Park Service's Chaco Center and others found that roadbeds were graded to level out small humps, were edged with earth or stone, and for long stretches were consistently 30 feet (9 meters) across for the primary roads closer to the great houses, or 15 feet (4.5 meters) across for the secondary roads.

Pueblo Bonito, largest of the great houses built along a 10-mile stretch of New Mexico's Chaco Canyon, covered almost two acres, contained nearly 700 rooms, and stood at least four stories high. The square and rectangular rooms were used for habitation and storage; the circular rooms, called kivas, probably were used for ceremonies. Shaped like a capital D, Pueblo Bonito was begun about A.D. 920. Estimates of the number of its inhabitants vary, since it is uncertain whether the site was occupied year-round. It may have stood empty for much of the year and been used only as a hotel by groups from around the region when they converged on the canyon at different seasons of the year to exchange goods and to renew relationships.

Chaco Canyon was the center of a network extending over at least 58,593 square miles (150,000 square kilometers) of northwestern New Mexico. Early on it was thought that outliers pumped food back to the canyon. But this idea seemed less plausible as the known Chacoan network grew, while evidence of food imports didn't. Hence the idea of great houses as hotels. Few lived in the harsh canyon, but groups converged there seasonally to renew ties and set up subsequent exchanges between groups having good years, and those not.

Perhaps. But Chaco's residents, archaeologist Gwinn Vivian of the Arizona State Museum responds, could grow enough corn, beans, and squash to support more than 5000 people. The trick was to capture rainwater spilling over the canyon's slick north walls, then channel it onto farm fields. And archaeological evidence shows that this was done. Great houses, mostly on the north side, may have controlled these runoff canals, and housed the farmers, never mind the apparent lack of habitation rooms. (The lack of habitation rooms, archaeologist Michael Adler of Southern Methodist University suggests, may be a bias in the archaeological record. Were the habitation rooms on the upper floors of these multistory great houses, as habitation rooms are in many modern pueblos, they would be less visible archaeologically, having collapsed in a confusing jumble of four or five floors of rubble. The bottom layer of rooms, which are often devoted largely to storage in modern pueblos, would naturally show up most clearly.) Perhaps only when intensive farming could no longer sustain house inhabitants did emigration and the establishment of outliers occur.

The workings of the Chacoan system remain a mystery. It is certain, however, that construction in the canyon halted during drought years in the mid-12th century A.D. But Lekson thinks the great houses, built to last, were used into the next century.

GOING TO POT

Meanwhile, in Eastern North America it looked as if the more things changed, the more they stayed the same. Plant and animal communities shuffled into

Near the confluence of the Arkansas and Mississippi rivers in Louisiana lies Poverty Point. The community thrived for 300 years on trade and fine lapidary work. A high-flying aircraft took this digitally processed, artifically colored mosaic of the one-square-mile complex *(right)*, which dates from 3500 B.P. The pink concentric ridges enclosing a central plaza may have been constructed as platforms for dwellings, as shown in the drawing *(below)*.

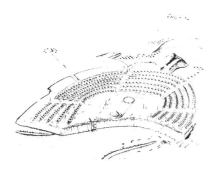

place and seas rose in the initial half of the Holocene, but local hunter-gatherers quietly went about their business, little altering toolkits or food types. Only in the millennia around 5000 B.P., after modern habitats were established, did the cultural changes—revolutions, some call them—begin.

First to change was the diet, which around 6000 B.P. expanded to include what Smithsonian archaeologist Bruce Smith calls "second-line" resources: fish and shellfish (such as mussels and mollusks) from river shoals and coastal estuaries. Some see that expansion as the work of skilled foragers, so familiar with their habitats that they could squeeze every ounce of available food out of them. Possibly. But then their world was filling up with people, too, so these hunter-gatherers may have had little option but to expand their diet to compensate for their decreasingly mobile lifestyle.

These groups also began experimenting with plants. Not tropical exotics, just local squash, sumpweed or marshelder, sunflower, and chenopod that sprouted in the areas they cleared around their semi-permanent, river-valley settlements. At first, Smith argues, these botanical "camp followers" were only dietary supplements and weren't really tended. But by 4000 B.P. they were being actively cultivated, used alongside plants and game collected in local forests, rivers, and lakes. It would be another 1500 years before domesticated plants played a major economic role.

A Poverty Point figurine head shows evidence of careful modeling. In fact, though many artifacts were found at Poverty Point, it seems unlikely that anyone actually lived there. Perhaps the center acted as a commodities exchange rather than a permanent settlement.

Artifacts left behind at the Poverty Point site include a wide variety of unusual shapes and decorative objects, some of which archaeologists believe were cooking stones.

Seeds selected from high-yield plants were carefully stored in below-ground silos and, increasingly after 4500 B.P., in clay vessels. The manufacture of pottery had humble origins along the South Atlantic Coast, initially patterned after the wooden bowls it presumably replaced. From there pottery spread to the Mississippi Valley (arriving around 3300 B.P.), the Northeast (3000 B.P.) and Midwest (2700 B.P.). In time, grass-tempered, thick-walled vessels gave way to thin-walled pots of many tempers, the better to hold water, withstand heat, or keep seed supplies dry and rodent-free. Like the latter-day Cuisinart, pottery revolutionized food processing.

Soapstone bowls and bottle gourds, possibly domesticated from gourds that floated from Africa on ocean currents, completed the "container revolution." Together they traveled across Eastern North America, Smith believes, in a complex trade web that sent Gulf and Atlantic coast shells inland, Appalachian slate and steatite in all directions, and copper artifacts, cold-hammered from nuggets found along Lake Superior, down as far as northern Louisiana.

There, at the crossroads of an exchange network and strategically located amid the confluences of major rivers—but, as Harvard archaeologist Stephen Williams points out, not near anything else of obvious value—the Poverty Point culture flared briefly (3600-2600 B.P.), then disappeared. The Poverty Point site is a large earthwork of six nested, semi-circular ridges, some 82 feet (25 meters) wide by 10 feet (3 meters) high, covering nearly 500 acres (200 hectares) with an outside diameter of almost 4000 feet (1200 meters). These ridges, and two nearby large mounds, consumed more than 1,236,000 cubic feet (35,000 cubic meters) of earth, all dug, carried, and shaped by hand. Or, rather, lots of hands: 1350 adults working 70 days a year for three years, by one estimate.

Artifacts left behind include miniature perforators, drills, needles (30,000 of these alone), highly polished beads, and exquisite animal effigies made of argillite, slate, copper, galena, hematite, steatite, and other stone imported nearly 625 miles (1000 kilometers). And there were millions of small (less than 2 inches in diameter), baked, clay balls. In the lower Mississippi Valley, where river deposits thickly bury local rock outcrops, these played the part of boiling and baking stones. They were heated, then tossed into pots of water or heaped over food in an earth oven.

Despite all the apparent activity, there are few floors or postmolds to indicate that anyone lived at Poverty Point. Perhaps traders came to this commodities exchange from the 150 or so small, Poverty Point-related sites clustered along Louisiana, Mississippi, and Arkansas waterways. In these hinterlands, groups exploited river floodplains, oxbow lakes, and uplands, a wide variety of plants and animals, and cultivated small gardens of bottle gourd and squash.

HOPEWELL MERCANTILE

The Poverty Point center and culture, so unlike anything in contemporary Eastern North America, disappeared without fanfare, but, farther north and a

Hopewell artisans produced extremely well-crafted and artistic work such as this exquisite bird's claw *(above)*, crafted from fragile sheets of imported mica, and a figurine of a kneeling man *(below)*. The knot over his forehead may represent the single horn that was the shaman's symbol.

few centuries later, earthworks and exchange on a far grander scale arose. By 2500 B.P. in the central Ohio Valley you could see it coming. There, Adena culture groups constructed earthen mounds, like Grave Creek (West Virginia), more than 65 feet (20 meters) high with a total volume of 2,472,000 cubic feet (70,000 cubic meters). Inside, often in carefully prepared log tombs, there were burials containing stone pipes, gorgets, polished and engraved stone tablets, imported mica, copper, marine shell, and, on occasion, wolf palates and oft-handled human skulls, the latter perhaps either enemies or revered ancestors.

The mounds were sometimes surrounded by circular earthen enclosures, averaging 328 feet (100 meters) in diameter, broken by gateways, ringed by "moats," and occasionally erected near earthen effigies like Serpent Mound in Ohio. Great effort went into constructing these features and the even more elaborate and richer mounds of the later Hopewell groups. These rivet archaeological attention, yet beyond them less spectacular but more profound developments were taking place.

In late Adena and throughout Hopewell times (2250 to 1800 B.P. or 250 B.C. to A.D. 400), high-yield and high-nutrition squash, sumpweed, sunflower, chenopod, along with knotweed, maygrass, and little barley, came to play a larger role in the diet. Growing one's own food, the obvious option to foragers whose mobility is restricted and who have already expanded their diets, buffers inevitable shortfalls in wild plant and animal foods.

Hopewell was launched from that foraging and small-scale farming base in the Ohio and (to a lesser degree) Illinois valleys, and its path was marked by some of the most intensive earthwork and mound construction ever done in Eastern North America. At the Hopewell (Ohio) site itself, there were nearly 3 miles (5 kilometers) of earthen embankments, up to almost 4 feet (1.2 meters) high, that enclose more than 111 acres (45 hectares) and 38 mounds. Elsewhere are elaborate circular, square, and octagonal earthen enclosures connected by wide, walled avenues and sprinkled with scores of burial mounds.

The mounds were rich in grave goods. Accompanying individual burials were thousands of sheets of North Carolina mica, hundreds of pounds of Missouri galena; obsidian from outcrops in Wyoming and Idaho; Great Lakes copper effigies, breastplates, beads, axes, and ear spools; assorted grizzly bear teeth, sharks' teeth, and barracuda jaws; marine shell and freshwater pearl; thousands of chert and ground stone disks; and Ohio-quarried pipestone platform pipes in a dazzling array of zoomorphic forms (pipes alone were exported on a large scale). That was conspicuous consumption.

But why? And why, after half a millennium of this, did the Hopewell exchange network, and Hopewell culture itself, collapse? There are the usual suspects: climate change, disease, violence, even new technologies. Yet, since none are supported by hard evidence, archaeologist David Braun, among others, offers another idea.

Hopewell foragers and part-time gardeners were pushing the limits of their environment, and often faced critical food shortages. Their exchange network, Braun and others believe, served to maintain alliances among families and groups as a form of insurance. In times of trouble those old friends could be called on to share their stores of food or their territory. Nowadays we call it foreign aid. Exchanged goods were tokens of those alliances, and perhaps were buried in elaborate earthworks when major trading partners died (which, incidentally, kept up demand for the goods themselves).

As Hopewell horticultural productivity increased, Braun argues, shortages in wild foods mattered less. Now there were reliable crops to fill out the diet. Since farming supports more mouths per acre than foraging, the shift into more intensive food production would, he feels, remove the incentive for exchange. Everyone could grow their own food, not needing to rely on other resources in another group's territories. As a consequence, the elaborate trade and earthworks system that facilitated access to those other resources and territories became obsolete.

A shift to intensive food production may have triggered the Hopewell collapse, but it wasn't corn-based farming. Not yet, anyway.

RISING UP FROM THE AMERICAN BOTTOM

Corn first appeared in Eastern North America around A.D. 200 but, Bruce Smith argues, only as a minor addition to the local domesticates. In the ensuing centuries many indigenous crops were supplanted by this one carbohydrate-rich and highly productive tropical plant. After A.D. 800 in Eastern North America, corn-based agriculture was the only game in town. Or at least in Mississippian towns.

Along the river valleys of the Southeast and Midwest, Mississippian groups appeared in the wake of post-Hopewell farmers who themselves neither trafficked in exotic artifacts nor built large earthworks. Mississippians reversed that trend and introduced a battery of innovations, many of which were associated with full-time corn agriculture.

Mississippians fashioned large tabular pieces of chert, and pressed them into service as hoes for tilling the soil. They improved ceramic manufacture, making lighter and stronger vessels, and creating an explosion of forms to serve many purposes. They cleared woodlands for fields, and dug large storage pits for seed and food. The corn grown on those fields and stored in those pits left a direct chemical signature on the bones of those who ate it, and studies show the amount of corn in the diet varied by area and, Smith adds, by an individual's status. Everyone supplemented their diet with deer, turkey, birds, fish, and wild and domesticated plants.

Mississippian sites had a new look, too. Planned and organized, they clustered around public plazas, communal storage features, and mounds. Sometimes they were surrounded by fortification walls. Their mounds served as platforms for buildings of timber, mud, and thatch, although occasionally were used for high-status burials and human offerings. There were haves and have-nots in Mississippian society. Those who had were healthier, ate more corn, worked and suffered less, and were accompanied in death by more elaborate grave goods, and sometimes other humans.

Mississippians lived in small hamlets and large towns, moving copper, shell, mica, galena, fluorite, and other exotics among them. Many of the commodities ended up at Cahokia (Illinois), a large site on the soggy floodplain of the American Bottom and home, archaeologist George Milner of Pennsylvania State University estimates, to many thousands of people.

At its peak, between A.D. 1050 and 1250, Cahokia spread over 5 square miles (13 square kilometers) though its satellite communities extended over 20 times that area. Back then Cahokia had more than 120 earthen mounds of various sizes, shapes and functions, the whole dominated by the 100-foot (30-meter) high, four-tiered, 14-acre (5.6-hectare) Monk's Mound, atop which sat a large stockaded building, likely a temple or council house. (The mound was named after a colony of Trappist monks who established a farm southwest of the mound in 1809, giving up a few years later after malaria decimated their number.)

South of Monk's Mound was a plaza flanked by platform mounds, the whole enclosed in a log palisade, with watchtowers and gates spaced at regular intervals. Although a formidable defensive work, its intent may have been merely to screen the central core from the remainder of the community.

Outside the wall were clusters of mounds and residences, large and small towns, and farming communities. These supported farmers, fishermen, hunters, and those whose days were partly devoted to less mundane pursuits: potters, flint knappers, engravers and sculptors, shell and metalworkers. Many watched the stars, too. A 410-foot (125-meter) diameter circle of evenly spaced logs, apparently aligned to mark the passing equinox and solstice, was erected just east of Monk's Mound.

Little is known of the political system that drove Cahokia, but occasionally we glimpse its leaders. In Mound 72, a male, perhaps in his mid-40s, was interred on a blanket of 20,000 conch-shell beads, accompanied by rolls of copper, two bushels of mica, and 800 projectile points of different styles and materials. Nearby were skeletons of 53 females, aged 15 to 25, all evidently strangled, and four decapitated males, side by side, arms overlapping.

The Cahokia decline after A.D. 1250 was not the Mississippian finale, merely an era's end on the American Bottom. Moundville (Alabama), Etowah (Georgia), and scores of Mississippian towns, too, had cycles of growth and decline, some (like the Natchez, who would be glimpsed historically) lasting into the 16th century. These cycles testify, Milner and Smith suspect, to the unstable political fabric binding these communities and, at Cahokia at least, severe resource depletion and an unforgiving river.

The mural at the entrance to Cahokia shows an artist's view of the main plaza with Monk's Mound rising at center rear. At its peak this Illinois site spread across five square miles.

A number of these chunky stones were found at Cahokia. Archaeologists theorize that they were made to be used in some kind of game.

MEETING IN THE THULES

In A.D. 1000 the Hohokam were cutting canals across the desert floor, the Chacoan were laying roads over mountain mesas, and Mississippians were building the largest pre-Columbian town north of Mexico. About that same time, thousands of miles to the north, seafaring hunters moving east *and* west first closed the circle, open since late Pleistocene times, between the Old World and the New. They encountered one another at various points and at different times along the Atlantic Coast of Greenland and northernmost North America. They were Thule Eskimo moving east, and Norse heading west.

Ancestral Thule Eskimo are spotted archaeologically on the Siberian shore and the islands of the Bering Strait and date back 2000 years. Back then they were coastal sea mammal hunters, preying on seal and walrus with distinctive polished slate, bone, and ivory tools, sinew bows, skin boats (kayaks and umiaks), and socketed toggle harpoons. Soon after A.D. 1000, they began to move east. Fast. Within 200 years they were nearly 2000 miles away on Ellesmere Island and in sight of Greenland. Archaeologist Robert McGhee of the Canadian Museum of Civilization thinks they were able to move quickly through the vast and ecologically homogeneous northern maritime region by following bowhead whales. These were warmer than average centuries, reducing the summer pack ice and opening the Beaufort Sea to whales and whalers who followed, leaving a trail of highly uniform artifacts (and languages) across the High Arctic from Alaska to Southwestern Greenland—where they met the Norse.

Thule and Norse groups first encountered each other in the 11th century, for it is then that iron, copper, and bronze tools from the Norse appear in Thule sites as far west as Bathurst Island. Closer to Greenland, Thule sites on Ellesmere Island yield a greater array and amount of trade goods: chain mail

The Thule on southern Baffin Island depicted a Norse figure in wood after their initial contact with the seafarers. Whether there was a single meeting or sporadic contact over many years is still uncertain.

armor, woolen cloth, smelted iron rivets, and a bronze bowl. They puzzled over each other too. The Norse wrote of the Thule in their sagas, while Thule on southern Baffin Island depicted a Norse figure in wood. All these items could have come from a single Thule-Norse meeting, but McGhee thinks there was wide-ranging and sporadic contact over a relatively long period of time. Yet unclear is whether this was peaceful trade (metal for ivory), mutual plunder, or both.

A century earlier, and farther south, Norse seafarers led by Leif Eiriksson had made landfall in North America. Their sagas speak of Helluland, perhaps Baffin Island, Markland, possibly Labrador, and Vinland, likely Newfoundland, where they wintered (some think Vinland was farther south). At Vinland, and on their return trip to Greenland, the Norse traded with "Skraelings." Likely, Smithsonian archaeologist William Fitzhugh thinks, Skraeling were Algonkian speakers, perhaps ancestral to the historic Beothuk people of Newfoundland.

Norse histories and the archaeological record intersect at the L'Anse aux Meadows site on the northern tip of Newfoundland, which is suspected, though not confirmed, to be Eiriksson's Vinland winter camp. Without question, the remains testify to a European presence. Excavations there produced a cluster of eight distinctly non-native, sod-walled structures (one a long house) on a terrace overlooking a shallow bay. Nearby was a smithy, what may have been a bath house, and four turf boat sheds. Norse artifacts, a spindlewhorl and needle hone, hearths, forges, and cooking pits, were found amidst the structures. The site was occupied briefly; according to the Norse sagas, only a few years.

The very same site had been used before, and after, by Native Americans, although there is no evidence they and the Norse were there simultaneously. Still, contact was made. A stone arrowhead, much like those made by natives of Newfoundland in the centuries around A.D. 1000, was recovered from below an eroding Norse graveyard in Greenland. Whether carried back to Greenland by hand or in someone's body is unknown. A perforated Norse coin, minted between A.D. 1065 and 1080, was found at the Goddard site on Maine's Penobscot Bay, where it arrived along with Nova Scotia chert via trade sometime in the 12th or 13th century. Altogether, however, the contacts were brief and ended often in violence.

EVE OF THE END

So A.V. Kidder was right. The grand sweep of New World prehistory was independent of any Old World stimulus. The only contacts made between Old World and New were very late, very isolated, and very local in reverberation.

Over the centuries of their sporadic encounters, Norse and Native Americans, whether Thule or ancestral Beothuk, were evenly matched. They were all hunter-gatherers, McGhee observes, and none possessed superior weaponry or technology. Their contacts, based either on mutual respect or

The Old World met the New again at L'Anse aux Meadows on the northern tip of Newfoundland. Distinctive sod houses, such as the one reconstructed at right, were discovered at the site where the Norse settled for a few years, along with a smithy and what may have been a bath house.

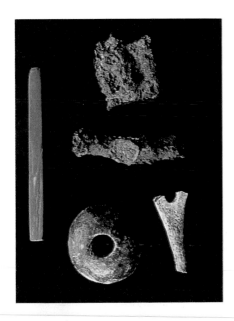

Norse artifacts from the L'Anse aux Meadows site include (from top, clockwise) a quartzite needle hone, the shank and rove of an iron rivet, part of a bone needle, and a soapstone spindlewhorl.

contempt, would never go much further than an exchange of goods, and that in the best of times, William Fitzhugh adds. The exchange was not vital to either party—the artifacts and scrap metal the Thule received from the Norse merely supplemented their own supplies of native copper and meteoritic iron. Each side likely had more to lose by contact than to gain.

The Norse most certainly lost. When Leif Eiriksson and his ship landed in North America in A.D. 1001, the New World and the Old met face to face. The Old World contingent got the worst of it, hamstrung—Fitzhugh observes—by their smaller forces, tenuous lines of support, lack of a technological edge, and the natives' superior homeland knowledge and survival skills.

Norse losses at the hands of the native Skraelings were a fatal blow to their intentions to gain a foothold in this land that was "so choice," as Eiriksson put it. All plans for western expansion died with their Vinland settlements. Thenceforth, contacts were limited to trade on Greenland. As Leif's brother Thorvald, fatally stricken in a clash with Skraelings around the Bay of Fundy, gasped in the end, "We have won a fine and fruitful country, but will hardly be allowed to enjoy it."

Those early North Atlantic contacts loomed large in the lives and deaths of the players. But for the overwhelming majority of Native Americans, living far from the front, pursuing antelope or collecting piñon in the Great Basin, hunting bison on the Great Plains, farming corn, beans, and squash in the Southwest and throughout the East, or doing a myriad of other activities in these and other places (not to forget all of Middle and South America), those brief northern encounters with strangers from another world were utterly unknown and thoroughly inconsequential.

All that would change with the next round of contact, beginning on that October night in 1492, when once again the Old World caught sight of the New.

Entitled *Mexico Prehispanico y colonial*, Mexican artist Diego Rivera's mural, completed in 1945, depicts life on market day before contact with the Old World and the deadly disease its people brought to Native Americans.

8

SIBERIA TO SMALLPOX

On March 11, 1835, Charles Darwin disembarked from H.M.S. *Beagle* at Valparaiso on the coast of Chile, and set off with "two Peons & 10 mules" on a geological trek over the Andes to the Argentinian town of Mendoza. The mountains were so spectacular that he "could hardly sleep at nights for thinking over [his] day's work." Best of all, what he saw of Andean geology promised "a very important fact in the theory of the formation of the world."

Little wonder that he ranked this brief excursion his most successful trip since leaving England three and a half years earlier. But in the end, his night in the "stupid town of Mendoza" meant so much more. There, on the edge of the Argentinean pampas on the night of March 26, 1835, Darwin was bitten by a giant, blood-sucking vinchuca bug (*Triatoma infestans*). He thought little of the attack at the time, and not at all later. He recrossed the Andes the next morning. Six months later Darwin was on the Galápagos Islands, where he glimpsed, but could not yet appreciate the meaning of, its wonderful variety of finches and turtles.

No matter. The idea of evolution by natural selection was planted on the *Beagle* voyage, and when it bore fruit a few years later, Darwin realized what a marvelous laboratory of evolutionary divergence the Galápagos Islands were. But it was a laboratory to which he could never return. Crippling headaches, dizziness and nausea, stomach pains, and fatigue began just a few years after his return to England, and dogged him the rest of his life. His night in Mendoza had caught up with him.

The bug that had bitten Darwin carried *Trypanasoma cruzi*, a microorganism causing Chagas' disease, which attacks the heart, stomach, and intestinal system. At first, those bitten hardly notice any effects. Ultimately, they cannot escape them. Chagas is a time bomb, the British scientist, Sir Peter Medawar, writes: Years afterward the victim suddenly drops dead or, like Darwin, becomes chronically ill with diagnosis-defying symptoms. It was worse in Darwin's case, for Chagas was then unknown and his physicians long suspected hypochondria.

Darwin fell prey to one of America's pathogens; he was a medical victim of the exchange between the Old World and the New. But he was an exception. Old World populations were not overrun by Chagas, nor any other New World pathogen. And through it all, freed by illness from society's distractions, Darwin produced his *Origin of Species* and more than a dozen other books that forever changed our view of life on earth and our understanding of human prehistory.

Not so fortunate were the untold millions of anonymous Native Americans who died from imported Old World pathogens. Why, asked a perplexed French missionary among the Mississippi Valley's Natchez people in the 1700s, should "distempers that are not very fatal in other parts of the world, make dreadful ravages among them?" Why, indeed?

THE BEHEADING OF PREHISTORY

In the decades and centuries after the last discovery of America, in 1492, Old World explorers and colonists brought an arsenal of deadly pathogens to America. Among the diseases, roughly ordered by disease historian Henry Dobyns of the University of Oklahoma, according to their mortality, were smallpox—the worst killer by far—measles, influenza, bubonic plague, diphtheria, typhus, cholera, scarlet fever, chicken pox, yellow fever, and whooping cough. They ravaged repeatedly, leaving widespread death in their wake. From the first epidemic in 1520 to the last major outbreak in 1899, Dobyns reckons that there were 41 separate smallpox epidemics in North America. Left in their wake were widespread death and irrevocably altered native lives.

Just how many Native Americans died from imported epidemic diseases is uncertain. Thomas Jefferson wondered about the answer in his *Notes on the State of Virginia*. He compared a tally of Virginia's 40 different tribes made in 1607, the year Captain John Smith made contact, with a count made in 1669 by the Virginia Assembly. The numbers were admittedly imperfect, but there was no mistaking their "melancholy" message. In those 62 years the tribes had been reduced to one-third their former numbers.

Jefferson believed smallpox and other diseases were not entirely to blame: "Spirituous liquors," war, and land grabbing might also have taken their toll. And they did. But as explorers Meriwether Lewis and William Clark discovered on their expedition west, disease usually arrived first. In April 1806, along the Columbia River in the Pacific Northwest, Clark came upon the large ruined village and the few, badly scarred survivors of a fierce smallpox epidemic that had roared through three *decades* earlier. The disease had reached this remote corner of America long before European liquor, war, or land grabs. For that matter, long before any Europeans had even arrived.

Disease, the enemy no one saw, traveled farther and faster than the conquistadors, explorers, and colonists who brought it to America. The reasons were deadly simple. Take smallpox, for example. Over its 10- to 14-day incubation period it readily spreads by breath or outside human hosts in a dried state—on infected blankets or clothing. When the first symptoms appeared in a native village, those who still felt healthy—but who were unaware that they too were already infected—would flee the stricken area, seeking refuge in neighboring villages, thus spreading the disease with deadly speed and efficiency.

Small wonder that by the time Europeans arrived on the scene, native populations were already devastated. Under the circumstances, European counts of native populations are highly suspect. Indeed, even where Europeans arrived before their diseases (Cortés in the Valley of Mexico, for instance), reliable numbers are elusive. Early explorers were notoriously bad census takers, often over- or underestimating native populations, depending on whether they were in the business of capturing souls (report high numbers as testimony of one's own good work) or land (report low numbers as justification to grab territory).

We may never know how many Native Americans lived here on October 12, 1492. Not that we haven't tried to guess. One school, championed by Dobyns, projects pre-contact populations based largely on the number of survivors. There are a couple of ways to do this. One is to look at recorded losses. Compare, for example, the Spaniards' count of natives in the Valley of Mexico *before* the first major smallpox epidemic with the census made a century *after*

European depictions of the October 1492 arrival of Christopher Columbus on the island he called San Salvador show a welcoming people ready to share their riches with the resplendent Columbus. What these highly romanticized works did not show were the irrevocable changes this contact would bring for both the Old and the New World.

that (and other) epidemics. The difference between pre-epidemic and post-epidemic totals measures relative population loss, and gives a depopulation ratio. Depopulation ratios in Mesoamerica and South America, Dobyns found, average 20:1 which, coincidentally, corresponds with a figure given by a New England cleric in 1621. In areas like North America where pre-epidemic populations went largely unrecorded, one can multiply the post-epidemic census by 20 to arrive at an estimate of native populations in 1492.

Alternatively, pre-contact populations can be projected back from historic census figures by determining how often the region was hit by an epidemic, and knowing what the disease and its mortality rates were. A surviving population of x individuals, having weathered over two centuries a dozen smallpox and measles epidemics with average mortality rates of, say, 75 percent, would have had—given certain additional assumptions about birth and death rates—an original population size of y.

Using these measures for want of something better, and fortifying them with assumptions about how many people could have lived in different regions given the richness of the environment, Dobyns calculates that 90 to 112 million people lived in the New World of 1492. Only 18 million occupied North America, which did not have the vast cities of Mesoamerica or South America.

Dobyns' astonishing figures are many orders of magnitude higher than all previous estimates, and they have their share of critics. Too many unsupport-

A 16th-century woodcut from a treatise by Fr. Bernardino de Sahajun entitled *General History of the Things of New Spain* deals with the aftermath of the Spanish contact as an Aztec medicine man ministers to smallpox victims. The ancestors of the first Americans had left the Old World before disease co-evolution there; the first Americans thus had no immunity to sicknesses that were often considered merely childhood illnesses in the Old World. Smallpox was the worst killer of all. By one estimate, it ravaged the New World with 41 separate epidemics in the 350 or so years after 1520.

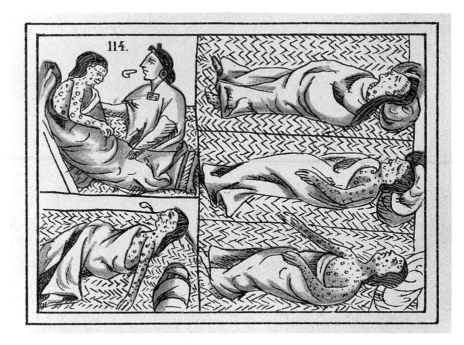

able assumptions, the detractors say, are behind the numbers. Who knows just how many epidemics there were, and of which diseases? It is better, the critics say, to tread cautiously, using direct historical evidence.

So Smithsonian Institution physical anthropologist Douglas Ubelaker, drawing on the most reliable of tribe-by-tribe census figures, and using available archaeological and physical anthropological evidence, totals native North American populations at the time of European contact at a mere 1,894,350 (this is his average estimate—he puts the range from 1.2 to 2.6 million).

Carefully and cautiously derived as they are, these figures are no less suspect than Dobyns', possibly having come in, Ubelaker freely admits, too low and too late. Take Southeastern North America. When the Spaniard Hernando de Soto explored the region from 1539 to 1542, he described a land teeming with people, communities, and towns. Yet a century later, when the French arrived, the region was virtually empty. Smallpox had struck. Gone were the descendants of Cahokia, the largest pre-Columbian town north of Mexico, along with hundreds of other towns and villages built by the children of Mississippian, Fort Ancient, Monongahela, and other groups, now known only by brief mention in de Soto's chronicles or from their rich archaeological remains. By the time reliable censuses were made, well after French settlement, only the few survivors were left to count, not the many who once had lived there.

Native American populations hit all-time lows between 1800 and 1940, the timing varying by tribe and area. At the nadir, generally accepted as 1900, there were roughly 530,000 Native Americans. Here lies the root of the claim that, from European colonization until the 20th century, more Native Americans died than were born. By Dobyns' figures that was a net population loss of 97 percent; by Ubelaker's figures, 72 percent. Either way, they were staggering losses.

LESS LUCKY AND DOWNRIGHT UNLUCKY

Because so much of the post-contact decline was historically invisible, University of New Mexico archaeologist Ann Ramenofsky argues that archaeology will provide the ultimate and direct testimony of demographic collapse. It will not be an easy task, given how cryptic archaeological clues are when it comes to population size. Yet, even lacking hard numbers, the archaeological record emphatically testifies to free-falling native populations beginning in the 16th century. It shows, too, that the burden of suffering was unevenly weighed.

Hardest and often earliest hit were those groups, generally farmers, living in densely populated permanent towns and villages along major water courses such as the Mississippi, Missouri, Ohio, Gila, and Rio Grande, where diseases spread easily, quickly, and widely. Their devastating effects were magnified by European slave raids, enemy attacks, and the forced neglect of crops and fields.

The post-contact history of Pecos Pueblo is probably typical (although atypical in that we have a record of it). Pecos was the archaeological site A.V. Kidder was excavating in 1927 when he and Frank Roberts received the news from Folsom. But just 400 years earlier, Pecos had been a thriving community at least 2,000 strong (by Spanish count). In the intervening years, the Pecos townspeople had been racked by repeated smallpox epidemics, and weakened by raids from mounted Comanches. By 1838, only 17 inhabitants were left. That year they packed up their belongings and abandoned the pueblo.

Groups like those on the Great Plains or Great Basin who were more mobile, who dispersed their populations into smaller groups seasonally or annually, and who were located far inland from major population centers, were generally hit later, and suffered relatively less. Relative is a loaded term. Individually they were just as vulnerable as their town-dwelling counterparts. But by virtue of their smaller group size, there were fewer of them dying at the same time.

THE CHILDHOOD OF DISEASE

The appalling mortality of Native Americans astonished Europeans. The natives were dying from what, in other parts of the world, were mere childhood ailments. Even during the 1700s, when smallpox was at its worst in western Europe, the disease accounted for just 10 to 15 percent of all deaths, 70 percent of which, University of Texas historian Alfred Crosby reports, took children under the age of two. The Old World had its epidemics, but their effects on Old World populations were slight.

This is so, University of Chicago historian William McNeill argues, because of the way populations and their diseases co-evolve. When diseases first appear, neither old nor young are spared a bout with the illness. Those who survive gain lasting immunity. Through time, as more susceptible individuals are eliminated from the gene pool, the hardier survivors mature and reproduce, and the population's gene pool becomes dominated by their descendants. Over time, epidemic diseases once deadly to both adults and children become childhood ills. As McNeill says, the more diseased a community—and Old World communities were riddled with disease—the less destructive its epidemics.

Epidemic diseases were absent the first few million years of human prehistory; when there were fewer of our species, they subsisted by hunting and gathering wild plant and animal foods, and they were fairly mobile. That had to have changed in order to have sparked the evolution of epidemic disease. There had to have been many more people, to insure a ready supply of new victims to sustain the chain of infection. The people also had to stay put—clearing the land, piling up filth, and fouling the water—in order to create the necessary breeding grounds for rats, lice, worms, mosquitoes, and all manner of disease-causing or carrying organisms.

And, then, there had to be domesticated animals, the major source for many of the most deadly epidemic diseases. It was only when humans began living with their newly tamed animals, drinking the same water, breathing the same air, and using animal waste to fertilize their crops and fields, that they unknowingly shared a volatile mix of pathogens from which sprang potent new diseases. Diseases like smallpox, which McNeill traces to cowpox; influenza, derivative of hog diseases; and measles, derived from rinderpest or canine distemper. In all, humans inherited dozens of diseases from animals.

That co-evolutionary process began close on the heels of settled village life and the beginnings of domestication, which can be traced back to roughly 9000 B.P. in Mesopotamia and the Middle East, where hunter-gatherers settled down and began to grow wheat and barley, lentils, and peas. Within a thousand years they had tamed wild cattle, sheep, pig, and goat, and the combination of farming and herding fueled a steep rise in human populations.

Through the middle Holocene, these Neolithic (New Stone Age) villages increased in size and population density. More mouths to feed demanded more farmland and pasture. Sanitary conditions declined: It was life cheek by jowl, as Alfred Crosby put it, with other people and domesticated animals. New diseases were born in these natural laboratories along the Tigris and Euphrates, and later the Nile, the Indus, and around the Aegean Sea. But if their arrival was noticed, it went unchallenged.

Epidemic diseases were present at least 3000 years ago, as testified by smallpox pustules on Egyptian mummies. Diseases figured as Biblical plagues. And they were spoken of by Hippocrates. They reached the British Isles in medieval times. By 1492, having lived for thousands of years in close proximity with more than a dozen species of domesticated animals, and having effectively covered their world with cities and empires, Old World populations had thor-

Once human beings began living with their newly domesticated animals in the Old World, they began to develop a host of new diseases brought about by drinking the same water and breathing the same air as the animals, and by using animal waste as fertilizer for crops. The beginning of animal domestication can be traced back to approximately 9000 B.P. to the region between the Tigris and Euphrates rivers.

oughly "domesticated" the pathogens that followed in their train. Occasionally they suffered spectacular epidemics like the Black Death of the 14th century, but their numbers always rebounded. Quite unlike the Native Americans.

ONLY IN AMERICA

In America, neither old nor young were spared. The fact that the native peoples were utterly defenseless against introduced epidemic diseases was taken by some as a sign of higher authority. "For the natives," Massachusetts governor John Winthrop wrote in 1634, "they are neere all dead of small Poxe, so as the Lord hathe cleared our title to what we possess." The natives themselves, discouraged by their losses and the stunning good health of the invaders, were often convinced that their own deities were no match for the European god.

Others blamed native health care: "When a nation is attacked by the small-pox," the French explorer Antoine Simon Le Page du Pratz wrote in 1758, "it quickly makes great havoc; for as a whole family is crowded into a small hut ... the distemper, if it seizes one, is quickly communicated to all." Du Pratz could not understand why native physicians, who were otherwise quite skillful, were unable to cope with these common ailments. Honed against long-familiar ills, native skills were no match for alien pathogens. Besides, in those pre-vaccination days no physician on either side of the ocean could have stemmed the assault of Old World diseases on New World populations. The pioneering English physician, Sir Edward Jenner, only began his successful efforts at developing a smallpox vaccine in the 1790s.

Native Americans suffered so terribly because they lacked immunity, and when a group with adult immunity spreads the disease to one without, mortal-

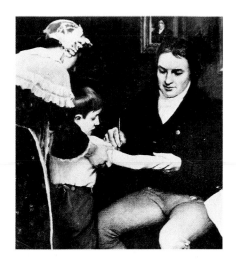

British physician Sir Edward Jenner pioneered vaccination when he realized that dairymaids around his home in Gloucestershire never fell victim to smallpox if they already had had cowpox. He began inoculating people with cowpox in order to provide immunity to smallpox in the 1790s. But for the first Americans, who domesticated few animals, there was no such natural immunity and—for three centuries after Contact— no vaccine.

ity is nearly universal. Crosby likens the process to a fire in a forest that has not burned for a very long time. When ignited, the forest burns swiftly and the destruction is total.

But *why* did Native Americans lack immunity? And why did they have no epidemic diseases of their own to plague the invaders? The answer is in the story of the first Americans, of where, when, and how they came, and what happened after they arrived.

BACK TO THE FIRST AMERICANS

The first Americans were descendants of Northeast Asian populations. We see this in the Sinodonty dental pattern, the shared mtDNA markers, and in at least certain elements of the languages of their modern descendants.

The port of entry of the first Americans was the Bering Sea region. During the Middle Wisconsin period and the early millennia of the Late Wisconsin, these first Americans would have had to cross by boat. That seems unlikely. They could have, and likely did, walk across in the Late Wisconsin, when the advance of continental ice sheets dropped sea levels worldwide and Beringia surfaced. Between 25,000 and 14,400 B.P. it was possible to cross the Mammoth steppe, then dotted by parkland and tundra, and grazed by mammoth, horse, and bison. It was also possible to do so during the subsequent few millennia when the breach was still narrow enough to freeze over in winter.

Going south from Beringia was another matter, tied to ice fluctuations along the shared margins of the Laurentide and Cordilleran glaciers. Passage was physically possible through virtually the entire Late Wisconsin, but perhaps biologically inhospitable much of that time.

The date when humans reached America south of the ice sheets is partly tied to the arrival of the first people in Siberia itself, now set no earlier than 20,000 B.P. It also depends on the timing of their departure from Beringia, perhaps around 14,000 B.P. It is yet unresolved whether they arrived in the Americas in time to reach Pedra Furada and Monte Verde (MV I) by 33,000 B.P. or even Monte Verde (MV II) at 12,000 to 13,000 B.P. Clovis Paleoindians on the High Plains are sure testimony that the first Americans arrived by at least 11,200 B.P., then possibly spanned the continent in a thousand years.

When they arrived, the North American landscape was a teeming zoo of megafauna, from mammoth to giant beaver, sabertooth tiger to giant skunk. By 10,800 years ago, however, all were extinct, though many may have disappeared before then. Paleoindians were contemporaries with these great beasts, and Paul Martin has argued vigorously, though not persuasively, for a human hand (or Clovis point) in their extinctions. More likely, the climate and environmental changes at the end of the Pleistocene, when the weather grew warmer, more seasonal, and summers lasted longer, finished off the megafauna.

These were the very same changes that, occurring halfway around the world, set the Neolithic stage for the domestication of cattle, goat, pig, sheep, camel, ass, elephant, horse, duck, goose, water buffalo, yak, dog, and cat. In sharp contrast, animal domestication was insignificant in the New World: a few species of South American camel, the turkey, and the guinea pig.

There are two reasons for that striking hemispheric imbalance. First, the New World fauna was impoverished. Pleistocene extinctions had wiped out 35 genera of megafauna—80 percent of North America's large mammals. Gone from North America were horses, elephants (mammoth and mastodon), and camels, upon whose Old World relatives Genghis Khan galloped to Empire, Hannibal crossed the Alps, and traders of the Persian Empire traversed vast seas of sand. All that remained of North America's large mammals were bison, moose, elk, caribou, deer, muskox, mountain goat, and pronghorn antelope—a very narrow pool from which to select potential animal domesticates.

Second, not all animals—especially not these North American survivors—are easily domesticated. Candidates for domestication, biologist Jared Diamond argues, must be social creatures and display dominant and submissive behaviors. They should not compete with humans for food and, better still, they should serve as food themselves if necessary. They cannot have an instant flight reflex when startled. They must breed readily in captivity. And, they must be adaptable to a wide range of environments.

Of the surviving New World large mammals, only bison come close to meeting those strict requirements. But penned bison are unruly animals. Besides, what's the incentive to domesticate? Domestication is partly a response to food shortages. But on the Great Plains, with the exception of the terrible drought of Altithermal times, bison were for more than 10,000 years an abundant, predictable, and reliable food source. There was no need to go to the trouble of corralling them. So no one did.

New World peoples did, of course, domesticate a cornucopia of plants (more than in the Old World, in fact). Hemisphere-wide, the list of American domesticates includes acorn squash, avocado, cocoa, chili pepper, cotton, gourd, lima bean, manioc, potato, peanut, pumpkin, sunflower, tomato, tobacco, and yams. But the most important was the triumvirate of corn, beans, and squash. These plants fed the great pre-Columbian towns of North America, and the Mesoamerican Olmec, Maya, Toltec, and Aztec peoples. Potatoes, peanuts, and yams did the same for South America's Chavin, Moche, Wari, and Inca. So successful was New World food production, that by 1492 there were cities and towns in the Western Hemisphere rivaling anything in the Old in terms of size and population. Tenochtitlán, the Aztec capital razed by Cortés, had a pre-contact population estimated at more than 200,000, with perhaps 1.5 million altogether in the surrounding valley. More people inhabited this one valley than *all* the British Colonies on the eve of the American Revolution. Even Boston, Massachusetts, 14 years after the revolution it helped ignite, had a population of only 18,000—just about the same as in Cahokia and the surrounding American Bottom 600 years earlier.

CROWDS, BUT NO CROWD DISEASES

The vast pre-Columbian cities existing throughout the Western Hemisphere testify that crowds are necessary, but not wholly sufficient, for the evolution of epidemic disease. By itself, a crowd cannot hatch a disease, though it will pass one along with deadly speed.

But until the arrival of Europeans, Native Americans had none to pass along. Their ancestors were not in the Old World when the diseases were born, and did not participate in the long co-evolutionary process. They left the Old World—Siberia, not Mesopotamia—thousands of years before the first cow or sheep was ever corralled, and well before the first epidemic diseases reared their heads. As one measure of just how far the first Americans were from the source of diseases, smallpox did not reach Siberia until 1630, Crosby reports, and only struck Kamchatka in 1768-1769. The rear flank of Native Americans was well insulated from Old World disease: by the vast distance from the source of diseases to eastern Siberia and the Bering Sea; by the small and scattered populations that lived in Siberia and Alaska; and by the low level of cross-Bering boat traffic. No ancestral American suffered through the many thousands of years of agony and illness as diseases grew potent and spread, though they paid dearly for those millennia of good health when pathogens finally arrived on their shores.

In the unlikely event the first Americans had carried diseases from the Old World, those would have been stripped away as they came across the "germ filter" that was Beringia. There, Smithsonian Institution physical anthropologist T. Dale Stewart argues, the harsh Arctic climate would have killed off disease germs (or their vectors, such as mosquitoes and worms). If migration to the Americas was a slow eastward drifting, he adds, diseased hosts would never have survived long enough to reach the New World. And if any disease did strike, there were few opportunities to pass it along. Beringia did not then, as the Arctic does not today, support any dense populations. An infected group would find itself naturally quarantined, wiped out with very little notice or widespread effect.

In like manner, the rising Bering Sea would have been an equally effective barrier in keeping New World diseases from reaching the Old, if, in fact, there had been any New World diseases to worry about. But, Pleistocene extinctions, combined with the difficulty or lack of incentive for domesticating the surviving mammals, gave no animal sources for mixing deadly new diseases. Only in South America, where camels were herded, was there a potential animal source for new disease strains. These camels and their herders, however, lived high in the Andes, in small and dispersed groups, and were too few and too isolated to sustain infections in the wild.

The New World had its native infections, including Carrion's disease, trichinosis, tapeworm, syphilis perhaps, and Chagas', the bane of Charles Darwin's later life. Although all were debilitating, few were deadly, and none seem to have flourished outside the hemisphere (with the possible exception of syphilis), or have affected European colonists.

A TALE OF TWO HEMISPHERES

Time and again, Alfred Crosby relates, European emigrants to America remarked on the healthiness of their new homes, and their claims are probably true, despite having a chamber of commerce ring. Statistics certainly bear them out: Even the first New England settlers averaged an astonishing lifespan of 71.8 years.

Indeed, their lives were often better in America than in the home country. For them, the New World was a rich land where their plants and animals thrived, where they and their descendants were free from overcrowding, had plenty of farm land and pasture, and enjoyed higher living standards than they had back home.

What a grim contrast to the fate of Native Americans, descendants of the true discoverers of America. Decimated in the decades and centuries after contact, it would take nearly 500 more years of exposure to repeated epidemics, and the advent of modern medicine, before their numbers would eventually begin to rebound. Only in the 1970s did Native American populations finally regain the million mark.

The reasons for the events that followed in Columbus' wake are tragically clear. The first Americans left the Old World early and far from the scene of disease co-evolution. They crossed a disease barrier to a New World whose large fauna were nearly wiped out, leaving little opportunity for animal domesticates and animal-originating diseases. They spent at least the next 11,000 years in complete isolation, save for a few inconsequential Norse landings. They were utterly defenseless against European diseases—though not necessarily the Europeans themselves.

In contrast to the Americas, the Old World saw no major Pleistocene-ending, mammalian extinctions, and had plenty of animal candidates for domestication. Neolithic farmers and town dwellers seized the advantage, and along the way began to ferment new diseases they could not, and did not, avoid. No germ filter here, and though its absence caused costly and repeated ills, over the long haul Old World peoples developed an immunity that helped them colonize the New World.

THE PAST IS THE KEY TO THE PRESENT

The contact between the Old World and the New was, of course, about more than just disease. Native American plants traveled to the Old World where they became vital staples—potatoes, corn, and tomatoes, for instance—or devilish vices—such as tobacco. Old World plants such as wheat, oats, and rye came to America, and thrived, as did dandelions, plantain, stinging nettles, crab grass, and other weeds.

After a hiatus of some 10,000 years, horses returned to the North American landscape—brought back by Old World peoples. As depicted in this 1846-1848 George Catlin painting, mounted Comanche (as well as Apache and other native hunters) were able to chase bison with increased mobility and speed. Population increased greatly in the Great Plains as a result.

Old World animals carried and fed European explorers and colonists, and revolutionized native lives on the Great Plains. Mounted on horses returned to America after a 10,000-year absence, Comanche, Apache, and other bison hunters were able to move as they never had before. Amid a continent where the overall population was falling, relative population density on the Great Plains rose dramatically as a result of the mobility and other advantages provided by the horse. Indeed, when horses came into the possession of farmers living on the edge of the Plains, the farmers often abandoned their fields and took up bison hunting.

Yet aside from these and other changes felt by peoples from both hemispheres, it was the tragic loss of 72 percent (perhaps as high as 97 percent) of the Native American population that most profoundly affected history's course. It was a cataclysm that still colors our understanding of the first Americans.

LIFE AFTER DEATHS

The Native Americans who did manage to survive the waves of disease and depopulation paid a price for that survival, as documented by Dobyns and other ethnohistorians. What happened in the centuries after contact varied considerably across the continent and among native groups themselves, but a few general trends are evident.

In the aftermath of epidemics, survivors abandoned old towns and regions: 16th and 17th century documents hint at extensive refugee movements. The refugees banded together with other survivors, often from previously unrelated communities, who perhaps were even speaking different languages. Naturally, as these heretofore ethnically and linguistically distinct individuals amalgamated, the social and political criteria that once governed their lives had to change. The old rules no longer applied among strangers. The Natchez of the Southeast, as archaeologist Jeffrey Brain realized, altered their definitions of

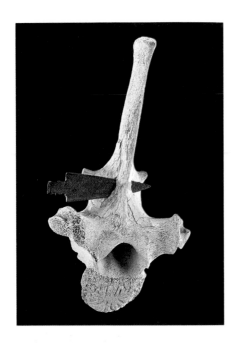

In the centuries after European contact, Native Americans gave up many of their traditional materials and artifacts. This buffalo vertebra with its embedded point tells the same story of the hunt as the early Folsom point found with bison bones. But knapped flint has been replaced by hammered metal.

status and rank, in order to permit intermarriage with unrelated Tunican-speaking refugees in the region.

Along the way there were also adaptive changes; some groups became economically dependent on European markets, while others adopted Old World plants and animals, and still others were forced onto reservations or into unfamiliar environments. Some native groups took up Old World religion, and others joined millenarian sects which, leavened with many religious roots, sprang up in the decades and centuries after contact.

Traditional architecture and settlements were abandoned. Most noticeably, the earthen mounds of Eastern North America, ubiquitous since Adena times, ceased to be built. Extant mounds, however, continued to have "considerable notoriety among the Indians." Jefferson reported that native people occasionally visited the mounds to express what he construed to be sorrow. There were so many apparently untended mounds that later European settlers, who saw too few Native Americans to account for such extensive constructions, were bewildered and attributed the work to a "Lost Race of Moundbuilders."

Native Americans abandoned many traditional artifacts and crafts in order to adopt European weaponry (swords and guns) and trade wares—especially those made of metal—and thus manufacture new artifact forms. Europeans created a demand for items not previously valued (furs, gold, and silver), and closed down markets for other goods (high quality chert, feather, and shell). The Goldilocks Assumption that people and their artifacts are relatively stable through time utterly fails in the centuries after contact.

A sharp and deep divide separates Native American history from prehistory. Groups whose customs and cultures were systematically recorded in the late 19th and early 20th century are the relatively few biological and cultural descendants of peoples known only archaeologically from pre-contact times. The ties across that great divide are anything but straightforward.

Yet it is the post-contact record of Native American history that archaeologists and anthropologists use to understand Native American prehistory. Consider what that may mean. In the process of depopulation and the amalgamation of survivors into new groups, one certain casualty was language.

SILENT SPEAKERS

Many languages simply expired along with their speakers in the centuries after contact. The explorers Lewis and Clark were explicitly charged to record what they could of the different languages they encountered on their way west, for President Jefferson, who sent them, well realized and deeply lamented "that we have suffered so many of the Indian tribes already to extinguish, without our having previously collected and deposited in the records of literature, the general rudiments at least of the languages they spoke."

Even where individual speakers survived, languages surely disappeared. To communicate with each other, refugees from different groups had to

Spanish horsemen ride across the walls of Canyon de Chelly. The Navajo pictograph may represent Spanish Cavalry. Another portion of the panel shows a Spanish priest.

adopt a single tongue, and over time lost their own. Broadly speaking, Native American linguistic diversity must have plummeted in the centuries that followed contact.

It is on this record of Native American languages that Joseph Greenberg's Amerind hypothesis is constructed. By itself, this says nothing of whether the word and grammatical links tying together the languages within his Amerind family are correct. That is for Greenberg, Lyle Campbell, and others to debate. Rather, it means that the relatively few surviving languages may not reveal the larger and more complex language families that once existed. There was surely much more to "Amerind" than now meets the ears.

Something else, too. In recent years a few archaeologists have attempted to use the number and distribution of Native American languages as a road map to the route of entry for the first Americans. The idea lurking behind this theory is that areas with the greatest number of languages—which happen to be the Pacific Northwest and California coasts—are those that were occupied the longest, and hence were the likely corridor of entry into the New World.

Yet, the number of languages is hardly a function of time alone. There are a greater number of languages known from the Pacific Northwest and California coasts simply because these areas of the continent were hit later and more lightly by epidemic disease than the natives of the Mississippi Valley. Pacific Coast speakers survived well into the late 19th century and talked with Franz Boas, Edward Sapir, and their students.

Of course, it is extremely doubtful whether the modern distribution of native languages bears any necessary relationship to transitory migration routes, particularly those taken tens of thousands of years earlier across a radically different, partly ice-shrouded landscape, perhaps by people who may have been historically and linguistically unrelated (except in the general sense all are ultimately Asian in origin). It is probably no more realistic to infer Pleistocene migration routes into North America by the number and distribution of modern native languages than it would be to infer de Soto's route in 1539-1542 by looking at the number and distribution of Spanish dialects in the Southeast today. And at least we know de Soto spoke Spanish.

THE NARROWEST BOTTLENECK OF ALL

If the linguistic ties from the historic to prehistoric periods are frayed, no less so are genetic links. Depopulation on the order of 72 percent, let alone 97 percent, would create a severe population bottleneck in the decades and centuries after contact, quite unlike any experienced by Native Americans since they left northeastern Asia more than 11,000 years earlier.

Genes carried by those Native Americans who survived contact are the product of a founder effect (although no literal "founding" was involved). They derive, as archaeologist Robert Dunnell of the University of Washington puts

At one time private secretary to Thomas Jefferson, Meriwether Lewis *(top)* left his desk to lead an expedition with his chosen co-leader, army officer William Clark *(bottom)*, to explore the newly acquired land of the Louisiana Purchase. Jefferson, in his instructions to Lewis in 1803, asked him to take note of the different languages they encountered on their journey west across the continent, realizing that many such languages already had disappeared.

it, from just a tiny fraction of the Native Americans living in the New World in the early 1500s. Most of the people responsible for the prehistoric archaeological record, he adds, have no living descendants.

What then of the genetic diversity of modern Native Americans, who today contribute their DNA to our efforts to understand their ancestry? Do those genes accurately represent the gene pool of America's founding populations, or just the survivors of the 16th century bottleneck? No one is certain.

But perhaps that uncertainty helps explain the discrepancy between Wallace's and Ward's mtDNA studies. Each may be right, and each may be sampling different post-contact "founding" populations. William Hauswirth, a geneticist at the University of Florida, is correct when he argues that in order to understand the genetics of the first Americans, our best bet is to use ancient, or at least pre-contact DNA, insofar as we can. Ultimately, places like Windover in Florida, with its spectacular preservation of ancient mtDNA, are vital to unraveling Native American genealogies.

REPLAYING THE TAPE OF PREHISTORY

There are rules that govern human lives. Broad principles, such as Darwin's natural selection, by which all human groups have flourished and failed over the long sweep of time. In these rules one understands the fundamental challenges and possibilities facing human populations as they grew and spread, explored new lands, hunted and gathered, or settled down to raise crops and build towns and cities.

Yet, as Harvard biologist Stephen Jay Gould reminds us, broad principles alone cannot explain why the human past looks precisely the way it does. For there are, within these principles, a wide range of options and outcomes, any one of which is as viable as the next. It is these options and outcomes that help determine the next set of options and outcomes, again within the broader rules. And the next set. And so on. The universe unfolds according to law, Darwin said, with the details, good or bad, left to chance—such as spending the night of March 26, 1835, in Mendoza, Argentina.

As a result, there is a contingency to prehistory and history, as each event is guided by broad principles but at the same time very much dependent on the previous sequence of options and outcomes. String the sequences together differently and you can get, Gould argues, a suite of outcomes "equally explicable, though massively different in form and effect."

One supposes it was "inevitable" that humans, once evolved (which, Gould shows, was hardly inevitable at all, at least when viewed from earliest geological time), would one day reach the Americas. But who the first Americans were, when they arrived, where they came from, and why they came, were not inevitable events at all. It only looks that way afterward, after a long and singular string of options and outcomes brought them to the western edge of Beringia at the end of the Pleistocene.

166

In this undated color lithograph, the great Aztec chief Moctezuma welcomes Hernan Cortés to Tenochtitlán (now Mexico City) in 1519. Little did he realize what lay in store for his people. Though the Aztecs defeated Cortés' first attempt to take their city, within a year their numbers were so decimated by the smallpox one of Cortés' men carried that the Spaniards were able to vanquish the city's inhabitants.

Replay the tape of history and, as Gould says, change a few of the quirky details, let their effects compound through time, and imagine what might have been. What if, for example, the first Americans hadn't left the Old World when they did? Or what if they brought diseases with them? Or if they had not come via Beringia? Or if 80 percent of America's megafauna had not become extinct at the end of the Pleistocene? Or if the remainder had been more readily domesticated, or there had been strong incentive to domesticate them? Or even if all those savants had been right, and the Native Americans really were the Lost Tribes of Israel, who carried with them an immunity conferred by Old World ancestry.

What might have been the case if Native Americans had not been devastated by disease?

Back to Tenochtitlán. Cortés had already lost the city in June 1520. Neither he, nor his horses, nor his pikes, nor his Tlaxcalan reserves, nor his grand strategies, formidable though they were, could, by themselves, have retaken Moctezuma's Aztec kingdom and its 1.5 million souls. But with smallpox he could—and did.

The impact of European disease rarely was so militarily decisive. Still, the triumphs of the conquistadors and all who followed were the triumphs of smallpox. Were it not for introduced epidemic diseases, American history would have been very different.

And the triumphs of smallpox and all the other introduced epidemic diseases had been foreordained more than 11,000 years earlier, when the first Americans stepped on to the western edge of the vast grassy plain of Beringia, then headed toward the rising sun.

REFERENCES

CHAPTER 1: OVERTURE

General and scholarly treatments of the first Americans abound. The most recent among them are listed below. One good way to keep current on the field is through *The Mammoth Trumpet*, a quarterly publication of the Center for the Study of the First Americans, Oregon State University.

CARLISLE, R. (EDITOR) 1988 *Americans before Columbus: Ice-Age origins.* Ethnology Monographs No. 12, Department of Anthropology, University of Pittsburgh.

DILLEHAY, T. AND D.J. MELTZER (EDITORS) 1991 *The first Americans: search and research.* CRC Press, Boca Raton.

FAGAN, B. 1987 *The Great Journey: The Peopling of Ancient America.* Thames and Hudson, London.

CHAPTER 2: THE GREAT ROUTE

The literature on this subject is immense. In preparing this chapter, I relied heavily on all these listed works, especially those written by a host of authors in the hefty volume edited by Ruddiman and Wright. For a good general treatment of the causes of the Ice Age, see Imbrie and Imbrie. Guthrie provides an excellent account of the environments of Beringia.

AGENBROAD, L., J. MEAD, AND L. NELSON 1990 *Megafauna and man: discovery of America's heartland.* Hot Springs: Mammoth site of Hot Springs, South Dakota.

GUTHRIE, R.D. 1990 *Frozen fauna of the Mammoth Steppe: The Story of Blue Babe.* University of Chicago Press, Chicago.

GRAYSON, D. 1991 Late Pleistocene mammalian extinctions in North America: taxonomy, chronology and explanations. *Journal of World Prehistory* 5: 193-231.

IMBRIE, J. AND K.P. IMBRIE 1986 *Ice Ages: Solving the Mystery.* Harvard University Press, Cambridge.

PORTER, S. 1988 Landscapes of the last Ice Age in North America. In *Americans before Columbus: Ice-Age origins,* edited by R. Carlisle, pp. 1-24. Ethnology Monographs No. 12, Department of Anthropology, University of Pittsburgh.

RUDDIMAN, W.F. AND H.E. WRIGHT, JR. (EDITORS) 1987 *North America and Adjacent Oceans During the Last Deglaciation.* The Geological Society of America, Boulder.

WRIGHT, H.E. 1991 Environmental conditions for Paleoindian immigration. In *The first Americans: search and research,* edited by T. Dillehay and D.J. Meltzer, pp. 113-135. CRC Press, Boca Raton.

CHAPTER 3: A HISTORY OF CONTROVERSY

The Willey and Sabloff volume remains the single most comprehensive source on the overall history of American archaeology. It covers in passing the human antiquity controversy; a more detailed treatment is in my cited paper, and will be the subject of my next book. The treatment of human antiquity in Europe is detailed in Grayson. Trigger provides a valuable overview of theoretical changes in archaeology worldwide, including a discussion of the significance of the human antiquity debates in both the Old and New Worlds.

GRAYSON, D.K. 1983 *The establishment of human antiquity.* Academic Press, New York.

MELTZER, D.J. 1991 On "paradigms" and "paradigm bias" in controversies over human antiquity in America. In *The first Americans: search and research,* edited by T. Dillehay and D. Meltzer, pp. 13-49. CRC Press, Boca Raton.

TRIGGER, B. 1989 *A history of archaeological thought.* Cambridge, Cambridge University Press.

WILLEY, G. AND J. SABLOFF 1993 *A history of American archaeology.* Third edition. San Francisco, W.H. Freeman.

CHAPTER 4: FINDING THE TRACES

There is a vast literature on the early archaeology of America. The most current compendium is Bryan's edited volume, but while published in 1986 the papers themselves date to a 1981 symposium. The best discussion on problems of artifact recognition can be found in Toth, and on dating in Taylor. Many of the sites mentioned in this chapter are discussed in a 14-part series published in *Natural History* (November 1986 to October 1987, and January-February 1988).

ADOVASIO, J.M. and R.C. CARLISLE 1984 An Indian hunters camp for 20,000 years. *Scientific American*, May 1984, pp. 130-36.

BRYAN, A.L. (EDITOR) 1986 *New evidence for the Pleistocene peopling of the Americas.* Center for the Study of Early Man, University of Maine, Orono.

DILLEHAY, T.D. 1984 A late Ice-Age settlement in southern Chile. *Scientific American*, October 1984, pp. 106-117.

TAYLOR, R.E. 1991 Frameworks for dating the late Pleistocene peopling of the Americas. In *The first Americans: search and research*, edited by T. Dillehay and D.J. Meltzer, pp. 77-111. CRC Press, Boca Raton.

TOTH, N. 1991 The material record. In *The first Americans: search and research*, edited by T. Dillehay and D.J. Meltzer, pp. 53-76. CRC Press, Boca Raton.

CHAPTER 5: WHO WERE THE FIRST AMERICANS?

The dispute over the Greenberg classification rattles on. To read the combatants before they directly engaged each other, consult the Greenberg (1987) and Campbell and Mithun (1979) volumes. The Greenberg, Turner, and Zegura (1986) paper is their most prominent and accessible joint statement, and in the commentary that follows is a sample of the criticism. As a participant, I benefitted from the arguments and yet-unpublished papers at the Greenberg Conference in Boulder, Colorado, in 1990. On matters of Native American languages, I relied on various authors in the invaluable *Handbook of North American Indians.* Turner's results have been detailed in a number of widely accessible places, and I only list two of the more recent ones. On mtDNA studies, the evidence is emerging fast, but so far only in the technical journals. Fortunately, there exist a few good general works, which serve as a guide to the literature, and they are listed here.

CAMPBELL, L. AND M. MITHUN (EDITORS) 1979 *The languages of native America: historical and comparative assessment.* University of Texas Press, Austin.

DUMOND, D.E. 1987 A reexamination of Eskimo-Aleut prehistory. *American Anthropologist* 89: 32-56.

EDELSON, E. 1991 Tracing human lineages. *Mosaic* 22: 56-63.

GREENBERG, J. 1987 *Language in the Americas.* Stanford University Press, Stanford.

GREENBERG, J. AND M. RUHLEN 1992 Linguistic origins of native Americans. *Scientific American* (November), pp. 94-99.

GREENBERG, J., C. TURNER, AND S. ZEGURA 1986 The settlement of the Americas: a comparison of the linguistic, dental and genetic evidence. *Current Anthropology* 27: 477-497.

LEWIN, R. 1991 The biochemical route to human origins. *Mosaic* 22: 46-55.

MELTZER, D.J. 1989 Why don't we know when the first people came to North America? *American Antiquity* 54: 471-490.

TURNER, C. 1986 The first Americans: the dental evidence. *National Geographic Research* 2: 37-46.
1989 Teeth and prehistory in Asia. *Scientific American* (February), pp. 88-96.

CHAPTER 6: NORTH AMERICAN PALEOINDIANS

The literature on North American Paleoindians is immense, but those sources listed below will provide access to the major sites and evidence of this period in prehistory. The most comprehensive papers on Pleistocene extinctions, and likely to stay that way for some time, are those in Martin and Klein's volume. Grayson's thoughtful summary chapter is especially valuable. A good recent summary of the Clovis occupation is Dennis Stanford's Introduction to the Bonnichsen and Turnmire volume. Later Paleoindian occupations are well treated in Frison, and Stanford and Day.

BONNICHSEN, R. AND K. TURNMIRE (EDITORS) 1991 *Clovis: origins and adaptations.* Center for the Study of the First Americans, Oregon State University, Corvallis.

FRISON, G. 1991 *Prehistoric hunters of the High Plains.* Second edition. Academic Press, New York.

HAYNES, C.V. 1982 Were Clovis progenitors in Beringia? In *Paleoecology of Beringia*, edited by D. Hopkins, J. Matthews, Jr., C. Schweger, and S. Young, pp. 383-398. Academic Press, New York.

MARTIN, P. AND R.G. KLEIN (EDITORS) 1984 *Quaternary extinctions.* University of Arizona Press, Tucson.

STANFORD, D. AND J. DAY (EDITORS) 1992 *Ice Age hunters of the Rockies.* University Press of Colorado, Niwot.

CHAPTER 7: THE LAST 10,000 YEARS

The Fagan and Jennings volumes treat all of North American prehistory; Kopper's work covers the same ground, but in a more general way accompanied by superb illustrations. Other cited papers provide detailed coverage of the sites and areas discussed in each of the snapshots. I relied on these heavily.

BRAUN, D. 1989 Coevolution of sedentism, pottery technology, and horticulture in the central Midwest, 200 B.C.-A.D. 600. In *Emergent Horticultural Economies of the Eastern Woodlands*, edited by W. Keegan, pp. 153-182. Southern Illinois University Press, Carbondale.

CROWN, P.L. 1990 The Hohokam of the American Southwest. *Journal of World Prehistory* 4: 223-255.

CROWN, P. AND W.J. JUDGE (EDITORS) 1991 *Chaco & Hohokam: prehistoric regional systems in the American Southwest*. School of American Research, Santa Fe.

FAGAN, B. 1991 *Ancient North America: the archaeology of a continent*. Thames and Hudson, London.

JENNINGS, J. 1989 *Prehistory of North America*. Third edition. Mayfield Publishing Company, Mountain View.

KOPPER, P. 1986 *The Smithsonian book of North American Indians: Before the Coming of the Europeans*. Smithsonian Institution Press, Washington, D.C.

LEKSON, S., T. WINDES, J. STEIN, AND W.J. JUDGE 1988 The Chaco Canyon community. *Scientific American* July 100-109.

MCGHEE, R. 1984 Contact between Native North Americans and the Medieval Norse: a review of the evidence. *American Antiquity* 49: 4-26.

MELTZER, D.J. 1991 Altithermal archaeology and paleoecology at Mustang Springs, on the southern High Plains of Texas. *American Antiquity* 56: 236-267.

MILNER, G. 1990 The Late Prehistoric Cahokia cultural system of the Mississippi River Valley: foundations, florescence, and fragmentation. *Journal of World Prehistory* 4: 1-43.

SMITH, B.D. 1986 The archaeology of the southeastern United States: from Dalton to de Soto, 10,500 to 500 B.P. *Advances in World Archaeology* 5: 1-92.

WILLS, W. 1988 Early agriculture and sedentism in the American Southwest: evidence and interpretations. *Journal of World Prehistory* 2: 445-488.

CHAPTER 8: SIBERIA TO SMALLPOX

A superb single volume treatment of the effects of European contact on the Americas is Crosby's book. Thomas' edited three-volume set provides rich first-hand archaeological and historical data. I depended on all the listed references.

CALDWELL, M. 1992 Vigil for a doomed virus. *Discover* 13: 50-56.

CROSBY, A. 1986 *Ecological imperialism: the biological expansion of Europe, 900 - 1900*. Cambridge University Press, Cambridge.

DOBYNS, H. 1983 *Their number become thinned*. The University of Tennessee Press, Knoxville.

GOULD, S.J. 1989 *Wonderful life*. W.W. Norton and Company, New York.

MCNEILL, W. 1976 *Plagues and peoples*. Anchor/Doubleday, Garden City.

RAMENOFSKY, A. 1987 *Vectors of death*. University of New Mexico Press, Albuquerque.

THOMAS, D. (EDITOR) 1989-91 *Columbian consequences*. Volumes 1-3. Smithsonian Institution Press, Washington, D.C.

UBELAKER, D. 1988 North American Indian population size, A.D. 1500 to 1985. *American Journal of Physical Anthropology* 77: 289-294.

INDEX

PICTURE CREDITS

Front cover photograph by Thomas Ives
Back cover photograph from The Great Lakes
Artifact Repository

9 Culver Pictures
10,11 Tom Bean
14, 15 *(left, lower)* The Smithsonian Institution
14, 15 *(upper)* The Smithsonian Institution,
   photo Chip Clark/SI
16, 17 Illustration © Greg Harlin/
   Wood, Ronsaville, Harlin
19 Mercyhurst Archaeological Institute
21 Great Lakes Artifact Repository
22, 23 E. Spiegelhalter/
   Woodfin Camp & Associates
24 *(upper)* Culver Pictures
24 *(lower)* The Bettmann Archive
25 *(both)* Tom Bean
26 Courtesy Vasco Milankovitch, Melbourne
27 *(upper)* Courtesy Ocean Drilling Program/
   Texas A&M University
27 *(lower left, lower right)* Eric V. Grave/
   Photo Researchers
29 Courtesy United States Geological Survey,
   Fairbanks
33 J. Richardson/Woodfin Camp & Associates
36 The Field Museum of Natural History,
   Neg. No. CK8T
37 TASS from SOVFOTO
38 The Peale Museum/
   Baltimore City Life Museums
39 Tom Bean
40, 41 The Denver Museum of Natural History,
   Neg. No. E-51
42 The Smithsonian Institution,
   photo Ed Castle
43 Courtesy Donald K. Grayson, Dept. of
   Anthropology/University of Washington
44 *(upper)* Culver Pictures
44 *(lower)* The University Museum/University
   of Pennsylvania, Neg. No. S4-138799
45 *(upper)* The Granger Collection, New York
45 *(lower)* University of Chicago
46 Peabody Museum/Harvard University
47 *(upper)* Oberlin College Archives
47 *(lower)* The Granger Collection, New York
48 The Bettmann Archive
51 Blackwater Draw Museum/
   Eastern New Mexico University
52 *(left)* The Smithsonian Institution Archives,
   photo Terry McCrea/SI
52 *(upper right)* The Denver Museum
   of Natural History
53 *(left)* Peabody Museum/Harvard University
53 *(upper right)* The Denver Museum
   of Natural History
56 Erwin Barbour, courtesy University of
   Nebraska State Museum

58 Texas Memorial Museum/
   The University of Texas at Austin
60,61 Paul G. Bahn
64 San Bernadino County Museum
65 *(left)* Don Lantz/
   San Bernadino County Museum
65 *(upper right)* San Bernadino
   County Museum
66 The Granger Collection, New York
68 UPI/Bettmann
70 Thomas Ives
71 Canadian Museum of Civilization, Ottawa,
   Neg. No. S91-913
73 Mercyhurst Archaeological Institute
74, 75 Illustration © Rob Wood/
   Wood, Ronsaville, Harlin
77 Niède Guidon & Anne Marie Pessis/
   Museu do Homem Americano
79 *(both)* Courtesy Tom Dillehay/
   University of Kentucky
82,83 James W. Lyle, courtesy Texas
   A&M University
84 Harold Cook, courtesy of Dorothy Cook
   Meade
85 Culver Pictures
91 *(all)* James W. Lyle, courtesy Texas
   A&M University
93 Courtesy Emory University,
   Department of Anthropology
97 Courtesy University of Alaska at Fairbanks
102 Courtesy Windover Archeological
   Project/Florida State University
104, 105 Tom Wolff
107 Library, The Academy of Natural Sciences
   of Philadelphia
110 Tom Wolff
114 *(all)* Kenneth Garrett
115 Courtesy University of Arizona,
   Department of Anthropology
116 University of Colorado Museum
117 Courtesy University of Wyoming,
   Department of Anthropology
118 Robert W. Parvin
119 *(left)* Kim Heacox
119 *(upper right)* Great Lakes
   Artifacts Repository
120, 121 Illustration © Rob Wood/
   Wood, Ronsaville, Harlin
123 *(left)* Courtesy Monahans
   State Park Museum
123 *(right)* Maxwell Museum of
   Anthropology/Werner Forman
   Archive/Art Resource
124 *(both)* Thunderbird Research Corporation
125 Courtesy University of Arizona,
   Department of Anthropology
128, 129 Superstock/Four by Five
131 Momatiuk-Eastcott/
   Woodfin Camp & Associates
132 *(both)* David J. Meltzer

133 *(left)* The Utah Museum of Natural
   History/Werner Forman Archive/
   Art Resource
133 *(upper right)* The Utah Museum
   of Natural History
134 Courtesy National Museum of the
   American Indian/Smithsonian Institution
135 Courtesy National Museum of the
   American Indian/Smithsonian Institution
136 *(both)* University of Michigan Museum
   of Anthropology
137 Arizona State Museum/University
   of Arizona
138 *(both)* Arizona State Museum/
   University of Arizona
140, 141 David Muench
142 *(left)* Reproduced from Jon L. Gibson,
   *Poverty Point: A Culture of the Lower
   Mississippi Valley*, Baton Rouge, LA
142 *(upper right)* NASA
143 *(both)* Pictures of Record
144 *(upper)* The Field Museum of Natural
   History/Werner Forman Archive/
   Art Resource
144 *(lower)* Peabody Museum, Harvard
   University/Werner Forman Archive/
   Art Resource
147 *(both)* Courtesy Cahokia Mounds
   Historical Site
148 Canadian Museum of Civilization, Ottawa,
   Neg. No. S91-996
149 *(both)* Courtesy L'Anse aux Meadows
   N.H.P./Canadian Parks Service
150, 151 Art Resource
154 Culver Pictures
155 Courtesy American Museum
   of Natural History
158 Roger Lemoyne
159 Culver Pictures
163 National Museum of American Art,
   Smithsonian Institution/Art Resource
164 Canadian Museum of Civilization, Ottawa,
   Neg. No. S91-2020
165 David Muench
166 *(both)* Courtesy Independence National
   Historical Park
167 The Bettmann Archive
176 Suzanne L. Seigel

Several maps and illustrations are based on the
research of individuals:

69 Herbert Haas, Southern Methodist
University; 87 Joeseph H. Greenberg, Stanford
University; 88 Christy G. Turner II, Arizona
State University; 99 Richard E. Morlan,
Archaeological Survey of Canada; 117 George C.
Frison, University of Wyoming; 131 Lawrence C.
Todd, Colorado State University.

AUTHOR'S ACKNOWLEDGMENTS

The great anthropologist, Alfred L. Kroeber, once protested having a symposium on the origins and antiquity of the first Americans at the annual meeting of the American Anthropological Association. "You will realize," he growled, "the sort of indefinite and aimless talk which would be brought out....Talk which would begin nowhere in particular, end nowhere, and chiefly furnish opportunities for individuals to occupy the floor."

It was hard to keep from thinking about Kroeber when I was asked to write a *book* on the subject. Those stronger than I would surely have resisted the temptation. But I succumbed. Partly, it was the gracious arm-twisting done by my friend, and series editor, Jerry Sabloff. "Think of the opportunity to launch preemptive strikes on your colleagues," he said.

And in part I succumbed because so much had changed since Kroeber hit that sour note 75 years ago. Back then, there was open warfare between disciplines, as archaeologists, paleontologists, linguists, physical anthropologists, and geologists fought over what they thought was a respectable antiquity for the first Americans. Almost annually there were new claims for very old sites, and without fail skeptics attacked those claims in meetings and in print. The future looked bleak: Controversy extended to the horizon, and there was no resolution in sight.

Come to think of it, things haven't changed all that much. Which was perhaps the best reason to take up Jerry's invitation. We now know more about the origins and antiquity of the first Americans than Kroeber ever imagined. We can probe the archaeological unknown with vastly more powerful tools. We possess a much deeper understanding of how the peopling of the Americas fits into human evolutionary history. Despite all this, the issue remains as lively and controversial as ever. Under the circumstances, it was hard to refuse to write a book on the topic.

I wrote this book for the general reader, and not my archaeological colleagues. The difference is largely a matter of style rather than substance, but also of coverage. The constraints of space and the demands of the narrative simply forbade me from mentioning every important site, researcher, argument, or claim. Sometimes, I confess, I was glad of it.

While the book wasn't written for them, I hope my fellow archaeologists find something of interest here; I am certain they will settle for a Zeppelin of a target. But, like Jerry says, I got to fire the first shot.

Before that starts, let me thank those who tried to keep me on the straight and narrow by answering my pesky questions or offering information or good advice: Michael A. Adler, James M. Adovasio, Lyle Campbell, Tom D. Dillehay, Dena F. Dincauze, Russell W. Graham, Donald K. Grayson, C. Vance Haynes, Jack L. Hofman, Vance T. Holliday, Jeffrey C. Long, Roger Lewin, Richard E. Morlan, Jeremy A. Sabloff, C. Garth Sampson, Bruce D. Smith, Dennis J. Stanford, Suzanne L. Siegel, David J. Weber, Ryk Ward, and especially Lewis R. Binford. It's a pleasure to share any of the credit, but I quickly and forever absolve them of any of the blame. I am grateful as well to all my colleagues who provided the photographs that grace this book.

For seeing this book to print, I'd like to thank the congenial and highly skilled editorial and production team led by Carolyn Jackson at St. Remy Press; Philippe Arnoldi and Chris Jackson who directed the illustrations and photography; also Patricia Gallagher and the editors at the Smithsonian Institution Press (including my friend Daniel Goodwin who, though he's been waiting for my promised history book almost as long as I have, refused to let me hide behind that commitment, thereby leaving me with no excuse but to accept this one). Robert C. Dunnell, Maxine and Seymour Garner, Donald S. Means and Joan O'Connor, Stephen and Florence Meltzer, and Ladislav P. Novak provided other important help along the way.

Portions of this book were written while I was on a Research Fellowship leave from Southern Methodist University, for which I am deeply grateful. Aspects of my archaeological field and historical research touched on here have been supported by grants from the National Science Foundation, the National Geographic Society, and The Potts and Sibley Foundation (whose support has also greatly facilitated my writing).

To any I have inadvertently omitted, my apologies and my thanks.

David J. Meltzer
Dallas, Texas